Intellectual Property Laws and Space Laws

Intellectual Property Laws and Space Laws

Emerging Frontiers of Innovation and Regulation

Edited by

Dr Parineet Kaur

Published in association with

The Indian Society of International Law
New Delhi

Vij Books
New Delhi (India)

First Published in India in 2026

Published by

Vij Books
(An imprint of Vij Books India Pvt Ltd)
(Publishers, Distributors & Importers)
4836/24, Ansari Road
Delhi – 110 002
Phones: 91-11-43596460, Mob: 98110 94883
e-mail: contact@vijpublishing.com
web : www.vijbooks.in

ISBN: 978-93-47436-82-6 (PB)

What matters is not the absence of imperfection, but how that imperfection is handled. Repair is the curriculum. When a parent circles back to acknowledge a misjudged reaction, to name their stress, to model self-accountability, they do more for a child's emotional literacy than any scripted lesson ever could.

And what's true in the home holds in the workplace. Leaders who regulate themselves, who maintain equanimity during crises, who make space for recovery rather than demanding constant performance, shape the emotional architecture of their teams. This is not "soft" leadership. It is operational strength. An organisation's resilience often hinges on what its leaders model—not in policy documents, but in the unscripted moments of uncertainty.

This chapter explores these ideas in full. Drawing from developmental psychology, cognitive behavioural science, and lived practice, it presents an invitation to rethink how resilience is formed—not just as an individual trait, but as a cultural process. It will spotlight real-world examples from parenting and leadership settings where psychological strength has been built through intentional exposure, meaningful limits, and compassionate guidance. You'll see how a child who's allowed to struggle, safely and reflectively, becomes a more robust thinker. How boredom becomes a workshop for insight. And how the adult nervous system—your own—becomes the ground on which others learn what it means to stay present in the storm.

This isn't just about children. It's about us. The impulse to over-manage, to over-protect, to soothe rather than strengthen, is not merely a parenting flaw—it is a cultural reflex. We are, in many ways, architects of fragility, even as we preach resilience. And so the question rebounds: Are we modelling what we hope to pass on? Or are we embodying the very fear-based behaviours we long to shield our young from?

same way a muscle strengthens through stress and repair, so too does the developing psyche.

This is not a call to withhold comfort or abandon empathy. Quite the opposite. It is a redefinition of support: not as rescue, but as resourcing. When we treat distress as something to be eliminated, rather than engaged, we rob children of the very capacities that make adulthood navigable—patience, discernment, delayed gratification. These traits are not taught in sweeping moral lessons but in mundane moments: the denied sweet at the checkout, the argument over toys, the frustration of a difficult homework assignment. These are the micro-rehearsals for future adaptability. Over time, tolerating small frustrations trains the brain to hold bigger ones without collapse.

Boredom deserves special mention. In our rush to optimise childhood—each minute scheduled, each silence filled—we've accidentally sterilised one of the most generative psychological states. Boredom isn't a problem; it's a portal. It's a crucible where imagination is forced to stretch and flex. When children are allowed to sit in that space—not rushed through it—they begin to source meaning from within rather than from constant external input. That's a seismic shift. One doesn't simply stave off boredom, they begin to engage it as a kind of creative resistance training.

Yet, even more powerful than any technique or tactic is the force of modelling. Children don't absorb values through instruction—they metabolise them through observation. They co-regulate. They watch. They imitate. A parent can lecture endlessly about calm, but if their own nervous system is erratic, reactive, or overly porous to stress, the message will not land. Children absorb what we do under pressure. Do we catastrophise when plans fall apart? Do we freeze when faced with conflict? Or do we breathe, recalibrate, and own our missteps with grace?

Cognitive resilience is not a given. It is cultivated—patiently, imperfectly, in countless small acts. This chapter won't offer quick fixes or silver bullets. What it offers instead is a durable framework—a lens and a set of tools that can reshape how we engage with those we are entrusted to guide. Whether you are raising children, mentoring the next generation, or leading teams, your influence extends beyond outcomes. It shapes the stories others will tell themselves when they encounter resistance. Will they collapse? Or recalibrate?

That difference, often, begins with you.

Let's begin the work of raising minds that don't just function—but endure. Not because it's easy. But because it matters more than ever.

The Inheritance of Emotional Wealth

It is tempting to measure legacy in numbers: the size of an estate, the contents of a portfolio, the presence or absence of financial security. But ask any psychologist, social worker, or adult reflecting on their upbringing, and a deeper truth becomes evident—*the most influential inheritance we receive is not monetary but emotional.* It is coded not in wills or trusts, but in tone of voice, patterns of response, and habits of self-regulation. Emotional wealth is not an abstraction. It is a transferable asset with real-world impact on how individuals think, relate, and recover.

This chapter challenges the cultural assumption that leaving financial stability is the ultimate parental success. While material resources do matter—they reduce stress, expand choice, and improve safety—they do not compensate for emotional illiteracy, chronic anxiety, or relational dysfunction. In many cases, financial inheritance passed down without emotional resilience *exacerbates* dysfunction rather than mitigating it. Emotional wealth, by contrast, compounds quietly but powerfully, shaping everything from conflict resolution skills to financial behaviour to mental health outcomes.

To understand this more clearly, we must first define what emotional wealth actually is. It is *not* about being cheerful or agreeable. It is the capacity to name emotions accurately, tolerate distress without collapse, and respond to difficulty with adaptive perspective. It includes empathy, boundaries, delayed gratification, emotional accountability, and the ability to self-soothe without destructiveness. These are capacities that allow individuals to *function effectively under pressure*, navigate relationships with maturity, and make decisions that align with long-term values.

Unlike material assets, emotional wealth cannot be transferred through paperwork. It must be modelled, mirrored, and reinforced in everyday interactions. A child who watches a parent apologise without defensiveness learns more about integrity than from any lecture. A teenager who sees an adult process grief without emotional shutdown is being taught how to metabolise pain. A young adult raised in a household where mistakes are met with calm inquiry rather than rage or shame carries forward a blueprint of psychological safety.

This modelling begins far earlier than most realise. Developmental neuroscience shows that children internalise emotional templates from caregivers well before they can articulate them. The patterns we demonstrate—whether we suppress, explode, avoid, repair—become part of a child's operating system. They learn whether emotions are safe to express, whether relationships can withstand conflict, and whether distress is a temporary state or a dangerous one. These lessons shape identity, coping, and even career paths.

Crucially, this emotional inheritance plays out directly in financial attitudes as well. A child raised in a home where financial stress was hidden but palpable may internalise money as a source of unspoken fear. Conversely, a child raised amid open, regulated discussions

Contents

Foreword

I am glad to write the preface for this book titled *Intellectual Property Laws and Space Laws: Emerging Frontiers of Innovation and Regulation*, being brought out by the Indian Society of International Law. The space era commenced with the successful launch of Sputnik I by the Soviet Union into outer space on 4 October 1957. This event also gave an impetus to the development of space laws. Space technology has been developing aggressively, and outer space has been explored not only for scientific purposes but also for commercial uses. Private enterprises have gradually expanded their involvement in space ventures during the last two decades. The space industry is rapidly transforming, with each month bringing news of a major space development from somewhere in the world. A report by the Space Foundation, a nonprofit organisation founded in 1983, reveals that the global space economy has reached an unprecedented $613 billion in 2024, reflecting strong 7.8 percent growth over the last year.

Space is not just a frontier for exploration; it is a cornerstone of our economy and security. Reaping the full benefits of future space innovations is associated with another complex question of intellectual property rights over space-related matters. Space activities have a significant impact on the welfare of humanity and society; it is a must that there exists clarity in the usage of outer space to enjoy beneficial impacts on society. The fact remains that the property laws were developed in association with territorial and sovereignty of a state, whereas outer space is outside any of such a state's territory, and is one of the several critical issues that need to be clarified now.

The international space law regime declares that no government can claim outer space or celestial bodies in outer space as its own. Private enterprises seeking to invest in potential space domains frequently point out that these provisions are a major barrier to the future commercial development of space. Such businesses contend that the absence of property rights prevents them from obtaining external financing, thus preventing the protection of their investments in space. The protection of intellectual property rights in outer space activities is necessary to serve and guarantee the interests of private enterprises.

In order to search for answers to the intellectual property rights in the space domain, a seminar-com-training session was held at the Indian Society of International Law on 16 May 2025. This book is an outcome of the papers presented at the seminar. I am sure this volume will be immensely useful to students, researchers and policy makers in searching for answers to the questions relating to the application of intellectual property law in outer space activities.

Prof (Dr) Manoj Kumar Sinha
President
The Indian Society of International Law,
New Delhi

15 July 2025

Preface

On September 8, 2016, the US launched a spacecraft, the Origins, Spectral Interpretation, Resource Identification, and Security-Regolith Explorer, or OSIRIS-Rex. The spacecraft travelled to a near-Earth asteroid named Bennu (formerly 1999 RQ36). It collected a sample of rocks and dust from Bennu's surface on October 20, 2020. The spacecraft delivered the sample to Earth on September 24, 2023, when it released a capsule with grains of Bennu (an estimated 8.8 ounces, or 250 gm) over Earth's atmosphere. Studies of rock and dust from asteroid Bennu have revealed molecules that, on our planet, are key to life, as well as a history of saltwater that could have served as the "broth" for these compounds to interact and combine. The findings do not show evidence for life itself, but they do suggest the conditions necessary for the emergence of life were widespread across the early solar system, increasing the odds that life could have formed on other planets and moons.[1] Later, NASA clarified that the visit to Bennu was a prelude for possible mining operations, with governments and private companies to extract water from asteroids to make rocket fuel, enabling further Space exploration.[2]

A few states have opposed the US plans for such exploration. These states pointed out that the 1967 Outer Space Treaty (OST) prohibits '*national appropriation of space assets*' and declares the exploration and use of Space to be '*the province of all humankind*'.[3] Further, why should only space-faring nations have the rights over space assets, which are '*common heritage*

1 OSIRIS-REx Mission, (NASA Science), available at: <https://science.nasa.gov/mission/osiris-rex/> accessed on 22 June 2025.

2 *A Gift from Space: UArizona-led OSIRIS-REx Mission Delivers Largest-ever Asteroid Sample to Earth*, *UArizona News* (Tucson), 24 September 2023, available at: <https://news.arizona.edu/news/gift-space-uarizona-led-osiris-rex-mission-delivers-largest-ever-asteroid-sample-earth> accessed on 22 June 2025.

3 Michael Byers and Aaron Boley, *Who Owns Outer Space? International Law, Astrophysics and the Sustainable Development of Space* (Cambridge University Press, Cambridge, 2023), p. 1.

of mankind' and national appreciation and exploration of space assets is prohibited under the existing space treaty system. And the larger question which emerges is: Who is the Owner of Outer Space and its Assets?

Physical property in outer space has been regulated under various international conventions, multilateral agreements, international principles and customary law. In addition, various soft laws such as UN General Assembly Resolutions, international commission initiatives and studies by INGOs provide states with basic guidelines to aid them in their approach to regulating physical property in space. States have framed domestic laws to regulate property rights within their territory. Rules for protecting property have to be framed considering the prevailing socio-economic-political background. Property rights under the domestic legal system typically include the rights to possess, control, develop, exclude, enjoy, sell, lease and mortgage properties.

The term "Intellectual Property" (IP) has been defined as a category of intangible rights protecting commercially valuable products of the human intellect. Intellectual property refers to creations of the mind, such as inventions; literary and artistic works; designs; and symbols, names and images used in commerce. Intellectual Property includes Copyrights, Trademarks, Patents, Trade Secrets, Industrial Designs, Geographical Indications, and Plant Variety Rights.[4] The relationship between property and IP is extremely complex, and views differ.[5] IP rights are private rights whose essential characteristic is to exclude third parties from using or

4 *Convention Establishing the World Intellectual Property Organization*, 14 July 1967, Article 2(viii), available at:<https://www.wipo.int/treaties/en/convention/> accessed on 22 June 2025. Article 2(viii) of the Convention Establishing the World Intellectual Property Organization of July 14, 1967 provides that "intellectual property" should include the rights relating to: literary, artistic and scientific works; performances of performing artists, phonograms, and broadcasts; inventions in all fields of human endeavour; scientific discoveries; industrial designs; trademarks, service marks, and commercial names and designations; protection against unfair competition; and all other rights resulting from intellectual activity in the industrial, scientific, literary or artistic fields. Thus, intellectual property covers a wide range of various creations of the human mind, which includes patent, trademarks, industrial design, copyrights and neighbouring rights.

5 Frank H. Easterbrook, "Intellectual Property is Still Property", *Harvard Journal of Law and Public Policy*, vol. 13 (1990), p. 108; Henry E. Smith, "Intellectual Property as Property: Delineating Entitlements in Information", *Yale Law Journal*, vol. 116 (2007), p. 1742; Peter S. Menell, "The Property Rights Movement's Embrace of Intellectual Property: True Love or Doomed Relationship?", *Ecology Law Quarterly*, vol. 34 (2007), p. 713; Hugh Breakey, "Two Concepts of Property: Property in Things and Ownership of Activities", *The Philosophical Forum*, vol. 42 (2011), p. 239; Kristen Carpenter, Sonia

exploiting the subject matter of IP belonging to another. IP rights are recognised internationally through a system of international treaties and organisations. The World Intellectual Property Organisation (WIPO), founded in 1967, is a specialised United Nations and administers most of the international treaties related to IP.

IP has unique characteristics and a purpose. It is built around the protection of intangible assets and their economic value. Certain key aspects of IP are as follows:

- IP is intangible creations of the mind, which include inventions, designs, and creative works. IP lacks a physical form but holds deep economic and cultural significance. For example, patented technologies, artistic compositions, and brand logos.
- IP rights confer exclusive legal rights upon creators and owners to control the use, sale, or license of their creations and also empower owners to earn financial benefits of their innovations and prevent unauthorised usage by others.
- IP rights are territorial and are enforceable within the jurisdiction where they are granted. For example, a patent registered in India is not automatically valid in other countries unless registered separately.
- IP rights are time-bound, and protection is available for a definite term, such as 20 years for patents or a creator's lifetime plus 60 years for copyrights. For example, the copyright protection for the work of Rabindranath Tagore, the Nobel Prize-winning poet, was initially held by Visva-Bharati University. It expired in December 2001. This means that his works are now in the public domain and can be freely published and used by anyone.[6]
- IP has economic value because innovation gives the edge to

Katyal and Angela Riley, "In Defence of Property", *Yale Law Journal*, vol. 118 (2009), p. 1022.

6 *The Indian Copyright Act, 1957*, Section 22; *Berne Convention for the Protection of Literary and Artistic Works*, adopted 9 September 1886 (as amended on 28 September 1979), available at: https://www.wipo.int/treaties/en/ip/berne/ accessed on 30 June 2025; *Government of India, Copyright (Amendment) Ordinance, 1991* (Ordinance No. 13 of 1991), later replaced by the *Copyright (Amendment) Act, 1992* (Act No. 13 of 1992), *Gazette of India*, Part II, Section 1, dated 12 May 1992; Ministry of Human Resource Development, *Public Notice on Expiry of Copyright in Works of Rabindranath Tagore*, Government of India, 1991.

commercial entities, enhances brand prestige, and contributes to global trade. Businesses utilise IP as a competitive edge, earning revenue through licensing, sales, or strategic partnerships.

- IP focuses on the rewarding of creativity and innovation, thereby encouraging people and businesses to invent new technologies, designs, or artistic expressions. Protecting the creation, IP encourages research and development.
- IP is dynamic and updated with the passage of technology, culture, and economic practices. The emerging areas of biotechnology and artificial intelligence (AI) have enhanced the coverage areas of IP protection.
- IP rights satisfy both private and public interests. Creators enjoy exclusive rights, and the public benefits from access to new technologies, artistic works, and cultural products. Some IPRs in the form of patents need public disclosure of technical information, as this ensures public availability and diffusion of the existing technical knowledge.
- IP may be transferred or licensed, enabling its owner to earn income by selling or granting license rights to use the IP. The licensing is a common practice in software development, music, and more technological industries. Laws on IP also protect their holders against infringement, plagiarism, or practices of counterfeiting.

The issue of IP rights and their protection is receiving more and more attention from participants in space activities. The legal status of physical property, such as spaceships and satellites in outer space, has been a recurring topic in UN agreements, proclamations of nations and intergovernmental organisations. However, there has been no international consensus on the status of intangible property, such as intellectual property, in outer space.

With the increase in patent and copyright claims to inventions or software created on the International Space Station (ISS),[7] there is a strong possibility

7 The *International Space Station (ISS)* was approved by the President of the United States in 1984. The Station was designed between 1984 and 1993 by NASA, and its elements were constructed across the United States, Canada, Japan, and Europe beginning in the late 1980s. In 1993, as the Station underwent redesign, Russia joined the partnership. The project proceeded in two phases: during Phase 1, NASA Space Shuttles carried astronauts and cosmonauts to the Russian *Mir* Orbital Station, and the United States assisted in modifying two Russian-built modules to accommodate international experiments. Phase 2, jointly led by the United States and Russia,

that, in the near future, more disputes will arise as regards IP rights in outer space. For instance, pharmaceutical companies are conducting research on the International Space Station (ISS).[8] Bristol Myers Squibb recently concluded a month-long experiment on the ISS to find out how monoclonal antibodies crystallise in microgravity, or extremely low gravity. Materials from the experiment and other space studies returned to Earth on a SpaceX spacecraft that splashed down in the Gulf of Mexico in January 2022. Astronauts with backgrounds in microbiology conducted the experiments. This research may impact future directions in drug development and manufacturing, and hopefully will provide important benefits to patients.

The Indian Air Force Officer, Group Captain Shubhanshu Shukla, was a part of the ISS Axiom-4 mission, where he completed several experiments to understand how to survive in space. His mission in June-July 2025 lasted 18 days, and a total of seven experiments, designed by Indian scientists, were conducted to study how living organisms behave and adapt in microgravity. These included studies on microalgae, seed sprouting, muscle regeneration, tardigrades (tiny resilient creatures), and human interaction with screens in zero gravity. These experiments are important

---

brought together contributions from all participating nations. The ISS is operated by five partner agencies—the *Canadian Space Agency (CSA)*, the *European Space Agency (ESA)*, the *Japan Aerospace Exploration Agency (JAXA)*, the *National Aeronautics and Space Administration (NASA)*, and the *State Space Corporation "Roscosmos"*—each responsible for the elements it provides. The Station's interdependent design relies on contributions from all partners to sustain its operations. As a collaborative scientific platform, the ISS symbolizes global unity in space exploration and serves as a hub for technological advancement and international cooperation. Although several components have exceeded their original design lifespans, regular safety assessments ensure continued habitation and operation. Modular construction allows for the periodic replacement of systems, ensuring the Station's viability as a working laboratory in orbit until at least 2030. National Aeronautics and Space Administration (NASA), International Space Station, available at: <https://www.nasa.gov/reference/international-space-station/> accessed on 22 October 2025; National Aeronautics and Space Administration (NASA), OSIRIS-REx Mission to Asteroid Bennu, available at: <https://science.nasa.gov/mission/osiris-rex/> accessed on 30 June 2025.

8 IP rights on the International Space Station (ISS) are governed by a complex, modular system based on the Intergovernmental Agreement (IGA). Each partner country retains jurisdiction over its modules, meaning national laws and courts apply to inventions created there. When an invention is a collaboration between partners, their respective IP laws must be navigated, and ownership is divided based on the agreement between the inventors. For details pertaining to *WIPO's work on patents and outer space* available at:< https://www.wipo.int/en/web/patents/topics/outer-space> accessed on 30 June 2025.

because they help scientists understand how life behaves in space, which is key for future missions to the Moon, Mars, and beyond. The findings could also lead to new solutions for health, food, and technology challenges on Earth. Shubhanshu studied the Indian strain of Tardigrades on the ISS to see how they survive, revive, reproduce, and respond to microgravity. Understanding how Tardigrades survive in space can help us develop new strategies for protecting living organisms in space missions. The study's findings could help us in (i) developing sustainable food systems for space missions, (ii) improving our understanding of plant growth in microgravity, and (iii) enhancing the nutritional health of astronauts on long-duration space missions.

There are five international treaties relevant to human activities in space. These are: (i) Treaty on Principles Governing the Activities of States in the Exploration and Use of Outer Space, including the Moon and Other Celestial Bodies, 1967.; (ii) Agreement on the Rescue of Astronauts, the Return of Astronauts and the Return of Objects Launched into Outer Space, 1968; (iii) Convention on International Liability for Damage Caused by Space Objects, 1972; (iv) Convention on Registration of Objects Launched into Outer Space, 1976; and (v) Agreement Governing the Activities of States on the Moon and Other Celestial Bodies, 1984. All of these treaties are widely accepted by the space-faring nations and most of the world, except for the Moon Agreement, which is a failure. The Outer Space Treaty establishes that the moon and other celestial bodies [are] not subject to national appropriation by claim of sovereignty, by means of use or occupation, or by any other means.

The principles governing outer space are as follows: (a) Declaration of Legal Principles Governing the Activities of States in the Exploration and Use of Outer Space, 1963; (b) Principles Governing the Use by States of Artificial Earth Satellites for International Direct Television Broadcasting, 1982; (c) Principles Relating to Remote Sensing of the Earth from Outer Space, 1986; (d) Principles Relevant to the Use of Nuclear Power Sources in Outer Space, 1992; and (e) Declaration on International Cooperation in the Exploration and Use of Outer Space for the Benefit and in the Interest of All States, Taking into Particular Account the Needs of Developing Countries, 1996. None of the above treaties contains a provision expressly dealing with intellectual property. **An explicit reference to IP rights is made in the 1996 Declaration, which provides:** "*States are free to determine all aspects of their participation in international cooperation in the exploration and use of outer space on an equitable and mutually acceptable basis. Contractual* *terms in such cooperative ventures should be fair and reasonable, and they should be in full compliance with the legitimate rights and interests of the parties concerned, as, for example, with intellectual property rights.*"[9]

In July 1999, a Workshop on IP Rights in Space was held in conjunction with the Third United Nations Conference on the Exploration and Peaceful Uses of Outer Space (UNISPACE III). It was a major intergovernmental conference for the purposes of creating a blueprint for the peaceful use of outer space in the 21st century. The recommendations made by the Workshop are as follows: (i) More attention should be paid to the protection of IP rights, in view of the growth in the commercialisation and privatisation of space-related activities. The protection and enforcement of IP rights should be considered together with the international legal principles developed by the UN in the form of treaties and declarations, such as those relating to the principle of non-appropriation of outer space, as well as other relevant international conventions. (ii) The feasibility of harmonising international IP standards and legislation in relation to IP rights in outer space should be further explored with a view to enhancing international coordination and cooperation at the level of both the State and the private sector. (iii) All States should provide appropriate protection of IP rights involving space-related technology, while encouraging and facilitating the free flow of basic science information. (iv) Educational activities concerning IP rights in relation to outer space activities should be encouraged.

Emerging fields in IP rights law are significantly shaped by advancements in technology, particularly in artificial intelligence, blockchain, and biotechnology. These fields, particularly in relation to space technology, are creating new challenges and opportunities for IPR, impacting areas like patent law, copyright, and trademark regulations. Pharmaceutical companies will very soon begin exploring more permanent ways to conduct research and development (R&D) in space, beginning on spacecraft, and eventually on the Moon and other bodies in space. They will also begin commercialising the products derived from their extra-terrestrial R&D efforts. They will seek all forms of IP protection and commercialise their products in all places where patients need medicines. A Geographical Indication (GI) tag is a label given to products that originate from a specific

9 *Declaration on International Cooperation in the Exploration and Use of Outer Space for the Benefit and in the Interest of All States, Taking into Particular Account the Needs of Developing Countries*, adopted by the United Nations Committee on the Peaceful Uses of Outer Space, 1996, Annex, para. 2.

region and are known for their unique qualities linked to that place; could a GI tag be given to products from the Moon or Mars?

These activities raise the issue of the applicable law, jurisdiction and enforcement of rights relating to IP in the space domain. For example, when companies seek to file patents covering their discoveries made in space, where should these patents be filed? What freedom to operate searches should be performed? However, there may be plans to use the trademark in space, as well as on Earth. Where should trademark protection be sought? What framework is the most efficient as a means of extending clearance and protection to brand names and related IP used in space? What sort of database should be created to track the use of trademarks in space to determine whether a mark is "available" for use and/or registration in space? Who should maintain this? Whether access to information will be free and available to every individual citizen worldwide? Since the existing regime for IP is relatively mature, a connecting point can be created to link outer space with the current IP regime.

The increasing involvement of private entities in the space domain provides impetus for states to provide a favourable legal environment for IP protection. It is important to examine whether the territorial nature of intellectual property can reconcile with the non-territorial nature of outer space. Keeping these issues in mind, a One Day Seminar (Online) on "*IP Laws and Space Laws: Emerging Frontiers of Innovation and Regulation*" was organised on 16 May 2025 by the Centre for Advanced Studies in Intellectual Property and Technology Law, ISIL.

The space economy is operating in a much different context today than what was ten years back. Today, more than 90 countries and scores of private companies are engaged in space activities.[10] Space-based systems support a large part of critical infrastructure and services such as transportation,

10 China has made sizable progress, outpacing Russia as the main competitor to the United States. Beijing aims to be the world's leading space power by the mid-2040s and has integrated its space activities in the army structure. China is planning to build a permanent research station on the lunar south pole and a solar power station in space. China and Russia are increasingly teaming up in space projects. India has shown the capability to perform low-cost missions, including the successful landing on the Moon in August 2023, making it the fourth country to achieve this. South Korea has a relatively recent space history, but aims to rank among the world's top five space powers by 2045. The United Arab Emirates (UAE) and Saudi Arabia have revealed ambitious space policies; the UAE aims to establish the first inhabitable human settlement on Mars by 2117. For details pertaining to "Asia's skyrocketing space race: A competition for peace?" (European Parliamentary Research Service Briefing, 2024) available at:

energy, water, food supply, communications and law enforcement. In due course of time, the importance of IP rights in outer space will increasingly become more prominent. Proactively addressing these issues will ensure that space exploration and commercialisation proceed smoothly, fostering innovation and economic growth. Hopefully, the issues brought out in this book, containing 17 chapters, will be helpful in safeguarding the interests of inventors and companies, encouraging further investment in space technologies in line with the principles established by the 1967 Outer Space Treaty.

The editor is grateful to Prof (Dr) Manoj Kumar Sinha, President, the Indian Society of International Law, New Delhi, for writing the Foreword for this book; and to Prof V G Hegde, Executive President, the Indian Society of International Law, for his constant encouragement. The Editor also expresses sincere gratitude to Wg Cdr (Dr) U C Jha, Secretary General, the Indian Society of International Law, for his valuable inputs to this book.

The editor thanks M/s Vij Books, New Delhi, for bringing out this edition.

15 July 2025
New Delhi

Dr Parineet Kaur
Assistant Professor

<https://www.europarl.europa.eu/ RegData/etudes/BRIE/2024 /762460/EPRS_BRI(2024)762460_EN.pdf>accessed on 30 June 2025.

Contributors

M V Chandramathi has done her LLM in International Law from Osmania University. She has done her Doctorate in Philosophy from the prestigious NALSAR University of Law. She has also contributed through her research articles published nationally and internationally, and received best paper awards too. Received Bharat ke Anmol in the year 2025. At present settled as Principal in a Law College.

Aishwarya Anand completed her Bachelor of Science in Life Sciences from Daulat Ram College, University of Delhi and obtained a Master of Science in Environmental Science from Nalanda Open University. She further pursued a Bachelor of Laws (LL.B. Hons.) from Banaras Hindu University. She completed a Master of Laws (LL.M.) in Intellectual Property Law at the National Law University, Delhi, as part of a joint LL.M. program offered in association with WIPO and CGPDTM, completed in July 2025.

Akshat Chopra is a Doctoral Researcher and UGC Junior Research Fellow at the Indian Law Institute, New Delhi. His research interests span constitutional and comparative public law, criminal justice, and emerging legal domains. He is actively involved in academic research, legal pedagogy, and interdisciplinary initiatives within the scholarly community.

Ajay Revansidha Tambulkar has secured a Master's in International Law and Human Rights from the Department of Law, Savitribai Phule Pune University, India. Presently, he is pursuing Doctoral research in International Space Law from the University of Delhi. He is serving as a faculty member at Army Law College, Pune, under Savitribai Phule Pune University. He has read, researched, published and delivered academic services in the domains of Constitutional Law, Jurisprudence, Research Methodology and Competence Development, International Law and its branches, like International Air, Space and Sea Law, International Economic Law, Humanitarian and Refugee Law, etc. He is associated with various academic and professional institutions in an inter-disciplinary manner, like, India Chapter of AI and Space Law Society, the Netherlands, Visiting Lecturer of the Indian Society of International Law, etc.

Amarendra Kumar is an Assistant Professor (Senior Scale) in Law Centre-II, Faculty of Law, University of Delhi, Delhi, India, since February 2018. Prior to this, he had been an Assistant Professor (Guest) at Campus Law Centre (CLC), Faculty of Law, University of Delhi, Delhi, India in the year 2017-18. He has been awarded with Ph.D. and M.Phil. Degrees from Centre for International Legal Studies (CILS), School of International Studies (SIS), Jawaharlal Nehru University (JNU), New Delhi, India. He has completed LL.M. Degree from the University School of Law and Legal Studies (USLLS), GGS Indraprastha University, Delhi, India; M.B.L. Degree from Professional and Continuing Education (PACE), National Law School of India University (NLSIU), Bengaluru, India, and LL.B. Degree from Law Centre-I, Faculty of Law, University of Delhi, Delhi, India.

Lakshmi Haritha Nakka is ***a*** Research Scholar of Dr. B.R. Ambedkar College of Law (South Campus) Andhra University, Visakhapatnam and is working as a Guest Faculty in Dr. B.R. Ambedkar College of Law; Lecturer in NBM Law College, Visakhapatnam, Affiliated to Andhra University for the past 3 years. She qualified APSET in 2019, and practised as an Advocate in the Visakhapatnam District Bar Association. Her papers were accepted in Scopus-indexed journals, and her articles were published in Web of Science-indexed book journal and other peer-reviewed journals, and she presented her papers in various International Conference and Seminars.

Pawan Kumar teaches at Amity Law School, Amity University, Noida. His major research area is international law and public law. He is on the editorial board of Chanakya Law Review, the International Institute of Justice and Police Sciences Journal and has published in Cambridge University Press, the Indian Journal of International Law, Indian Law Review, Kathmandu School of Law Review, CNLU Law Journal, Sri Lanka Journal of Legal Studies, and AALCO Journal of International Law.

Simar Kumar is an Advocate at Lume Legal, where she primarily focuses on Intellectual Property Rights and International Law. Her work reflects a deep engagement with the evolving intersections of law, technology, and global governance. Through her research and practice, she seeks to contribute to developing nuanced legal frameworks that address emerging challenges in these domains.

Ancy P Anto is an Assistant Professor and Research Scholar at Alliance School of Law, Alliance University, Bengaluru, and specialises in Space Law and teaching International Law, Property Law, and Intellectual Property Law. Her academic and research interests lie in public international law and emerging legal regimes shaping contemporary global governance.

Abhishek Thommandru *is* Ph.D. (Law), and specialises in FinTech Legal Mechanisms, teaching Technological, Business, and Banking Laws. He is a Research Fellow at URD Iran and TSUL Uzbekistan, with credentials from Aristotle University, DSNLU, Andhra University, and VIT-AP University (2023). His research centres on Anti-Money Laundering in India.

Animesh Pratap Singh is a JRF and PhD Scholar at Dr. RMLNLU, Lucknow. Prior to this he was an Assistant Professor at Law School of Kanpur University and has done his LLM from NALSAR, Hyderabad. His research interests lie in IPR, and Law and Technology.

Anand Kumar Singh is a doctoral scholar currently enrolled at Dr Ram Manohar Lohia National Law University, Lucknow. His area of expertise is International Trade Law. Currently, his research is aimed at studying the implications of use of trade remedial measures on overall global trade.

Lini Priya Vasavan is an Associate Professor of Law at Government Law College, Thrissur, under the Department of Higher Education, Government of Kerala. With over 14 years of teaching experience across fifteen law subjects, she specialises in Constitutional Law and Criminal Law. [He/She/They] has published nine research papers, a book chapter, and a policy paper for the Government of Kerala. She is also a Member of the Kerala State Legal Services Authority (KELSA) and serves on the Board of Studies, University of Calicut.

Saumya Tripathi, a Ph.D. Scholar at the Indian Law Institute, New Delhi, serves as Associate Editor of the Indian Law Institute Law Review. Specialising in Criminal and Security Law, her research spans Women's, Cyber, and Child Law. She has published and presented papers at national and international seminars.

Shreeni Jaiswal is a BA LL B (Integrated) student at Banasthali Vidyapith with strong academic and research engagement in contemporary legal issues. She focuses on international law, human rights, and global governance, with experience in an internship at the ISIL and coordinating legal aid initiatives.

***Shivangi Trivedi* is a** BA LL B (Integrated) student at Banasthali Vidyapith with strong academic and research engagement in contemporary legal issues. Her interests include corporate law, arbitration, competition law, and emerging developments in space law, strengthened through internships at the Department of Legal Affairs and the Rajasthan High Court. She actively participated in moot courts, debates, and community legal awareness programs.

Neha Singh is an Assistant Professor of Law, Galgotias University and a Doctoral Researcher at Banaras Hindu University, specialising in Space Law and Intellectual Property Rights. A graduate of NUJS Kolkata and UPES Dehradun, she has published on AI, digital rights, and IPR in reputed journals and presented papers internationally on AI regulation and outer space law.

Shivang Tripathi is an Assistant Professor of Law at Bennett University, pursuing his PhD at Banaras Hindu University. A former advocate at the Allahabad High Court, he specialises in IPR and Constitutional law, with numerous publications in peer-reviewed journals on AI, digital rights, and space law.

Yasser Shabir Chowdhary is an Advocate at the Delhi High Court, specialising in Intellectual Property, Corporate, and International Human Rights Law. He holds a B.Sc. from the University of Jammu and an LL.B from the Faculty of Law, University of Delhi. Hailing from a tribal background in Jammu and Kashmir, he is devoted to advancing marginalised communities through legal and literary work.

Abhishek Mohanpuria is an Advocate practising at the Delhi High Court with expertise in Intellectual Property Law, Technology Law, and Securities Law. He holds a BBA LL B and is also experienced in Legislative Drafting and Research. He has also built a strong reputation for his initiatives supporting accessibility for persons with disabilities and promoting education.

Sakshi is currently pursuing her LLM in International Law at the South Asian University, New Delhi. Her primary research interests lie in Outer Space Law and Intellectual Property Rights (IPR). She holds a Bachelor of Laws (LLB) degree from the Campus Law Centre, University of Delhi. Sakshi has also gained practical experience as an Associate at Jeta Legal, a law firm based in New Delhi, and as an intern at the Asian-African Legal Consultative Organisation (AALCO) and the Indian Society of International Law (ISIL).

Modi Umangkumar Champaklal is an Assistant Professor of Law at The Maharaja Sayajirao University of Baroda. His research spans intellectual property, space law, data protection, and constitutional governance. He has advised policy initiatives, published widely, and mentors students on interdisciplinary legal research bridging technology, rights, and regulation in India and beyond, globally.

Saneh Kumari, a Research Scholar at the Indian Law Institute (ILI), is a Gold Medallist in LL.M. Her research portfolio critically examines core areas including national security, juvenile justice and contemporary issues in criminal law, with several paper presentations and publications.

Hritwik Ravi is a Research Scholar at the Indian Law Institute with a strong focus on criminal law and contemporary legal issues. His research covers national security, election laws, juvenile justice, POCSO, and the Indian Knowledge System, with several publications and conference presentations contributing to academic discourse.

Ranjini B.V. holds a BA LLB and an LLM in Intellectual Property Rights, and is NET qualified. She is currently pursuing her PhD at the Tamil Nadu Dr Ambedkar Law University (TNDALU). Ranjini is an Assistant Professor at the Crescent School of Law, Chennai.

Part I

Conceptual and Theoretical Foundations

Chapter 1

Conceptual Framework of Outer Space Law and Intellectual Property Rights

---

-M. V. Chandramathi

Abstract

The intersection of outer space activities and intellectual property law marks a new legal frontier. Outer space was once the domain of governments alone is now increasingly commercialised by private companies like SpaceX, Virgin Galactic, and Blue Origin. This shift presents serious legal questions about the ownership and protection of inventions made or used in space. Existing space treaties, including the Outer Space Treaty, 1967, and the Moon Agreement, 1979, emphasise the idea of space as a common heritage of mankind. However, intellectual property rights by nature demand territorial exclusivity and ownership, which directly conflict with outer space governance frameworks. This research paper aims to examine and compare national frameworks like those of the United States and India with international space law instruments. It identifies gaps where current regimes fail to protect innovations adequately while maintaining international cooperation ideals. The paper analyses how national laws like the U.S. Patents in Space Act try to extend patent law into extra-terrestrial domains, and how emerging Indian space policies approach similar issues. Challenges in enforcement, ownership over inventions in multinational missions, and a lack of a uniform legal standard make the current system fragmented and uncertain. Using a doctrinal research methodology, the study draws from treaties, national statutes, scholarly articles, and relevant judicial decisions. It also considers solutions proposed by institutions such as WIPO and INTA. The paper ultimately argues for the creation of a harmonised international legal framework that balances the protection of private innovation with the principle of outer space as the common province of humanity. Without such reforms, legal uncertainties will hinder technological advancement and equitable exploration of outer space resources.

Key Words: Outer Space Law, Intellectual Property Rights, International Frameworks, Indian Space Law, Commercialisation.

Introduction

Space activities historically began under exclusive state control after the launch of Sputnik-I in 1957.[1] The race intensified with subsequent missions by the USA, USSR, and China. However, the twenty-first century saw private companies like Virgin Galactic and SpaceX entering outer space.[2] The growing involvement of the private players necessitated robust intellectual property protection to foster investments. Intellectual property law, traditionally, protects rights within territorial boundaries.[3] Outer space, declared res communis under the Outer Space Treaty, exists beyond any national sovereignty.[4] This extraterritorial nature creates friction between the intellectual property law's foundation of territoriality and the universal character of space law.[5] Consequently, states, corporations, and international organisations struggle to balance private rights with collective heritage principles enshrined in treaties like the Moon Agreement of the 1979.[6] Collaborative international missions such as the International Space Station (ISS) further complicate ownership rights, especially over inventions made jointly in orbit.[7] This convergence of the laws demands

1 KD Raju, "Issues in Protection of the Intellectual Property Created in Outer Space: An Indian Outlook", Current Developments in Air and Space Law, p. 224.

2 Jewel Ali, "From Earth to Orbit: Converging Space Law and Intellectual Property Rights to Safeguard Innovation beyond Earth", *International Journal of the Legal Science and Innovation,* vol. 6, issue 5 (2024), p. 210.

3 WIPO, "Intellectual Property and Space Activities", Issue Paper (April 2004), p. 2.

4 Outer Space Treaty, 1967, Art. II.

5 KP Abitha, "Intellectual property and outer space: The need of the international harmonized legal framework", International Journal of the Law, vol. 6, issue 1 (2020), p. 1.

6 Agreement Governing Activities of the States on Moon and Other Celestial Bodies, 1979, Art. 11.

7 INTA, "IP in Space", Report (2022), p. 9.

critical analysis to protect innovations without violating the principle that space belongs to humanity as a whole.[8]

There exists a stark legal vacuum concerning intellectual property protection in outer space.[9] Most space treaties, including the Outer Space Treaty and the Moon Agreement, avoid addressing IPRs explicitly. National laws, such as U.S. Patents in Space Act, attempt to extend patent jurisdiction into space. However, such extensions create jurisdictional overlaps, uncertainties, and potential diplomatic tensions.[10] Inventions made in space, particularly on multinational platforms like ISS, lack clear rules about patent ownership.[11] The absence of international IP enforcement frameworks further exacerbates risks, discouraging innovation and investments in space technologies. Thus, a comprehensive harmonised mechanism for securing intellectual property rights in space remains a pressing need for the global community.[12]

Case laws are cited where applicable, and a critical analytical approach is adopted. The research triangulates international instruments, national statutes, and judicial trends to frame coherent analysis and propose viable solutions.[13]

Understanding Outer Space: Definition and Characteristics

Outer space remains officially undefined under international treaties or national law frameworks.[14] Scholars and organisations loosely agree it begins beyond Kármán Line, approximately 100 kilometres above sea level.[15] No nation can claim sovereignty over any part of outer space

8 RiteshMehra, "Intellectual Property Protection in Outer Space – An Overview", *ILI Law Review*, vol. II (2019), p. 145.

9 WIPO, "Intellectual Property and Space Activities", supra, p. 4.

10 United States Patents in Space Act, 1990, Sec. 105.

11 INTA, "IP in Space", supra, p. 17.

12 Jewel Ali, "From Earth to Orbit", supra, p. 212.

13 INTA, "IP in Space", supra, Appendix II.

14 KD Raju, "Issues in Protection of the Intellectual Property Created in Outer Space: An Indian Outlook", Current Developments in Air and Space Law, p. 224.

15 Jewel Ali, "From Earth to Orbit: Converging Space Law and Intellectual Property Rights to Safeguard Innovation beyond Earth", *International Journal of the Legal Science and Innovation*, vol. 6, issue 5 (2024), p. 211.

according to Article II of the Outer Space Treaty.[16] This principle mirrors the maritime concept of the *res communis*, barring occupation or ownership. Outer space has been declared "province of the all mankind," ensuring exploration benefits all humanity equally.[17] Resources discovered on celestial bodies are intended to serve global interests rather than national profits. Thus, unlike territorial domains governed by sovereignty, outer space embraces collective ownership of humankind, without partition, sale, or appropriation.[18]

Principles of the Outer Space Law

The Outer Space Treaty, 1967, sets fundamental norms for outer space activities. It prohibits national appropriation and demands that activities benefit all countries.[19] Article I establishes freedom of exploration; Article II forbids claims of sovereignty; Article III subjects activities to international law standards.[20] The Treaty requires that states bear responsibility for national activities in space, whether governmental or private, under Article VI.[21] Liability for damage caused by space objects is outlined under Article VII, emphasising peaceful use and accountability. The Moon Agreement, 1979, extends OST principles to Moon and other celestial bodies.[22] It declares Moon's resources "common heritage of the mankind" under Article 11. No ownership or sovereignty claims are permitted. However, very few states have ratified the Moon Agreement. Major space powers like USA, Russia, and China have declined, limiting its enforceability.[23]

---

16 Treaty on Principles Governing Activities of the States in Exploration and Use of the Outer Space, Including Moon and Other Celestial Bodies, 1967, Art. II.

17 Ibid., Art. I.

18 KP Abitha, "Intellectual Property and Outer Space: The Need of the International Harmonized Legal Framework", *International Journal of the Law*, vol. 6, issue 1 (2020), p. 2.

19 Outer Space Treaty, 1967, supra, Art. I.

20 Ibid., Art. III.

21 Ibid., Art. VI.

22 Agreement Governing Activities of the States on Moon and Other Celestial Bodies, 1979, Art. 11.

23 Ritesh Mehra, "Intellectual Property Protection in Outer Space – An Overview", *ILI Law Review*, vol. II (2019), p. 145.

Intellectual Property Rights (IPR): Basic Concepts

1. Patents grant exclusive rights to inventors to make, use, and sell inventions for fixed term.[24] In space context, patents protect technological advancements like spacecraft components, satellite designs, and propulsion systems.
2. Copyrights safeguard creative expressions, including technical manuals, scientific software, and satellite imagery.[25] Satellite data, if sufficiently original, may attract copyright protection under national laws.
3. Trademarks identify commercial origin, protecting logos, mission names, and services in outer space commerce, like "SpaceX" or "Blue Origin".[26] Trademarks build branding essential for space tourism industry.
4. Trade secrets protect confidential technical know-how, manufacturing processes, or mission-critical data from public disclosure.[27] In space activities, trade secrets maintain competitive advantages, particularly where patents are too risky to disclose.

Challenges in Applying IP Law to Outer Space

Intellectual property rights have traditionally been territorial, enforceable only within a nation's jurisdiction.[28] Each country grants, administers, and enforces rights independently through its domestic legal machinery. Outer space, by contrast, is an extraterritorial domain where no state exercises sovereignty.[29] Enforcing territorial IP laws over activities conducted in outer space becomes legally ambiguous and technically difficult. Ownership of the inventions created aboard multinational platforms like the International Space Station involves complex jurisdictional issues.[30] The ISS uses an Intergovernmental Agreement allocating patent jurisdiction based on the module where invention occurs. Moreover, infringement actions under national patent laws may fail because activity happens outside enforcing

24 WIPO, "Intellectual Property and Space Activities", Issue Paper (April 2004), p. 2.

25 Ibid.

26 INTA, *"IP in Space"*, Report (2022), p. 14.

27 Ibid., p. 17.

28 Prashanti Upadhyay, "A Comparative Study of the Intellectual Property Rights Issues in Space Activities in U.S.A., Canada and India", p. 3.

29 Outer Space Treaty, 1967, supra, Art. II.

30 INTA, "IP in Space", supra, Appendix II.

state's territorial scope.[31] The territoriality principle clashes with shared ownership regime envisioned under space treaties.

International Legal Framework for Outer Space IP Protection

Space Treaties and IP Implications

The Outer Space Treaty, 1967 (OST) remains the cornerstone of space governance. It mandates that space must benefit all mankind, prohibits national sovereignty, and prescribes peaceful exploration.[32] However, it leaves intellectual property protection almost entirely un-addressed. The Moon Agreement, 1979, extends principles of the OST. It introduces the concept of the Moon and its resources as "common heritage of the mankind".[33] However, major space-faring nations like United States, Russia, and China have not ratified it, limiting its effectiveness. The Rescue Agreement, 1968, deals with return of the astronauts and space objects. It implies that technological objects recovered must respect IP rights of the ownership states, although it does not explicitly mention intellectual property.[34]The Liability Convention, 1972 elaborates state responsibility for damages caused by space objects. While it focuses on physical damages, infringements related to proprietary technologies carried on-board remain ambiguous.[35]The Registration Convention, 1976 requires states to maintain registry of the objects launched into space. It indirectly influences IP rights by connecting space objects with launching states' jurisdictions for regulatory purposes.[36]

WIPO's Role and Initiatives

The World Intellectual Property Organisation (WIPO) recognised early rising intersection between IP and space activities. Its 2004 Issue Paper

31 WIPO, "Intellectual Property and Space Activities", supra, p. 5.

32 Treaty on Principles Governing Activities of the States in Exploration and Use of the Outer Space, 1967, Art.I and II.

33 Agreement Governing Activities of the States on Moon and Other Celestial Bodies, 1979, Art. 11.

34 Agreement on Rescue of the Astronauts ,Return of the Astronauts and Return of the Objects Launched into Outer Space, 1968, Art. 5.

35 Convention on International Liability for Damage Caused by Space Objects, 1972, Art. II and III.

36 Convention on Registration of the Objects Launched into Outer Space, 1976, Art.II.

on "Intellectual Property and Space Activities" outlined unique challenges posed by extraterritorial activities.[37] WIPO emphasised the critical importance of adapting existing IP regimes to cover inventions, trademarks, and copyrights generated during space missions. It urged that traditional territorial IP models must evolve. WIPO promotes using international mechanisms like the Patent Cooperation Treaty (PCT) and Madrid System for trademarks to register IP rights across multiple jurisdictions.[38] WIPO also linked TRIPS Agreement to space IP issues, pointing out that TRIPS-mandated protections must extend into domains like Low Earth Orbit, Lunar bases, and inter-planetary missions, demanding international cooperation.[39]

INTA's 2022 Report Recommendations

The International Trademark Association (INTA) in its 2022 "IP in Space" report took a pioneering step. It recommended creation of the Outer Space Intellectual Property Office (OSIPO).[40] This body would administer registrations and resolve disputes relating to IP created or used beyond Earth. The report proposed" quasi-territorial" approach where space objects registered by a particular country could become proxies for jurisdiction in IP matters.[41]It also advocated for Outer Space Treaty Version 2.0, updating 1967 OST to directly address intellectual property, commercialisation, enforcement mechanisms, and harmonised dispute resolution pathways for space ventures.[42] Importantly, INTA underscored that practical, incremental steps towards space IP governance must precede ultimate adoption of the comprehensive treaties. Private contracts between entities must initially bridge gap.

Emerging International Mechanisms

Arbitration and alternative dispute resolution (ADR) models are gaining traction for space-related IP disputes. WIPO's Arbitration and Mediation Centre provides customised mechanisms for cross-border IP disputes, including potential disputes arising from inventions created in

37 WIPO, "Intellectual Property and Space Activities", Issue Paper (April 2004), p. 2.

38 WIPO, "Intellectual Property and Space Activities", supra, p. 5.

39 WIPO, "Intellectual Property and Space Activities", supra, p. 6.

40 INTA, "IP in Space", Report (2022), p. 9.

41 Ibid., p. 10.

42 Ibid., p. 17.

space missions.[43] The UNIDROIT Space Protocol attempts to develop a framework for financing and asset-based protection of the space property, albeit more focused on physical assets rather than intellectual assets.[44]New private initiatives propose establishing specialised space arbitration tribunals, based on virtual hearings, to manage disputes arising from cross-jurisdictional collaborations in outer space projects.[45]The future trajectory lies in combining treaty-based obligations with efficient, adaptable, and internationally neutral private dispute settlement frameworks.

National approaches to IP protection in outer space

United States

The U.S. Patents in Space Act, 1990 explicitly extends American patent law into outer space activities.[46] It considers inventions made, used, or sold in outer space aboard U.S.-registered space objects as being made within U.S. territory.[47] This approach allows American patent holders to enforce their rights even for extraterrestrial inventions without needing additional treaties. However, where space objects are registered under foreign states or governed by international agreements, Act's reach is limited.[48] In such cases, jurisdictional conflicts may arise unless there is prior agreement between states concerned. NASA's IP Management Policies support a strong pro-patentee framework. NASA's New Technology Reporting System requires contractors and grantees to disclose inventions promptly.[49] NASA retains non-exclusive, irrevocable license to use such inventions for governmental purposes without payment. NASA actively licenses its patented technologies under Technology Transfer Program, enabling commercial space industries to flourish while maintaining innovation

43 WIPO Arbitration and Mediation Center, "Arbitration Rules", available at: <https://www.wipo.int/amc/en/arbitration/rules/> accessed 23 April 2025.

44 UNIDROIT, "Space Protocol toCape Town Convention", available at: <https://www.unidroit.org/instruments/security-interests/space-protocol/> accessed 23 April 2025.

45 INTA, "IP in Space", supra, Appendix II.

46 United States Patents in Space Act, 1990, Public Law 101–580, 104 Stat. 2863.

47 Ibid., Sec. 105.

48 WIPO, "Intellectual Property and Space Activities", Issue Paper (April 2004), p. 7.

49 NASA New Technology Reporting System, 14 CFR § 1245.

incentives.[50] IP rights thus form critical pillar of the NASA's public-private collaboration model.

Canada

The Canadian Space Agency (CSA) promotes international collaboration in space exploration and research. However, Canada lacks legislation equivalent to U.S. Patents in Space Act.[51] Instead, Canada uses co-operative agreements to ensure clarity regarding ownership of the intellectual property generated in space missions. Under CSA contracts, ownership of the IP arising from Canadian space projects is often retained by contractor, subject to a license in favour of the Government of the Canada.[52] This encourages private innovation while safeguarding public interests. Canada's Remote Sensing Space Systems Act, 2005 regulates satellite imaging data. It mandates licensing, security controls, and ownership conditions for remote sensing systems.[53] However, it does not create new IP rights but ensures national security and responsible data dissemination. The Act indirectly influences IP protection by ensuring that distribution and use of the satellite data respect licensing and confidentiality restrictions.[54]

India

The Indian Space Research Organisation (ISRO) encourages patenting of the indigenous technologies and protects its intellectual property assets through internal policies.[55] ISRO's Technology Transfer and Industry Collaboration (TTIC) unit oversees licensing agreements and commercial partnerships. ISRO retains rights to inventions made by its scientists and contractors unless specific agreements provide otherwise. However, enforcement and regulatory frameworks for space-related IP remain fragmented. The draft Indian Space Activities Bill, 2017 proposes establishing licensing mechanism for private sector participation in

50 NASA Technology Transfer Program, Technology Transfer Portal, available at: <https://technology.nasa.gov> accessed 23 April 2025.

51 Prashanti Upadhyay, "A Comparative Study of the Intellectual Property Rights Issues in Space Activities in U.S.A., Canada and India", p. 5.

52 Canadian Space Agency, "IP Management Framework for Space Collaborations", CSA Official Policy Document (2020).

53 Remote Sensing Space Systems Act, 2005 (Canada), S.C. 2005, c. 45.

54 Ibid., Sections 7-12.

55 ISRO, "*Technology Transfer and Industry Collaboration Manual*", ISRO Headquarters, Bengaluru, 2021 Edition.

space activities.[56] Clause 15 of the Bill envisages regulatory framework to safeguard proprietary rights over inventions made during licensed operations. However, Bill remains pending, and India currently lacks specialised space IP legislation comparable to U.S. or Canada's focused policies. Inventions made in space are governed under Patents Act, 1970, and general copyright laws without space-specific modifications.[57] This absence of the dedicated legal framework creates uncertainty for private space start-ups seeking IP protection for inventions created in orbit or on future Indian-operated stations.[58]

Key Issues and Comparative Analysis

Jurisdiction and Enforcement Problems

Intellectual property rights are territorial by nature, confined within state's legal boundaries.[59] Outer space law, particularly OST, rejects sovereign appropriation and extends no territorial jurisdiction over space.[60]This divergence between terrestrial IP frameworks and extraterritorial character of the outer space activities creates enforcement gaps.[61] Courts may decline to adjudicate IP infringements occurring on foreign-registered space objects or multinational platforms. Jurisdictional ambiguities persist when inventions originate aboard structures like International Space Station where multiple nations exercise partial jurisdiction under separate agreements.[62] The INTA 2022 Report proposed resolving conflicts by assigning jurisdiction based on registry of the launching state, offering practical solution for IP enforcement in space missions.[63]

56 Draft Indian Space Activities Bill, 2017, Clause 15, Ministry of the Space, Government of the India.

57 The Patents Act, 1970 (India), Section 48; Copyright Act, 1957 (India), Section 13.

58 KD Raju, "Issues in Protection of the Intellectual Property Created in Outer Space: An Indian Outlook", Current Developments in Air and Space Law, p. 226.

59 WIPO, "Intellectual Property and Space Activities", Issue Paper (April 2004), p. 2.

60 Treaty on Principles Governing Activities of the States in Exploration and Use of the Outer Space, 1967, Art.II.

61 KD Raju, "Issues in Protection of the Intellectual Property Created in Outer Space: An Indian Outlook", Current Developments in Air and Space Law, p. 225.

62 INTA, "IP in Space", Report (2022), Appendix II.

63 INTA, "IP in Space", supra, p. 17.

Ownership and Licensing Challenges

Ownership rights over inventions made during collaborative space missions are complex and unclear.[64] The OST mandates international cooperation but offers no blueprint on apportionment of the intellectual property arising from joint ventures.[65] ISS operations follow Intergovernmental Agreement, allocating IP rights based on nationality of the inventor or module used.[66] However, conflicts still emerge when multiple parties from different jurisdictions contribute to single invention. Without pre-negotiated licensing agreements, disputes over usage rights, royalties, and commercial exploitation frequently arise.[67] The lack of the uniform licensing standards increases risks for private entities investing in multinational space collaborations.

Patentability of the Space Inventions

Space inventions must satisfy universal patentability criteria: novelty, inventive step (non-obviousness), and industrial application.[68] Novelty demands that invention must be new globally, not merely on Earth. Non-obviousness remains challenging where microgravity-induced phenomena, although predictable, create marginal technical advantages.[69] Questions arise whether such advances merit patents under TRIPS Agreement standards. Industrial application requires functionality, but space-specific inventions often find limited utility on Earth. Different jurisdictions interpret industrial applicability diversely, affecting cross-border protection of the space technologies.[70] The US Patents in Space Act addresses these issues partly by deeming inventions aboard US space objects as occurring within US jurisdiction, thus satisfying domestic patent filing standards.[71]

64 Jewel Ali, "From Earth to Orbit: Converging Space Law and Intellectual Property Rights to Safeguard Innovation beyond Earth", International Journal of the Legal Science and Innovation, vol. 6, issue 5 (2024), p. 213.

65 Outer Space Treaty, 1967, Art. I.

66 Intergovernmental Agreement on International Space Station, 1998, Art. 21.

67 WIPO Arbitration and Mediation Center, "Contract Clauses for Collaborative R&D Projects", available at: <https://www.wipo.int/amc/en/> accessed 23 April 2025.

68 TRIPS Agreement, 1994, Art. 27.

69 Prashanti Upadhyay, "A Comparative Study of the Intellectual Property Rights Issues in Space Activities in U.S.A., Canada and India", p. 6.

70 Ibid.

71 United States Patents in Space Act, 1990, Public Law 101–580, Sec. 105.

Copyright in Remote Sensing and Space Data

Satellite imagery and remote sensing data trigger complicated copyright and database protection concerns.[72] Copyright law generally protects original compilations like thematic satellite maps, but raw remote sensing data often lacks originality. The WIPO Issue Paper noted that originality criteria must evolve where automated systems produce massive datasets without direct human authorship.[73] Canada's Remote Sensing Space Systems Act ensures that security, licensing, and data usage policies apply, although it does not itself create new IP rights over data.[74]In India, copyright protection under Copyright Act, 1957 extends to original works but lacks space-specific adaptations, leading to uncertainties over remote sensing materials' protectability.[75]

Trade Secrets and Confidentiality in Space Research

Trade secrets play vital role in protecting valuable technical knowledge developed during space missions. Unlike patents, trade secrets do not require public disclosure.[76] Multinational collaborations complicate trade secret protection as participating entities must trust each other's confidentiality commitments across different legal systems. Without binding confidentiality agreements, critical know-how shared between parties may leak, causing irreparable harm to innovation strategies.[77] WIPO Arbitration and Mediation Center's model clauses for space collaborations recommend specific confidentiality clauses embedded in contracts to mitigate such risks.[78]

72 INTA, "IP in Space", supra, p. 14.

73 WIPO, "Intellectual Property and Space Activities", supra, p. 6.

74 Remote Sensing Space Systems Act, 2005 (Canada), Sections 7-12.

75 The Copyright Act, 1957 (India), Section 13.

76 WIPO Arbitration and Mediation Center, "Protection of the Trade Secrets", available at: <https://www.wipo.int/amc/en/> accessed 23 April 2025.

77 Ibid.

78 Ibid.

Gaps, Challenges, and Emerging Trends

Absence of a Uniform Definition of the "Space Object" and "Space Activity"

International treaties fail to define "space object" and "space activity" clearly and uniformly.[79] The OST broadly mentions "space objects" but without establishing technical parameters for classification.[80]Different nations interpret "space activity" variably, complicating regulatory control and IP allocation.[81] The Moon Agreement defines space activities partially, but its limited adoption weakens uniformity.[82]Emerging technologies like small satellites and autonomous space vehicles further stretch traditional definitions.[83] Absence of the clarity hinders IP enforcement, jurisdiction assignment, and liability assessment in transnational collaborations.

Lack of the Harmonisation in National Laws

National laws governing IP protection in space differ significantly between countries.[84] The U.S. Patents in Space Act extends territoriality to U.S.-registered space objects, but no similar laws exist in most nations.[85] India relies on Patents Act, 1970, which does not address outer space inventions separately.[86] Canada uses contractual licensing under CSA policies without statutory extension into space.[87] This lack of the harmonization causes uncertainties over applicable laws, enforcement rights, and recognition of the IP titles across jurisdictions.[88] Private space entities face risks of the non-recognition and forum shopping.

79 Outer Space Treaty, 1967, Art.I and II.

80 Ibid., Art. VIII.

81 KD Raju, "Issues in Protection of the Intellectual Property Created in Outer Space: An Indian Outlook", Current Developments in Air and Space Law, p. 225.

82 Agreement Governing Activities of the States on Moon and Other Celestial Bodies, 1979, Art. 1.

83 INTA, "IP in Space", Report (2022), p. 9.

84 WIPO, "Intellectual Property and Space Activities", Issue Paper (April 2004), p. 5.

85 United States Patents in Space Act, 1990, Sec. 105.

86 The Patents Act, 1970 (India), Sec. 2(1)(j).

87 Canadian Space Agency, "IP Management Framework", 2020.

88 Prashanti Upadhyay, "A Comparative Study of the Intellectual Property Rights Issues in Space Activities in U.S.A., Canada and India", p. 6.

Technological and Commercial Developments: New Threats to IP

Rapid technological innovations introduce new threats to space IP protection frameworks. Artificial intelligence-driven space inventions challenge traditional inventorship criteria.[89] Commercialisation of the lunar mining, asteroid resource extraction, and orbital manufacturing raises IP ownership dilemmas.[90] Blockchain technology, used for satellite data authentication, demands new forms of the copyright and database rights.[91]Failure to update legal systems risks leaving innovative space enterprises unprotected, thus discouraging investments and technology diffusion.

Privatisation, Commercialisation, and Need for New Governance Mechanisms

Space activities are shifting rapidly from state-centric to private-commercial operations.[92] SpaceX, Blue Origin, and Virgin Galactic exemplify private leadership in space missions and tourism ventures. Existing treaties designed for government actors poorly address privatisation-driven IP issues.[93] The OST principles of the non-appropriation and peaceful use complicate commercial exploitation.[94]Thus, new governance mechanisms must balance public interests with private innovation incentives. Legal vacuum threatens future collaborations and commercial certainty.

Recommendations and Proposed Legal Reforms

Need for International Outer Space IP Treaty

A dedicated treaty for outer space intellectual property protection is urgently required. The treaty should define "space object," "space activity," and "invention in space".[95] It must recognise jurisdiction based on

89 Jewel Ali, "From Earth to Orbit", *International Journal of the Legal Science and Innovation*, vol. 6, issue 5 (2024), p. 212.

90 Ibid.

91 INTA, "IP in Space", supra, Appendix II.

92 WIPO Arbitration and Mediation Center, "Space ADR Mechanisms", accessed 23 April 2025.

93 Outer Space Treaty, 1967, Art. I.

94 Ibid., Art. II.

95 WIPO, "Intellectual Property and Space Activities", supra, p. 6.

registration of the space objects or national origin of the inventors.[96] The treaty should allow creation, registration, enforcement, and licensing of the IP rights across space platforms.[97]It must balance territorial principles with extraterritorial realities, harmonising IP protections globally while respecting outer space commons doctrine.

Strengthening National Laws

India must amend its patent laws to extend their applicability to space inventions explicitly.[98] The pending Indian Space Activities Bill should incorporate clear provisions protecting innovations created during licensed operations.[99]India can model reforms after U.S. Patents in Space Act, which creates clarity over jurisdiction and ownership of the inventions aboard space objects.[100]Similar amendments must define liability, enforcement procedures, and priority of the rights between private licensees and state. Judicial training programs should be developed to handle space IP disputes sensitively.

Establishment of the Outer Space IP Registry

An international Outer Space Intellectual Property Registry (OSIPR) must be created under WIPO's supervision.[101] Space inventors should be allowed to file registrations mentioning invention location, object registry, and national affiliation.[102] Registry entries must serve as public notice to all space-faring nations and parties. Territorial extensions must be facilitated to recognise registered rights globally through a harmonised mutual recognition model. This will strengthen innovation security and reduce conflicts.

Role of the Arbitration and Alternative Dispute Resolution (ADR)

Arbitration must become the preferred mechanism for resolving space IP disputes. WIPO Arbitration and Mediation Center's flexible rules

96 INTA, "IP in Space", supra, p. 14.

97 Ibid., p. 17.

98 Draft Indian Space Activities Bill, 2017, Clause 15.

99 Ibid.

100 United States Patents in Space Act, 1990, Sec. 105.

101 INTA, "IP in Space", supra, Recommendation 1.

102 Ibid.

provide strong model for quick, neutral outcomes.[103] Space contracts must mandatorily include arbitration clauses recognising institutional competence over cross-border disputes.[104] UNIDROIT's Space Protocol could evolve to create specialised panels for commercial space-related IP arbitration. ADR methods must also cover disputes between states, private entities, and multinational consortia to avoid diplomatic standoffs over technology use.

Balancing Innovation Incentives with Global Public Interest

New legal models must encourage private sector innovation while ensuring fair access and sustainable space use. Treaties must re-affirm outer space common heritage principle while incentivising R&D through strong IP protections.[105] Licensing structures should ensure that developing countries access critical space technologies on fair terms. Mandatory technology-sharing obligations in public missions can balance innovation profits with public welfare.[106]Environmental sustainability principles must govern patented space technologies' deployment, especially those involving resource extraction or orbital installations.[107] This ensures that commercial space activities remain inclusive, equitable, and environmentally responsible.

Conclusion

Outer space activities have evolved dramatically, shifting towards privatisation, commercialisation, and multinational collaboration. Current legal frameworks under OST and national laws fail to adequately address the unique challenges posed by intellectual property rights in space. Key issues include jurisdictional ambiguity, inconsistent national practices, fragile enforcement mechanisms, and gaps caused by emerging technologies. Space actors today confront a critical legal vacuum. The urgency for a harmonised global legal framework is more pronounced than ever. An international treaty dedicated to space IP, coupled with

103 WIPO Arbitration and Mediation Center, "Arbitration Rules for Space IP", available at: <https://www.wipo.int/amc/en/> accessed 23 April 2025.

104 Ibid.

105 Moon Agreement, 1979, Art. 11.

106 WIPO, "Intellectual Property and Space Activities", supra, p. 7.

107 INTA, "IP in Space", supra, Appendix III.

strengthened national laws and practical mechanisms like OSIPR and ADR, can fill existing gaps. Balancing private innovation incentives with the principle of the space as a province of the all humankind remains guiding star. Sustainable, inclusive, and innovation-driven governance models are crucial to realising humanity's future beyond Earth.

Chapter 2

Beyond Earthly Boundaries: Rethinking Intellectual Property Rights in the Age of Commercial Space Exploration

---

-Aishwarya Anand

Abstract

The evolution of space exploration from a government-led scientific endeavour to a commercially driven enterprise marks a turning point in human progress. With private entities increasingly launching satellites, exploring space tourism, and envisioning manufacturing in orbit, a new set of legal challenges has come into focus—particularly the question of how intellectual property rights (IPRs) will be governed beyond Earth's jurisdiction.

TRIPS has played a crucial role in standardising IPR protection across nations, but it does not offer guidance for activities conducted in the unique legal environment of outer space. This gap becomes all the more significant as research and development in space shift into the hands of private stakeholders, raising questions about ownership, enforcement, and innovation incentives.

This paper explores the limitations of TRIPS and the broader international legal landscape, including treaties like the Outer Space Treaty, which lack explicit provisions on IPRs. I argue that the World Intellectual Property Organisation (WIPO), as the principal body responsible for international IPR governance, must proactively engage in shaping a forward-looking framework. The aim is not only to offer legal certainty to innovators venturing into space but also to foster an equitable and collaborative environment that supports scientific progress and technological development, as well as harmonising the technical advancements with its commercial exploitation.

Keywords- IPR, WIPO, TRIPS, Outer space, WTO

Introduction

The twenty-first century has ushered in an unprecedented era of innovation and ambition—one that reaches far beyond the boundaries of our planet. What was once the exclusive domain of state-sponsored scientific missions has evolved into a flourishing ecosystem of commercial activity in outer space. Today, private companies are not only deploying satellites and conducting research in microgravity but are also preparing for space tourism, planning lunar settlements, asteroid mining, and envisioning factories orbiting Earth. As we move from the age of exploration into the era of economic activity in space, the legal infrastructure governing this new domain must evolve accordingly.

One of the most significant legal blind spots in this transition concerns the protection, enforcement and regulation of intellectual property rights (IPRs) in outer space. Innovation lies at the heart of space activity—whether in the form of patented technologies, copyrighted software, or proprietary research processes envisaging trademark-related aspects. WIPO deals in the regulation of these rights in terrestrial jurisdictions, while the trade-related aspects are dealt with under the TRIPS agreement, and there is a need to regulate and protect IPR in harmonisation with their trade, as these IPs are expected to be exploited commercially. However, the legal frameworks we currently rely on, particularly the Agreement on Trade-Related Aspects of Intellectual Property Rights (TRIPS) under the World Trade Organisation (WTO), are designed with Earth-bound jurisdictions in mind. TRIPS have been instrumental in harmonizing IPR standards across nations, yet it offers no guidance on the application or enforcement of these rights in extraterrestrial settings.

This paper contends that the time is ripe for a serious re-examination of how intellectual property is treated in space. In particular, the World Intellectual Property Organization (WIPO being the custodian of IPR regulation and protection- must take the lead in facilitating international dialogue, drafting guidelines, and eventually developing treaty-based solutions tailored to the realities of space commerce. Only by anticipating these legal challenges now can we ensure a fair, innovative, and cooperative framework for the future.

In what follows, this research explores the limitations of the current legal regime, assesses the risks of inaction, and proposes a way forward for integrating space into our global IPR architecture. As we prepare to extend human presence and enterprise beyond Earth, we must be equally prepared to extend our legal imagination.

Laws and Treaties Governing Outer Space

The Committee on the Peaceful Uses of Outer Space is the forum for the development of international space law. The Committee has concluded five international treaties over time, and these are generally referred to as the "Five United Nations Treaties on Outer Space". The five treaties and the principles underlying them are listed as follows:

The Outer Space Treaty 1967

Formally known as the *Treaty on Principles Governing the Activities of States in the Exploration and Use of Outer Space*, including the Moon and Other Celestial Bodies. This pioneer treaty serves as the cornerstone of international space law. It was adopted by the General Assembly in its resolution, opened for signature on 27 January 1967, and entered into force on 10 October 1967.

The principles entailed within the treaty are:-

- The exploration and use of outer space shall be carried out for the benefit and in the interests of all countries and shall be the province of all mankind;
- Outer space shall be free for exploration and use by all States;
- Outer space is not subject to national appropriation by claim of sovereignty, by means of use or occupation, or by any other means;
- States shall not place nuclear weapons or other weapons of mass destruction in orbit or on celestial bodies or station them in outer space in any other manner;
- The Moon and other celestial bodies shall be used exclusively for peaceful purposes;
- Astronauts shall be regarded as the envoys of mankind;

- States shall be responsible for national space activities whether carried out by governmental or non-governmental entities;
- States shall be liable for damage caused by their space objects; and
- States shall avoid harmful contamination of space and celestial bodies.

The Rescue Agreement 1968

Formally known as the *Agreement on the Rescue of Astronauts, the Return of Astronauts and the Return of Objects Launched into Outer Space.* It was adopted by the General Assembly in its resolution 2345 (XXII), opened for signature on 22 April 1968, and entered into force on 3 December 1968.

The Agreement, elaborating on elements of articles 5 and 8 of the Outer Space Treaty, provides that States shall take all possible steps to rescue and assist astronauts in distress and promptly return them to the launching State, and that States shall, upon request, provide assistance to launching States in recovering space objects that return to Earth outside the territory of the Launching State.

It obligates signatory states to assist astronauts in distress and promptly return them to their launching state (Articles 1–3). Additionally, it requires nations to recover and return space objects that land unintentionally on Earth (Article 5). While primarily focused on safety and cooperation, the agreement indirectly touches on jurisdiction by reinforcing the role of launching states—a concept that could inform future IPR disputes involving spacecraft or patented technology recovered after accidents.

The Liability Convention 1972

Formally named the *Convention on International Liability for Damage Caused by Space Objects*, The Liability Convention was considered and negotiated by the Legal Subcommittee from 1963 to 1972. An agreement was reached in the General Assembly in 1971and the Convention entered into force in September 1972. Elaborating on Article 7 of the Outer Space Treaty, the Liability Convention provides that a launching State shall be absolutely liable to pay compensation for damage caused by its space objects on the surface of the Earth or to aircraft, and liable for damage due to its faults in space. The Convention also provides for procedures for the settlement of claims for damages.

It establishes that a launching state is *absolutely liable* for damage caused by its space objects on Earth or to aircraft (Article II) and *fault-based liable* for damage occurring in outer space (Article III). The convention also outlines procedures for claiming compensation (Articles VIII–X), providing a legal pathway for resolving conflicts arising from collisions or debris-related incidents.

The Registration Convention 1975

Formally named the *Convention on Registration of Objects Launched into Outer Space*, the Registration Convention was considered and negotiated by the Legal Subcommittee from 1962. It was adopted by the General Assembly in 1974, opened for signature on 14 January 1975 and entered into force on 15 September 1976.

Building upon the desire expressed by States in the Outer Space Treaty, the Rescue Agreement and the Liability Convention to make provision for a mechanism that provided States with a means to assist in the identification of space objects, the Registration Convention expanded the scope of the United Nations Register of Objects Launched into Outer Space that addressed issues relating to States Parties responsibilities concerning their space objects. The Secretary-General was, once again, requested to maintain the Register and ensure full and open access to the information provided by States and international intergovernmental organisations.

The Registration Convention mandates that states maintain a national registry of launched space objects and submit orbital parameters to the United Nations (Articles II–IV). This system aims to promote transparency and mitigate conflicts over ownership or jurisdiction.

The Moon Agreement 1979

Formally known as *Agreement Governing the Activities of States on the Moon and Other Celestial Bodies*, The Moon Agreement was adopted by the General Assembly in 1979 and entered into force in July 1984. The Agreement reaffirms and elaborates on many of the provisions of the Outer Space Treaty as applied to the Moon and other celestial bodies, providing that those bodies should be used exclusively for peaceful purposes, that their environments should not be disrupted, that the United Nations should be informed of the location and purpose of any station established on those bodies.

It designates the Moon and its resources as the "common heritage of mankind" (Article 11) and proposes an international regulatory regime for resource exploitation. However, it's restrictive approach—requiring profit-sharing and centralised governance—has deterred major space-faring nations from ratifying it, India being one of them.

United Nations Declarations and Legal Principles: Relevance to Intellectual Property Rights in Outer Space

The legal architecture of outer space is primarily grounded in soft law instruments, including a set of declarations and principles adopted by the United Nations General Assembly. While not binding treaties, these declarations offer interpretive guidance and establish global expectations for responsible behavior in space. They also provide the ethical and policy context within which any legal regime—including intellectual property rights (IPRs)—must be situated. The five key declarations relevant to space law each touch upon issues directly or indirectly associated with IPRs. This section examines their implications for the various categories of intellectual property.

The "Declaration of Legal Principles" (1963) (General Assembly resolution 1962 (XVIII))

The 1963 Declaration of Legal Principles Governing the Activities of States in the Exploration and Uses of Outer Space laid the foundational framework for international space law. Most notably, it articulated that outer space, including the Moon and other celestial bodies, is not subject to national appropriation and must be used for the benefit of all humankind.

This principle presents a conceptual tension with patent law and other exclusive IP regimes. Patents, by their very nature, grant monopoly rights to inventors, which could be perceived as conflicting with the principle that the "use of outer space shall be carried out for the benefit of all countries." For example, if a private company patents a technology developed exclusively in orbit—such as a process enabled by microgravity—it may limit other actors, particularly those from developing states, from accessing or using that technology without a license. This raises questions of equitable access versus incentivization of innovation, making it essential that IPR regimes in space respect the spirit of shared benefit while protecting innovation.

The "Broadcasting Principles" (1982) (General Assembly resolution 37/92)

The Principles Governing the Use by States of Artificial Earth Satellites for International Direct Television Broadcasting emphasise the right of all nations to receive and disseminate information through satellite broadcasting without discrimination. These principles highlight the importance of respecting national sovereignty, cultural integrity, and prior consent in cross-border broadcasts.

The broadcasting principles bear relevance primarily to **copyright** and **trademark law**. Copyright protects the creative content transmitted via satellites—such as TV programs, music, and audio-visual works. Trademarks may also appear in satellite-broadcast advertisements and media. The principle of prior consent implies that content transmitted from space must comply with the IP laws of receiving states, thereby reinforcing the importance of respecting territorial copyright frameworks. Additionally, in cases of unauthorised re-broadcasting, IP enforcement mechanisms must ensure that creators retain control over how and where their content is disseminated globally.

The "Remote Sensing Principles" (1986) (General Assembly resolution 41/65)

The Principles Relating to Remote Sensing of the Earth from Outer Space are especially relevant to **database protection**, **copyright**, and emerging **sui generis rights**. The declaration defines "primary data" (raw data directly sensed by satellites) and "processed data" (enhanced data that allows further analysis), laying the groundwork for distinguishing between data that may or may not be eligible for IP protection.

From an IP perspective, this principle intersects with the commercialisation of geospatial and environmental data. The principle promotes transparency, the sharing of benefits, and the provision of remote sensing data to sensed states, especially developing countries. However, when commercial entities compile or process such data into proprietary databases or analysis tools, they may seek copyright or sui generis database protection. This creates a potential conflict: protecting proprietary interests versus ensuring equitable data access. Thus, any IP regime covering remote sensing data must be carefully tailored to promote innovation while honouring the spirit of open access and fairness embedded in these UN principles.

The "Nuclear Power Sources" Principles (1992) (General Assembly resolution 47/68)

The Principles Relevant to the Use of Nuclear Power Sources in Outer Space focus on the safety, environmental risks, and international liability associated with deploying nuclear-powered systems in orbit. While the primary emphasis is on environmental and technical standards, the use of advanced nuclear technologies in space inevitably intersects with **patent law** and **trade secrets**.

Entities developing novel nuclear technologies for space propulsion, energy storage, or long-duration missions may seek patent protection or maintain confidential know-how. However, due to the sensitive nature of such technologies—often dual-use or defence-related—these IP rights are often tightly controlled under national security laws. The principles' call for transparency, prior notification, and international cooperation could conflict with the secrecy surrounding patent applications or classified trade secrets. As such, a delicate balance must be struck between protecting proprietary rights and meeting the transparency obligations required for the safe and responsible use of nuclear technologies in space.

The "Benefits Declaration" (1996) (General Assembly resolution 51/122)

The Declaration on International Cooperation in the Exploration and Use of Outer Space for the Benefit and in the Interest of All States, Taking into Particular Account the Needs of Developing Countries, is perhaps the most directly relevant to contemporary debates on IP in space. It emphasises that the exploration and use of outer space must benefit all countries, regardless of their economic or scientific development, and explicitly references **intellectual property rights** in the context of international cooperation.

This declaration introduces a strong equity dimension into space law, urging that access to space technology and its benefits not be monopolised by technologically advanced nations. It recognises that contractual terms in cooperative ventures—such as joint missions or shared data projects—should be fair and not undermine the legitimate interests of the parties, including their IP rights. However, it also implies that rigid enforcement of IPRs—especially patents and trade secrets—could potentially hinder equitable technology transfer to developing countries. Thus, this principle supports incorporating flexibilities into IP law, such as licensing conditions, public-private partnerships, and technology-sharing frameworks, to ensure inclusivity in the global space economy.

Space-Based Creations and Intellectual Property Rights: A Detailed Analysis

The rapid commercialisation of outer space has transformed it from a domain of scientific exploration into a frontier of economic opportunity. As private and public actors increasingly engage in activities such as satellite communication, Earth observation, space tourism, and orbital manufacturing, a wide range of intellectual creations arise—each invoking protection under different branches of intellectual property (IP) law. However, the traditional territorial foundation of IP regimes poses unique challenges when applied to outer space, which remains legally non-sovereign and governed by principles of collective use. This section examines the types of creations that emerge from space activities, the relevant categories of IP they engage, and the specific legal challenges that arise in ensuring their protection and enforcement.

Patents: Inventions in Outer Space

Inventions are central to space activities. These include novel apparatuses such as propulsion systems, life-support technologies, zero-gravity manufacturing techniques, and biomedical innovations resulting from research conducted in microgravity environments. Patent law offers inventors exclusive rights to exploit their inventions for a limited period, typically 20 years, in exchange for public disclosure of the innovation.

According to Article 27(1) of the TRIPS Agreement, patents shall be granted "without discrimination as to the place of invention"—thereby extending protection to inventions made in outer space. However, enforcement depends on the territorial reach of national laws. The United States addressed this by enacting 35 U.S.C. §105, which deems inventions made on U.S.-registered space objects to have been made within U.S. territory[1].

The **Outer Space Treaty (OST)** affirms non-appropriation of celestial bodies (Article II) but permits jurisdiction over objects registered by a state (Article VIII)[2]. On multinational platforms like the **International**

1 35 U.S.C. §105 – "Inventions in Outer Space", United States Code.

2 Treaty on Principles Governing the Activities of States in the Exploration and Use of Outer Space (1967), Articles II & VIII.

Space Station (ISS), jurisdictional ambiguity is resolved through the 1998 **Intergovernmental Agreement (IGA)**, which applies the principle of quasi-territoriality—each module of the ISS is treated as the territory of the state that registered it[3]. However, in cases where inventions span multiple modules or involve international collaboration, complex issues of co-ownership, applicable law, and enforcement arise. Despite some harmonisation efforts, the absence of a global space-patent treaty continues to leave gaps in legal certainty.

Copyright: Software, Creative Works, and Processed Data

Space missions generate numerous copyrightable works, including mission software, audio-visual recordings, telemetry visualisations, digital art, and photographs taken aboard spacecraft. Copyright protects original expressions fixed in a tangible medium, and under the **Berne Convention**, protection is automatic and does not require formal registration[4].

The **WIPO Copyright Treaty (WCT)** clarifies that computer programs and databases may also be protected, provided there is originality in their selection or arrangement[5]. This is especially relevant in space missions where data from remote sensing satellites is processed and visualised using software to produce maps, models, and simulations. While raw telemetry data often lacks protectable originality, it's processed and creatively curated versions may qualify for protection.

Jurisdictional issues arise in determining which national law applies—especially when works are co-created by international crews or published through global channels. The author's nationality, habitual residence, and place of first publication become key factors in determining applicable copyright law[6]. Given that most copyright disputes are adjudicated under national regimes, space-originated works often fall into grey areas where enforcement may be impractical or unclear.

3 Agreement among the Government of Canada, Governments of Member States of ESA, the Government of Japan, the Government of Russia, and the Government of the United States concerning Cooperation on the Civil International Space Station, Article 21

4 Berne Convention for the Protection of Literary and Artistic Works (1886), Articles 3–5

5 WIPO Copyright Treaty (1996), Article 4 and 5

6 WIPO, *Intellectual Property and Space Activities*, 2004, para. 46.

Remote Sensing Databases and Sui Generis Protection

Remote sensing and Earth observation missions yield vast quantities of structured data, which may not always meet the originality requirement for copyright. Nonetheless, the economic value and the investment in compiling such databases merit protection. This is where **sui generis database rights** come into play, particularly in the **European Union under Directive 96/9/EC**[7].

As WIPO observes, there is no globally harmonised framework for non-original database protection, though it is being actively discussed[8]. Remote sensing data processed by satellites or sensors—especially when arranged for commercial use—requires safeguards against unauthorised copying and resale. However, access to such data is also regulated by soft law instruments such as the **1986 UN Principles on Remote Sensing**, which encourage equitable distribution of data for the benefit of developing nations[9].

This dual mandate—protection of commercial interests and facilitation of global access—creates a tension between IP rights and broader ethical obligations under international space law. A fair and balanced regime must ensure that innovation is rewarded without obstructing the equitable use of space-derived data for sustainable development.

Trademarks: Branding and Commercial Use in Space

The rise of space tourism, commercial launches, and private satellite networks has introduced branding into the space economy. Trademarks—distinctive symbols, names, or logos—are used to distinguish goods and services and build consumer trust. Companies may place logos on spacecraft, issue branded merchandise, or advertise in orbit.

Trademark protection is governed by national or regional laws and is contingent on use in commerce. However, in the space context, identifying the relevant jurisdiction can be difficult. As noted by WIPO, future disputes may involve unauthorized use of trademarks on orbital platforms,

---

7 Directive 96/9/EC of the European Parliament and of the Council of 11 March 1996 on the legal protection of databases.

8 WIPO, *Copyright and Databases* available at: <https://www.wipo.int/copyright/en/activities/databases.html>.

9 UN Principles Relating to Remote Sensing of the Earth from Outer Space (1986).

especially where the use occurs in or from space but targets consumers on Earth[10].

Currently, no international treaty addresses trademark rights in outer space. If a mark is used aboard a spacecraft registered by one country, but the commercial impact is felt in another, the question of which law governs infringement is unclear. In the future, orbital advertising and space-based branding will necessitate the extension or adaptation of trademark principles to outer space contexts.

Industrial Designs: Aesthetic and Functional Space Products

In addition to functionality, the visual and aesthetic aspects of space products are becoming commercially significant. This includes the design of spacecraft interiors, tools, wearable technologies, and consumer-facing space habitats. Industrial design law protects the ornamental features of such articles, including shape, color, and configuration.

Design rights are typically territorial and limited in duration. As WIPO points out, applying them in space raises questions similar to those under patent law. If a product is designed and used on a space object registered by one state, is that state's law sufficient to protect against unauthorised replication on another space object registered by a different country?[11]

Further, the distinction between aesthetic and functional elements is more nuanced in space. For example, a specific curvature on a tool might simultaneously serve ergonomic and aesthetic purposes, making it difficult to determine whether patent or design protection is more appropriate. As space commercialisation expands, industrial design law will require clear principles to address multi-jurisdictional use and cross-border enforcement.

Trade Secrets: Confidential Know-How and Sensitive Information

Much of the knowledge developed for space missions is not published or registered but instead maintained as confidential know-how. Examples include mission-specific protocols, proprietary algorithms, and technical processes used in manufacturing or navigation. Such information is typically protected through trade secret law, which relies on internal confidentiality measures and contracts.

---

10 WIPO, *Intellectual Property and Space Activities*, paras. 18–20.

11 Ibid., para. 45.

However, trade secrets are especially vulnerable in outer space. As the ILI Law Review notes, space platforms like the ISS host personnel from multiple countries, increasing the risk of unintentional disclosure or espionage[12]. Moreover, without an international treaty or enforcement mechanism, parties have limited recourse if their trade secrets are misappropriated in space.

The ISS IGA provides a partial solution by allowing partners to establish rules regarding confidentiality and IP use (Article 21), but it only applies to the participating states[13]. As more private actors enter the field, reliance on such inter-governmental agreements will be insufficient. Trade secret protection in space must be backed by uniform standards and dispute resolution frameworks that transcend national borders.

Towards a Coherent Regime: Reconciling International IP Law with Space Governance

The dynamic interplay between intellectual property law and space law reflects a legal frontier still in its formative stages. While space activities are governed by international principles rooted in equity, demilitarisation, and collective benefit, intellectual property (IP) regimes—codified through multilateral trade agreements and national laws—are fundamentally grounded in exclusivity, territorial sovereignty, and commercial incentive. The previous discussions on IP-relevant space-based creations and the guiding UN declarations reveal both synergies and frictions that must be reconciled to support a legally coherent and economically viable space ecosystem.

The space-specific declarations—such as the 1963 Declaration of Legal Principles and the 1996 Benefits Declaration—emphasise that outer space is the "province of all mankind" and that its exploration must serve the interests of all countries, particularly developing ones. These principles reflect the ethos of global inclusion and shared technological advancement. However, this normative foundation is placed under stress by the enforcement of exclusive IP rights, particularly patents and trade secrets, which are inherently monopolistic and favor the jurisdictional reach of technologically advanced states.

12 Ritesh Mehra, "Intellectual Property Protection in Outer Space - An Overview", *ILI Law Review*, Vol. II, Winter Issue 2019.

13 IGA, Article 21.

In contrast, the TRIPS Agreement under the World Trade Organisation (WTO) sets out binding minimum standards for the protection and enforcement of intellectual property rights. It requires WTO members to grant patent protection for any invention, whether products or processes, without discrimination as to the "place of invention" (Article 27.1). On its face, this provision supports the inclusion of space-originated inventions within national IP regimes. However, TRIPS is silent on how its provisions apply when inventions or creative works originate in non-sovereign domains such as outer space. As a result, the current international IP infrastructure lacks the jurisdictional clarity necessary to uniformly apply and enforce IP rights in extraterrestrial contexts.

The World Intellectual Property Organization (WIPO), as the specialized UN agency for intellectual property, is well-positioned to address these gaps. WIPO has acknowledged the challenges posed by space activities, notably in its 2004 issue paper on "Intellectual Property and Space Activities." The paper stresses the need for legal predictability, especially regarding the jurisdiction over space-based inventions, copyrightable content, remote sensing data, and trademarks. WIPO also supports the development of frameworks to manage cross-border IP rights, including collaborative enforcement mechanisms and dispute resolution options. However, unlike TRIPS, WIPO instruments are typically non-binding unless adopted through treaties, and no existing WIPO convention expressly extends its scope to extraterrestrial domains.

When juxtaposed, the space law principles and international IP treaties reveal several legal tensions. The principle of non-appropriation under the Outer Space Treaty (OST) and the mandate for equitable benefit-sharing under the UN Benefits Declaration may be compromised if IP rights are used to deny access to critical space technologies. Simultaneously, withholding IP protection could discourage private investment in space innovation. This dilemma is particularly pronounced in cases involving remote sensing databases and satellite telecommunications—areas where data exclusivity is commercially valuable but contradicts principles advocating for shared access and transparency.

Furthermore, enforcement mechanisms under TRIPS—such as the WTO Dispute Settlement Body—are not designed to resolve IP disputes originating in space. National courts cannot exercise jurisdiction over activities occurring beyond Earth unless those activities can be "deemed" to occur within a sovereign registry, as is done under the ISS Intergovernmental Agreement (IGA). While this quasi-territoriality model offers a partial solution, it only applies to specific cooperative arrangements and does not offer a universal framework for space-based IP governance.

In moving forward, a possible solution lies in the development of space-specific IP instruments under the joint leadership of WIPO and the Committee on the Peaceful Uses of Outer Space (COPUOS). These instruments could establish:

- Clear jurisdictional rules for registering and enforcing IP rights aboard space objects;
- Model clauses for cooperative ventures that balance exclusive rights with equitable access;
- Protocols for database protection and satellite data sharing;
- Mechanisms for confidential know-how and trade secret protection in multilateral environments.

Finally, incorporating TRIPS flexibilities—such as technology transfer obligations (Articles 7 and 66.2) and safeguards for public interest—into space-related IP policies can ensure that innovation does not come at the cost of exclusion or inequality. These flexibilities, when aligned with the normative aspirations of UN space principles, offer a legal pathway to balance proprietary interests with global development goals.

Conclusion

As humanity enters a new epoch of space exploration, the governance of intellectual property in outer space emerges as both a legal imperative and a moral challenge. The evolution of outer space from a domain of scientific discovery to one of economic opportunity has brought intellectual property to the forefront of legal discourse. From patented technologies and proprietary satellite data to copyrighted software and space-branded services, the creations born of space activities demand protection. Yet, the traditional frameworks of IP law—grounded in territorial jurisdiction and national enforcement—are ill-equipped to operate in the extra-territorial, multi-jurisdictional environment of outer space.

Through the preceding analysis, it becomes clear that a legal vacuum exists at the intersection of space law and intellectual property. While instruments like the TRIPS Agreement offer a globally harmonised structure for IP protection, they fall short of addressing the unique challenges posed by the extraterrestrial setting. Conversely, the United Nations' declarations and space law principles prioritise inclusivity, cooperation, and shared benefit—often standing in philosophical tension with the exclusivity inherent to intellectual property rights.

Institutions such as the World Intellectual Property Organisation (WIPO) and the World Trade Organisation (WTO) must take proactive steps to bridge this divide. Legal harmonisation, jurisdictional clarity, and policy innovation are urgently required to ensure that space-based inventions and creative works are protected in ways that align with both commercial interests and the collective aspirations of humanity.

Ultimately, intellectual property rights in outer space must be designed not only to incentivise innovation but also to reflect the fundamental principles of equity, sustainability, and peaceful cooperation. Only through a balanced and globally coordinated legal framework can we ensure that the benefits of space exploration are shared, the rights of innovators are respected, and the promise of space as a common heritage of mankind is preserved for generations to come.

Chapter 3

Constitutionalism in Outer Space: Reconciling Intellectual Property with the Common Heritage of Mankind

-Akshat Chopra

Abstract

Outer space is often considered the "province of all mankind", a realm beyond national sovereignty intended for the benefit of all peoples. This principle, encapsulated in the Common Heritage of Mankind (CHM) doctrine, sits awkwardly alongside the rise of private commercial space activities and the assertion of intellectual property rights (IPRs) in space-related innovation. This chapter examines outer space through a constitutional lens, treating the foundational space treaties as an emerging constitutional order. It explores the Common Heritage principle in space law and the expanding role of intellectual property in space activities. The chapter analyses points of tension between exclusive private rights and the shared interests of humanity, and it proposes pathways to reconcile IPR with the Common Heritage concept. Ultimately, a "space-constitutional" framework is advocated, one that balances innovation incentives with the equitable sharing of the benefits of outer space, ensuring sustainable and inclusive space governance.

Introduction

Outer space presents humanity with a frontier where law as a concept and a tool faces unpredictable challenges and opportunities. As human activity increases in the arena of space, ranging from satellite constellations to space tourism and asteroid mining, there is a growing recognition of the fact that the principles established during the Cold War have become increasingly obsolete.[1] The Outer Space Treaty (OST) is often regarded as the *de facto* constitution of outer space, which embodies the principles governing the exploration and use of resources in space.[2] The core idea is that space shall be used only for peaceful purposes, benefit, and in the interest of all nations, thereby transforming it into one of the global commons.[3] This idea later solidified into the doctrine of "Common Heritage of Mankind" (CHM), which simply means that outer space and the resources in it are not the property of any single nation-state, but are to be understood and taken care of by all of humanity.[4]

However, at the same time, the legal framework must grapple with the increasing role of the private sector and commercial enterprises in space. Private companies and institutions are developing vital technology, including pharmaceutical research and designs for habitats in space. Naturally, such actors seek to secure their intellectual property rights to protect their hard-earned innovations. This raises a complex question. How can the current legal order with respect to space reconcile the idea of exclusivity of intellectual property rights (IPRs) with the idea that space constitutes a part of the Common Heritage of Mankind (CHM)?

To answer this question, we require a nuanced understanding of constitutionalism in outer space. More specifically, constitutionalism in the context of international law refers to the application of fundamental rules that limit powers, much like a national constitution governs a nation and limits the state's power. Applied to outer space, the constitutionalism lens helps identify and establish common principles such as peace, cooperation, and the common benefit of mankind in space law.[5] However,

1 Treaty on Principles Governing the Activities of States in the Exploration and Use of Outer Space, including the Moon and Other Celestial Bodies, 1967, art. I.

2 The Treaty on Principles Governing the Activities of States in the Exploration and Use of Outer Space, including the Moon and Other Celestial Bodies (Outer Space Treaty, 1967).

3 Adam S. Bower, "Global Constitutionalism and Outer Space Governance", in A. Lang and A. Wiener (eds.), *Handbook on Global Constitutionalism* 656 (2023).

4 Manasa S. Venkatachalam, *No Rocket Science!: Outer Space, Intellectual Property Rights, and the International Court of Justice*, Völkerrechtsblog, April 15, 2021, available at https://voelkerrechtsblog.org/no-rocket-science/ (last visited on September 3, 2025).

5 S.F. Khan, "Intellectual Property and Space Activities: A Legal Perspective", in *Proceedings of the International Institute of Space Law* 553, 560-562 (Eleven International Publishing, 2019)

unlike a national constitution, space law, being a part of international law, lacks comprehensive and inherently strong institutions and mechanisms to resolve conflicts that naturally emerge. Tensions are bound to grow as the number and the seriousness of stakeholders involved increase.[6]

This chapter seeks to examine these tensions with a focus on IPR in outer space, and their compatibility or lack thereof with the principle of CHM. The subsequent parts will also delve into how the core space treaties further the idea of constitutionalism and where they fall short of the ideal. It also seeks to explore the development of the CHM principle from its foundation in the OST's declaration of space as the "province of all mankind" to its explicit entrenchment in the 1979 Moon Agreement. It will also examine the status and challenges of IPRs in space activities, ranging from the issue of the territorial nature of the rights and how the present agreements and laws address this issue. Finally, it argues for the development of a space-constitutional framework that integrates and tries to reconcile the values of both exclusivity of innovation and protection of the CHM. In making these arguments, the chapter will draw from scholarly works, treaties, provisions, and relevant case law to illustrate how space governance could be achieved, which focuses on mankind at the centre, while remaining innovative, progressive, and inclusive.

The Constitutionalism Lens in Outer Space

The Outer Space Treaty is often considered a foundational document of international space law, establishing the core principles of space exploration, which include its status as a global common for peaceful use, the benefit of all, and an explicit prohibition on national appropriation of resources from celestial bodies.[7] These principles are considered the bedrock as far as the legality of space activities is concerned and are analogous to a domestic constitution, but without the overarching state power.

Despite these rather wide-ranging and strong principles, the constitutional framework of space law, as of today, is weak due to a lack of robust institutions and enforcement mechanisms, which are acceptable to all stakeholders concerned. Unlike a national constitution, the OST did not create a judicial wing, like a "space court" or a separate enforcement body. International forums like the United Nations Committee on the Peaceful Uses of Outer

6 *Ibid.*

7 P.J. Blount, "Peaceful Purposes for the Benefit of All Mankind: The Ethical Foundations of Space Security", in Cassandra Steer and Matthew Hersch (eds.), *War and Peace in Outer Space: Law, Policy, and Ethics* 109-122 (Oxford University Press, Oxford, 2021).

Space (COPUOS) lack binding adjudicatory power and operate by the practice of consensus only.[8] The limited nature of the jurisdiction of these institutions makes it practically difficult to resolve new questions which have emerged, including the regulation of commercial resource extraction in space.

The governance of space under international law has largely stalled since the 1979 Moon Agreement; no major treaties have been signed thereafter, despite rapid technological progress in space exploration. This lacuna has led some states to adopt unilateral mechanisms using national laws, which raises concern as to whether the future of space governance will be established through international agreement at all or will be an oligarchy of a select few developed states.[9]

Ultimately, all lines of constitutionalism highlight the pressing need for a timely, robust, and agile framework for space law. The rules to be made under such a treaty or international framework must be consistent with the foundational principles of peaceful use and common benefit, which have been underscored by the OST.[10] Any new institutions must ensure proper accountability and provide effective dispute resolution as space activities evolve rapidly.

The Common Heritage Principle vis-à-vis Space Law

The CHM principle in space law postulates that outer space and its resources are supposed to be used for the benefit of all, not just a few. This concept gained prominence in the 1960s and 1970s with the Outer Space Treaty (OST) laying the groundwork by declaring space exploration is for the benefit and interest of all countries and prohibiting national appropriation. The key elements that outline the CHM Principle include:

- Non-Appropriation

---

8 United Nations Committee on the Peaceful Uses of Outer Space (COPUOS), available at https://www.unoosa.org/oosa/en/ourwork/copuos/index.html (last visited on September 4, 2025).

9 R. Dickey, "Commercial Normentum: Space Security Challenges, Commercial Actors, and Norms of Behaviour" (Aerospace Corporation, Washington D.C., 2022), available at https://csps.aerospace.org/papers/commercial-normentum-space-security-challenges-commercial-actors-and-norms-behavior (last visited on September 4, 2025).

10 T. Masson-Zwaan and R. Cassar, "The Peaceful Uses of Outer Space", in Simon Chesterman, David M. Malone and Santiago Villalpando (eds.), *The Oxford Handbook of United Nations Treaties* 181-200 (Oxford University Press, Oxford, 2019).

- Common Management via an International Authority
- Equitable Sharing of Benefits
- Peaceful Use
- Sustainability for Future Generations

Despite the lofty ideals, the CHM principle's legal standing in space law rather emanates from the inherent weakness of international law in itself.[11] The agreement, which embodies the set principle, the Moon Agreement, has been ratified by only 18 states, and none of the major spacefaring nations, including the United States (U.S.), China, and Russia, are on that list.[12] These states, citing national interests, resisted the agreement, expressing apprehension that profit-sharing, if socialised, would negatively impact commercial investment and private sector interest in space resource extraction.[13]

This lack of a multilateral treaty has led to unilateral national laws that challenge the very foundation of the CHM principle. Countries like the US, through the Commercial Space Launch Competitiveness Act[14], Luxembourg[15] and Japan[16] have created laws that recognise private ownership of resources which have been extracted from space. Supporters argue that this does not violate the OST's ban on national appropriation of territory; however, it would be difficult to deny that these statutes enable nations, through private entities, to achieve indirectly what they are prohibited from doing directly.

In response, the US launched the Artemis Accords, a non-binding set of agreements which have been signed by more than 45 nations, which promote the principles for lunar exploration but avoid the use of the term

11 R.S. Jakhu and P.S. Dempsey (eds.), *Routledge Handbook of Space Law* (Routledge, Abingdon, Oxon, 2016).

12 Agreement Governing the Activities of States on the Moon and Other Celestial Bodies, December 5, 1979, 1363 U.N.T.S. 3 (Moon Agreement), arts. 11(1), 11(5)-11(7).

13 P.B. Larsen, "Outer Space Arms Control: Can the USA, Russia and China Make this Happen" 23 *Journal of Conflict and Security Law* 137-159 (2018).

14 U.S. Commercial Space Launch Competitiveness Act, 2015, Pub. L. No. 114-90, 129 Stat. 704 (2015).

15 Law on the Exploration and Use of Space Resources, 2017 (Luxembourg).

16 Act on the Promotion of Business Activities Related to the Exploration and Development of Space Resources, 2021 (Japan).

"Common Heritage".[17] This has created a dichotomy on one side, the CHM principle seeks collective management, while on the other, a "first-come, first-served" approach is favoured by spacefaring nations. The legal aspect of space resource ownership remains contested, but the recent trend points towards national commercialisation instead of international governance.

Intellectual Property Rights and Space Activities

Intellectual property rights (IPRs) have become increasingly vital in space exploration, as private entities now play a larger role. These companies invest heavily in research and development for niche technologies, including life support systems and new materials, and need a certain level of guarantee to protect their investments in these inventions. This has led to greater emphasis on patents, copyrights, and trade secrets for innovations in the area of space technologies and commerce.[18] The legal protection afforded to these creations is important for encouraging further developments in the ever-expanding space economy.

A key challenge is that IP laws are traditionally territorial in nature; however, international space law, as it stands today, provides a solution for this. According to art. VIII of the OST, a state retains jurisdiction and control over the space object that it registers. This would imply that a spacecraft is treated as an extension of the territory of the state that launched it, analogous to how a ship at sea is considered under the jurisdiction of the state under whose flag it is sailing.[19]

The 1998 Intergovernmental Agreement on the International Space Station (IGA) explicitly states this principle for intellectual property.[20] It states that an invention made on an ISS module is deemed to have occurred on the territory of the partner state that owns that module. For example, an invention made in the U.S. segment of the ISS would be subject to U.S. patent law. The U.S. Patents in Space Act further lends credence to this by stating that an invention, use, or sale on a U.S.-registered space object

17 Artemis Accords: Principles for Cooperation in the Civil Exploration and Use of the Moon, Mars, Comets, and Asteroids for Peaceful Purposes, October 13, 2020, s. 11.

18 World Intellectual Property Organization, "Inventions in Space" (2022), available at https://www.wipo.int/about-ip/en/frontier_issues/inventions_in_space.html (last visited on September 4, 2025)

19 *Supra* note 3, art. VIII.

20 Intergovernmental Agreement on the International Space Station, Jan. 29, 1998, TIAS No. 12927, art. 21(2).

will be deemed to have occurred within U.S. territorial jurisdiction.[21] This law prevents companies from using a rather glaring legal loophole to avoid patent infringement by operating in space.[22]

Despite these frameworks, significant challenges remain in enforcing IP rights in space.

A company could register its space vehicle in a country with a lax IP enforcement regime, creating what could be referred to as a "flag of convenience" situation to avoid infringement claims.

Detecting and ultimately proving IP infringement in orbit is difficult for natural reasons, such as the difficulty in observing a competitor's activities.[23] Enforcement of remedies, such as injunctions or seizures, could occur only when the infringing party or the product returns to Earth.

There is no international IP title valid in space itself as of today; inventors must file patents in individual countries, as is the current practice. This highlights the lack of a special global regime for space law within the overarching lacuna of international space governance.[24]

These challenges emphasise the potential conflict between the assertion of IP rights, which, by their very nature, are exclusive, and the foundational principles of space law, which include but are not limited to common benefit and freedom of exploration.

Reconciling IP with Common Heritage

IPRs and the CHM principle, at first glance, appear to be at odds with each other at first glance. IPRs grant an exclusive temporary monopoly to innovators, while CHM talks about common management and benefit-sharing with respect to outer space. However, they can be reconciled if the application of both these concepts is properly managed. The key here is to ensure that IPRs do not become a tool to undermine the fundamental

21 United States Code, 35 U.S.C. § 105 ("Inventions in outer space") (Public Law 101-580, 1990).

22 *Nemitz* v. *United States*, No. CV-N-03-0599, 2004 U.S. Dist. LEXIS.

23 Lauren Peterson, "Governing the Unknown: How the Development of Intellectual Property Law in Space Will Shape the Next Great Era of Exploration, Exploitation, and Invention" 19 *Northwestern Journal of Technology and Intellectual Property* 1, 4-5 (2021).

24 Alexandra M. Davidson, "To Explore Outer Space: The Intellectual Property Frontier for Patents" 47 *Hofstra Law Review* 645, 647-659 (2019).

freedom and principles of access, which are supposed to be guaranteed by international space law.

IPRs, by their very design, are made to incentivise innovation and promote investment, which in the long run benefits everyone. For instance, a patent of a new space mining tool would not give ownership of the asteroid itself but only protect the specific design and layout of the tool. So long as the patent is not generic or overbroad and allows for an alternative method, it can coexist with the CHM principle. At the same time, if the patent were so extensive that it effectively gave its holder real control over an entire lunar region, for example, through expansive claims, it would come into conflict with the principle of non-appropriation of the global commons.[25] To prevent this from happening, legal safeguards, such as the application of the "Public Trust Doctrine"[26] or public policy exceptions at the international level, could be applied to limit the scope of intellectual property rights when they threaten the common interest of mankind.[27]

Several mechanisms can reconcile IPRs with CHM:

- **Benefit-Sharing Requirements**: A part of the profits from space-based inventions and resources extracted could be contributed towards an international fund akin to a revenue-sharing model used in deep seabed mining, and also to fight climate change under the "common but differentiated responsibilities" principle. This would ensure that the benefits from development flow back towards all of humanity, aligning with the spirit of the "Moon Agreement".
- **Technology Transfer Mechanisms**: While the idea of forced disclosure of IP is controversial in itself, a rather softer approach could be established in the form of voluntary technology pools or licensing agreements under UN oversight. This could allow critical ideas and technologies to be licensed and developed on fair terms which otherwise developing nations could not access.
- **Preservation of Basic Research**: A clear differentiation needs to

25 S. Neil Hosenball, "The Common Heritage of Mankind: An Element of Law for the Development of Outer Space" 4 *Journal of Space Law* 125, 131-133 (1976).

26 *M.C. Mehta* v. *Kamal Nath* (1997) 1 SCC 388.

27 Christopher Mirasola, "Common Heritage as Public Trust: A Property Law Approach to Managing Resources Beyond National Jurisdiction" 97 *Southern California Law Review* 393 (2024).

be made between scientific knowledge, which is fundamental in nature and needs to be freely shared, for example, geological data and its commercial application, which can and should be protected by IPR regimes.[28] This would ensure that IP does not hinder real scientific progress, while at the same time, it does its core job of promoting innovation and research.

- **International Dispute Resolution**: An international forum is needed, which could be established to resolve disputes where nation-states or any private entity believe that an IPR is violating the common interest. A specialised space tribunal provides a constitutional check on the potential abuse of IP.[29]
- **Redefinition of Patent Scope**: Patent offices and office bearers should ensure that space-related patents are defined and accepted, narrowly to prevent over broad claims that could monopolise an entire category of activities. This would encourage a diversity of approaches and prevent a single patent holder from cornering an entire arena for personal exploitation.

Efforts are underway to address the issues discussed above. A working group within the UN is exploring models for space, resource governance, including benefit-sharing, taking inspiration from a similar mechanism used for genetically modified organisms. Also, a proposal for a mining license system under the UN auspices could provide enterprises with legal authorisation in exchange for their continued compliance with the rules, which would ultimately serve the common interest. Thus, ensuring that all nation-states see the tangible benefits of space exploration is crucial for maintaining international peace as mankind expands its frontiers.

Way Forward: Towards a Space-Constitutional Framework

The challenges of space governance require a space constitutional framework which balances the common interest of mankind and the role of private enterprises in a way that is both equitable and conducive to innovation at the same time.

28 Maeve Dineen, "For the Betterment of All Mankind: Claiming the Benefits of Outer Space Through Intellectual Property Rights" 13 *UC Hastings Science and Technology Law Journal* 73, 75-78 (2022).

29 I. Kealotswe-Matlou, "The Rule of Law in Outer Space: A Call for an International Outer Space Authority", in Cassandra Steer and Matthew Hersch (eds.), *War and Peace in Outer Space: Law, Policy, and Ethics* 91-106 (Oxford University Press, Oxford, 2021).

A future "space-constitutional framework" should involve codification of a set of principles, balanced in nature, which acknowledge both common interest in space and the role of corporations. Key principles would include:

- Reaffirming that space activities should benefit all of humanity
- Regulating resource extraction in a manner which promotes equitable access and benefit-sharing
- Recognising IP as a necessary incentive for innovation, but ensuring that they do not lead to unfairness, exclusion, or appropriation
- Fostering cooperation for technology transfer to enable all nations to participate

This would set up a precedent that avoids both extreme libertarian and collectivist undertones, ensuring that a proper balance is achieved between progress and inclusion.

To institutionalise these principles, new strengthened bodies are needed. One is an International Space Resource Authority (ISRA). ISRA would not control mining but serve as a clearinghouse for registration, ensuring transparency and mediating conflicts. It could also manage a fund for benefit-sharing and set guidelines for best practices. Another approach is to strengthen the United Nations Committee on the Peaceful Uses of Outer Space (COPUOS) by giving it a larger mandate to oversee the implementation of these new guidelines and serve as a forum for resolving disputes. The Permanent Court of Arbitration has already created rules for space-related disputes. States could use this forum for resolving disputes related to the subject matter of space.[30]

As far as the technical steps are concerned, states can update their national IP laws to explicitly cover outer space in a manner which is consistent with international principles discussed above. This would include implementing explicit provisions for inventions in space, as the U.S. has done.[31] And possibly, including provisions for compulsory licenses in case of overarching public interest or missions of critical importance. This

30 Permanent Court of Arbitration, *Optional Rules for Arbitration of Disputes Relating to Outer Space Activities* (2011), available at https://pca-cpa.org/en/services/arbitration-services/optional-rules-for-arbitration-of-disputes-relating-to-outer-space-activities/ (last visited on September 4, 2025).

31 United States Code, 35 U.S.C. § 105 ("Inventions in outer space") (Public Law 101-580, 1990).

could ensure that IP regimes do not obstruct the vital needs of society or scientific progress in general.

The legitimacy of any such framework would depend on the inclusive participation of all stakeholders. A United Nations (UN)-led diplomatic process would be needed to negotiate the updates to the present space law, which would include inputs from all states, including those which have not developed spacefaring capabilities but have an unequivocal stake in the global commons. Such a process would address the concerns of developing nations, perhaps by a mechanism in which private ownership of resources is exchanged for assured benefit-sharing and capacity building. Naturally, any novel framework must also preserve the core values of the space law as they exist today, such as peaceful use, astronaut rescue, and the freedom of scientific investigation.

Ultimately, the balance of IPRs with the CHM principle is a test case and an important one at that for building a stable, predictable and inclusive legal regime and ultimately an environment in space. Such a framework would prevent unnecessary conflicts, and ensure that as mankind expands its presence, it does not do so arbitrarily but rather guided by the principle of the rule of law, benefiting all shades of humanity, irrespective of their corresponding status as developed, developing or least developed nations.

Part II

Technology Transfer, Innovation and Commercialisation

Chapter 4

The Commercial 'Spin-Off' of Space Technology and IPR in Outer Space Regime: A Critical Study of Space Technology Transfers in Asia

-Ajay Revansidha Tambulkar and Amarendra Kumar

Abstract

The proliferation of space technology is transforming planet earth into the nucleus of expeditions aimed at exploration, use, application and legal claims over outer space resources. The intellectually fueled inventions of space technology and its applications have led to claims on space resources with proprietary intent; this has emphasised the necessary relation of Space Law with Intellectual Property Rights. The rise in private players with enormous investments in space technology has ushered the present era of commercialisation of space, ranging from research and development of reusable launch vehicles, multi-utility satellite constellations, permanent space stations, placing humans in space for commercial gains and inventions aboard in space-vehicles, etc. These developments shall be analysed through the lens of Intellectual Property Rights (IPR) in the context of space inventions and cross-border transfer of such inventions to facilitate 'common good'.

Technology transfers have grown in recent decades as an important source of innovation, growth and employment, and the space sector is also witnessing this techno-transformation i.e. ISRO has transferred over 400 technologies to around 235 industries. The technology transfers in the commercial space technology domain from national space agencies to the private sector is a distinctive feature of the space industry that needs a strong governance ecosystem. The transfer of technology shall be analysed from the standpoint of fundamental principles of Outer Space Treaty (OST), like space activities shall be pursued "for the benefit and in the interests of all countries.

This chapter attempts to critically analyse the existing regulatory framework under OST, TRIPs and relevant technology transfer agreements that govern the commercial space technology transfers. Further, research work aims to study the need for a robust policy-legal framework for the promotion of space technology transfers in the Asian region to equitably bridge the gap between top space-faring nations and other resource deficit nations.

Keywords: Space technology, spin-off, technology transfer agreements, Intellectual Property Rights, Space governance

Space as a New Frontier with New Space Economy and Technological Innovations

The vast expanse of space consisting of stars and planets has been part of human narratives, and now they are on the agenda of ambitious space missions. This transformation is a result of human intellect and enthralling scientific inventions. Space has emerged as an advanced frontier of competition and commercialisation; it is the responsibility and duty of States and non-state actors to ensure that the outer space shall remain the domain of sustainable cooperation for the benefit of all.

Today, global space economy[1] is thriving as a New Space Economy[2] with features like, increasing number of frequent multi-sized satellite launches from state and non-state actors, avant-grade technology innovations

1 OECD (2023), The Space Economy in Figures: Responding to Global Challenges, OECD Publishing, Paris,available at: <https://doi.org/10.1787/fa5494aa-en>.; United Nations Conference on Trade and Development (UNCTAD), Exploring Space Technologies for Sustainable Development, 2021, United Nations; OECD (2023), OECD Science, Technology and Innovation Outlook 2023: Enabling Transitions in Times of Disruption, OECD Publishing, Paris, available at: <https://doi.org/10.1787/0b55736e-en.>

2 Landry Signe and Hanna Dooley, How Space Exploration Is Fueling The Fourth Industrial Revolution, Brookings, Available at: <Https://Www.Brookings.Edu/Articles/How-Space-Exploration-Is-Fueling-The-Fourth-Industrial-Revolution/#Top1>

like use of Artificial Intelligence[3] and Aerospike Engines[4], low-cost of manufacturing and launches due to pioneering methods like Additive Printing[5] and Reusable Launch Vehicles[6] (RLVs) and rise in end user requirements for commercial purposes like satellite-based data and internet services. Innovation is the precursor that boosts the space value chain, and it is driving growth in the space industry. Further, technology transfer from the space industry across sectors and nations ensures the dissemination of such innovation to a larger section of humanity. In light of these developments, analysing convergence of space technology innovations, Technology Transfer (TT) and Intellectual Property Rights becomes ad rem.

Technology Transfer and Space Technology Transfer: Conceptual Overview

Innovation and technology are two dynamic wheels of sustainable development of the global economy. Technology can be described as industrial know-how, resulting from the combination of knowledge, human resources and technical management, necessary to develop new equipment or expertise for certain purposes. Such technology is an outcome of inventions and to ensure that the application of technology benefits the masses and improves their standard of life, often innovations are protected through a series of legal measures, such as patents, licenses, and trademarks, that are usually referred to as Intellectual Property Rights. Space technology is also categorised as one of the 'emerging technologies'[7];

3 Aahaan Anand, The role of AI in space mission planning and simulation: Transforming space exploration with advanced computing, International Journal of Computing and Artificial Intelligence 2024; 5(2): 220-224; UNCTAD 2025 Technology and innovation report, By 2033,the frontier technology with the largest market size is likely to be AI, at around $4.8 trillion ,accounting for 30 percent of the overall market, available at : <https://unctad.org/system/files/official- document/tir2025_en.pdf.>

4 Qing Sun, Xiamen University, Design of Aerospike Engines: Overcoming challenges to revolutionise spaceflight, Journal of Aeronautics and Aerospace Engineering, Vol. 12, 2023.

5 Mao Mao,3D printing in space: from mechanical structures to living tissues, International Journal of Extreme Manufacturing, available at: < https://iopscience.iop.org/article/10.1088/2631-7990/ad23ef/pdf.>

6 Bushnell, Dennis M, Commercial Space in The Age Of "New Space", Reusable Rockets and The Ongoing Tech Revolutions, Langley Research Centre, 2018, available at< https://ntrs.nasa.gov/citations/20180008444.>

7 Rotolo D., Hicks D., and Martin B. R., "What is an Emerging Technology?" Research Policy, Volume 44, Issue 10 (2015):1827- 1843, ISSN 0048-7333.

scholars have determined five vital features of such emerging technology, like, radical novelty, relatively fast growth, coherence, prominent impact, and uncertainty and ambiguity. These factors make regulation of space technology more complex. Here, it is pertinent to understand that categorising space innovations or products, or services itself is a task undertaken by national IP regulatory bodies and therefore it lacks uniformity in the international space market. Further, the domestic laws intending to safeguard national interest often regulate cross-border flow of such emerging technology through export control regime.

UNCTAD Draft Transfer of Technology Code (draft TOT code) defines 'technology' as systematic knowledge for the manufacture of a product, for the application of a process or for the rendering of a service.[8] Whereas, 'Technology transfer'[9] (TT) means the process by which commercial technology is disseminated across sectors with a larger utilitarian approach. This technology diffusion takes the form of a technology transfer transaction, which may be covered by a legally binding contract; this involves the communication, by the transferor, of the relevant knowledge to the recipient.

World Intellectual Property Organisation (WIPO), states that, Knowledge and technology transfer (K&TT) is a collaborative process that allows scientific findings, knowledge and intellectual property to flow from creators\, such as universities and research institutions, to public and private users.[10] In present research context, state-sponsored space agencies as well as private space-tech entities are the creators of such knowledge and technology; for example, ISRO has transferred technology of more than 400 techno-innovations having utility in other sectors.

The arm of the Government of India's Department of Space, New Space India[11] treats Technology Transfer as a process by which knowledge acquired by an entity while developing a particular technology is transferred to an external entity, including public-private sector, academia, etc. For example, recently, New Space India Limited (NSIL) transferred the IMS-1 Satellite

8 UNCTAD Draft Transfer of Technology Code, 1985 Chapter 1 Para 1.2.

9 Blakeney, M., Legal Aspects of Technology Transfer to Developing Countries, Oxford: ESC Publishing,1989.

10 Maskus, K.E. (2004), Encouraging International Technology Transfer (Vol.7), Geneva: International Centre for Trade and Sustainable Development.

11 ISRO Transfers IMS-1 Satellite Bus Technology to a Private Industry, August 04, 2023, available at: <https://www.isro.gov.in/ISRO_Transfers_IMS1SatelliteBus.html>

Bus Technology developed by ISRO to M/s Dhruva Space Pvt. Ltd. (Dhruva Space). [12] Further, 'Space Technological Transfers and Commercialisation (TTCs),[13] are defined as the movement of know-how, skills, technical knowledge, procedures, methods, expertise or technologies from one public research organisation (e.g. national space agency- ISRO) to another organisation (e.g. private entity-Skyroot, Dhruva Space, etc.), generating value and economic development outside the space sector. International technology transfer (ITT)[14] is referred as a process whereby a party from one country gains access to a foreign party's information and successfully learns and absorbs it into their production function. International trade and foreign direct investment (FDI) are two important channels of ITT.

The technological 'spin-off'[15] is conceived as transfer of technology, primarily it was discussed in the context to transfer of knowhow and technology from public agencies like ISRO, NASA, JAXA, etc. to other entities with the intention to promote application and at times to commercialise the same. A number of space agencies define[16] 'spin-off' as technologies initially created to meet the agency's objectives, which incorporated internal expertise, and then were commercialised as a product or service to serve other uses outside of the agency.

Technology-transfers in space domain: A technical, economic and legal outlook

Space technologies primarily consist of satellite earth observation, satellite communication and satellite positioning. The multi-pronged applications of space technology are, weather forecasting, remote sensing, global positioning systems, satellite television, internet broadband and communications, etc. The Organisation for Economic Co-operation and Development (OECD) emphasized[17] three key activities in the space economy. Firstly, fundamental space activities like space manufacturing and launch called as the upstream space segment. Secondly, activities that depend on the exploitation of space data and signals, for example, satellite

12 Ibid.

13 OECD Space Technology Transfers and their Commercialization-Science, Technology and Industry Policy Papers, July 2021 No. 116.

14 Ibid

15 OECD(2016), Space and Innovation, OECD Publishing, Paris, available athttps://dx.doi.org/10.1787/9789264264014- en.

16 Ibid.

17 OECD Handbook on Measuring the Space Economy

television, internet, voice communication, etc. as well as the manufacturing of associated equipment, are called as the down-stream segment. Finally, applications and activities that are derived from space technologies but not dependent on them to function are termed as space-derived activities, for example, air bag deployment technology, Lithium Ion Battery, 3D Li DAR camera, etc. These three categories of activities are common among all space-faring nations with variations in scale, frequency and inter-sectoral technology transfers.

Some of the most frequently used business models[18] for technology transfer are: outright sale and assignment agreement, Patent licensing agreement, Research and Development (R&D) Contracts, Joint Ventures, Corporate Partnership agreement and Marketing and distribution agreements. Technology transfer takes place broadly through three types of channels[19] that allow the flow of technologies from inventor to recipient. The channels are; General Channel, Reverse Engineering and Formal Channels. Further, Formal Channel is effected through multiple means like, Licensing, Franchise, Joint Venture, Turn-Key Project, Foreign Direct Investment (FDI) and Technical Consortium on R&D Projects, etc. Whenever technology is transferred through these modes compliance with national and international regulations becomes an essential condition to sustain and develop economic prospects of such commercialisation. Technology transfers are often subjected to export control laws, antitrust regulations, and other legal frameworks that vary by jurisdiction.

International Governance of Space: An overview

Since the dawn of space age, with the launch of first satellite the international community responded in a resolute manner, for instance, the United Nations established the Committee on the Peaceful Uses of Outer Space (UNCOPUOS) and this UN body played pivotal role in the development of international space law through UN Declarations, Resolutions and Treaties. The five core space treaties have all been negotiated and drafted with the initiative of this committee.

---

18 S Sudha Rani, Dr B Madhusudan Rao, Dr Prahlada Ramarao and Sunil Kumar, Technology Transfer - Models and Mechanisms International Journal of Mechanical Engineering and Technology (IJMET) Volume 9, Issue 6, June 2018, pp. 971–982, Available online at <http://iaeme.com/Home/issue/IJMET?Volume=9&Issue=6;> Tarek Khalil & Ravi Shankar, "Management of Technology", McGraw Hill Education (India) Pvt Ltd , 2nd edition, 2016, p 372- 380

19 Ibid.

The '*Magna Carta* of space law'[20] in its very first Article provides that, 'The exploration and use of outer space, including the Moon and other celestial bodies, shall be carried out for the benefit and in the interests of all countries, irrespective of their degree of economic or scientific development, and shall be the province of all mankind.'[21] Further, the treaty provides for fundamental principles of space law like; the notion of space as the province of all human kind[22], the freedom of exploration and use of outer space by all states without discrimination[23], responsibility of States[24], and the principle of non-appropriation of outer space. Article VIII of OST provides that a space object's State of registration "shall retain jurisdiction and control over such object, and over any personnel thereof, while in outer space or on a celestial body."[25] This is analogous to the floating island theory of jurisdiction in maritime law.

The Registration Convention[26] implements the Outer Space Treaty's registration requirements. Article II of the Registration Convention provides that the launching state is responsible for registering a space object. Article I (a) defines "launching State" as;

(i) The State that launches or procures the launching of the space object or

(ii) The State from whose territory or facility a space object is launched.

Generally, patent laws do not extend to activities in space since they are territorial, but the Outer Space Treaty and the Registration Convention together enable launching States to extend their laws, including patent laws, to space objects they register.

20 Radhhakrishna Rao, "Space Technology and Soft Power", *Institute of Peace and Conflict Studies*, 2009, *available at*<http://www.ipcs.org/focusthemsel.php?articleNo=3025>,(last visited on 5th September,2019); Taylor Dinerman,"NASA and Soft Power, again", *The Space Review*, 2009.

21 Outer SpaceTreaty,1967,Art.1.

22 Ibid.

23 Ibid.

24 Outer Space Treaty, 1967, Art. 6

25 Treaty on Principles Governing the Activities of States in the Exploration and Use of Outer Space, including the Moon and Other Celestial Bodies, 1967.

26 Convention on Registration of Objects Launched into Outer Space, 1975

The Moon Agreement[27] last one to develop in five core treaties provides for significant principles like moon is province of mankind, principle of cooperation and mutual assistance[28], common heritage of mankind[29], etc. The five core treaties and certain other international instruments govern wide range of space activities, from R&D to removal of space debris after completion of space mission or end of the life of satellite. However, neither OST nor Liability Convention or Moon Agreement provides clear norms about intangible property rights and their regulations in space industry, activities off the earth in orbits or outer space.

Commercialisation of Space and Application of Intellectual Property Rights

Space 4.0 represents the evolution towards a new era of space activities. International Space Law prescribes, Principle of non-appropriation, stating no government can claim outer space or celestial bodies in outer space as its own.[30] Outer Space Treaty aims to ensure that outer space activities are pursued 'for the benefit and in the interests of all countries' and are "the province of all mankind." This collective spirit is shared by later treaties concerning outer space.

Article 2 (viii) of the Convention Establishing the World Intellectual Property Organization of 1967 provides that "Intellectual Property" should include the rights relating to: literary, artistic and scientific works; performances of performing artists, phonograms, and broadcasts; inventions in all fields of human endeavor; scientific discoveries; industrial designs; trademarks, service marks, and commercial names and designations; protection against unfair competition; and all other rights resulting from intellectual activity in the industrial, scientific, literary or artistic fields.

A patent protection under national and international law, enhances the rights of an inventor over invention for twenty (20) years, making it an exclusive right ensuring economic products of such invention through use, sell or manufacture the same invention. On the planet earth, national

27 Agreement Governing the Activities of States on the Moon and Other Celestial Bodies, 1979.

28 The Moon agreement, Art. 4.

29 The Moon agreement, Art.11(1).

30 Treaty on Principles Governing the Activities of States in the Exploration and Use of Outer Space ,including the Moon and Other Celestial Bodies (1967),Art. 2, (hereinafter Outer Space Treaty).

patent authorities grant licenses in municipal sphere whereas the Patent Cooperation Treaty regulates patenting issues at international level; however, the extension of such laws to outer space is a pertinent question. Issue of inventions in outer space poses more difficulties, which a number of legal mechanisms endeavour to alleviate. At present there exist framework like the Madrid System which permit registration of trademarks internationally, however, there no dedicated instrument covering protection of trademark relating to any activities conducted in outer space. Scholars argue the need to expand the scope of terrestrial IP regime to outer space.

Intellectual property (IP) is viewed as a significant instrument at different stages of innovation and commercial activities, like, at primary research and development stage, IP helps to create secure legal claim through ownership over intellectual findings and further it creates right in creation to control the use of IP. Whereas at secondary commercial stage, IP serves as a tool to acquire market and retain exclusivity over a new product or process. Further, IP attracts investment through development collaboration or licensing deals and leverages economic advantages Space industry.

At present juncture when space technology is contributing to the transformation of global market, frequent debate and discussion on (physical/material) property rights and claims over resources in space has been part of UNOOSA and other international forums. However, no international consensus on the legal status of intangible property like intellectual property in outer space has reached so far. The generic approach in State practices regarding applicability of national intellectual property laws indicates that, national patent and other industrial IP governing laws are applicable up to internationally recognised Karman Line, set at 100 kilometers above Earth. Whereas, demarcation of Earth from outer space in terms of the applicability of national laws is not universally accepted and this raises questions about the uniform protection of intellectual property in the outer space domain and as space activities become more cross-border.

The Registration Convention of 1975 reaffirmed international agreements that gave individual states responsibility over national activities where objects were launched from that State's territory into outer space. According to international space law the state where a space object is registered retains jurisdiction over it. This raises the question of whether national intellectual property laws extend to object\s registered and launched into outer space. In the absence of explicit international rules, under several international agreements concluded with respect to international space projects, registered space objects are treated as quasi-territory for the purposes of intellectual property.

International instruments and principles concerning Intellectual Property and Outer Space

The Paris Convention[31]: The Paris Convention for the Protection of Industrial Property, which is the basic international treaty in the field of industrial property, does not expressly consider the question of inventions in outer space. However, Article 2 of it contains provisions establishing the national treatment principle. Whereas, the right of priority of international patent protection is prescribed in Article 4 and common rules, including certain measures for the enforcement of intellectual property rights, which all the Member States must follow. These provisions primarily underline the legal standpoint that members States of Paris Convention need to revisit the text of treaty and ensure that the scope of present convention covers activities in outer space.

The Berne Convention[32]: The Berne Convention for the Protection of Literary and Artistic Works is the basic treaty in the field of copyright and related rights. As the Paris Convention, the Berne Convention does not expressly consider the question of intellectual property rights in outer space. However, it contains provisions establishing basic principles such as national treatment, the "independence" of protection and the principle of automatic protection, i.e., copyright protection may not be subject to any formality.

WIPO Copyright Treaty (WCT) [33]: The WCT provides, among other things, for the protection of (i) computer programs, whatever may be the mode or form of their expression, and (ii) the compilation of data or other material ("databases") in any form, which by reason of the selection or arrangement of their contents constitute intellectual creations. In particular, Article 8 assures the authors' right to enjoy the exclusive right to authorise any communication to the public of their works, including the making available to the public of their works in such a way that members of the public may access these works from a place and at a time individually chosen by them. This Article is also applicable to transmissions to and from a spacecraft.

31 The Paris Convention for the Protection of Industrial Property, 1883.

32 Berne Convention for the Protection of Literary and Artistic Works, 1986.

33 WIPOCopyrightTreaty,1996.

TRIPS Agreement[34]: TRIPS in Article 7 provides that IPR regime shall be deployed for, 'the promotion of technological innovation and to the transfer and dissemination of technology'. Perhaps, protection of IPR is viewed from the bigger utilitarian approach of dissemination of invention through systematic legal mechanism. The TRIPS Agreement states that the protection and enforcement of intellectual property rights should contribute to the promotion of technological innovation and to the transfer and dissemination of technology, to the mutual advantage of producers and users of technological knowledge and in a manner conducive to social and economic welfare, and to a balance of rights and obligations.

The obligation for developed countries to provide incentives for technology transfer is in Article 66.2. Least-developed countries want this requirement to be made more effective. In Doha in November 2001, ministers agreed that the TRIPS Council would "put in place a mechanism for ensuring the monitoring and full implementation of the obligations". Further, according to Article 27.1, patents must be available and patents rights enjoyable without discrimination as to the place of invention. Therefore, national law has to ensure that, with respect to inventions created in outer space, patents must be granted and enforceable in the territory in which it applies under the same conditions applicable to inventions created elsewhere.

Space technology transfers in Asian region: trend and bridging the developing gap

Studies about space technology transfers have often overlooked the potential of Asia, perhaps it is recently reported by international forums like World Bank, IMF, WIPO, UNCTAD and OECD, that Asian economy is the potential axis of global economy. In 1970s the developing nations from Asian region expressed aspirations to access foreign technology and develop capability to harness such technological break throughs for their national development, in this trajectory, technology transfer was conceived as an effective tool to bridge developmental gap between global north and south.

34 The Agreement on Trade-Related Aspects of Intellectual Property Rights, 1994.

Experts insights[35] provided through a report titled, New Space in Asia[36], clearly emphasise that revolutionary trends in space industry are at work in Asian countries as a product of both determined public strategies and fast-developing commercial space ecosystems. Asian New Space, encompasses a wide range of diverse and interrelated trends leading the space sector towards a more business and service-oriented step, certain key features of Asian trend in space domain are as follows;

- New public schemes for space programmes, procurement and support to innovation involving new arrangements with the private sector and the development of new public instruments.
- New entrants, including emerging space-faring nations and new business ventures from space companies and start-ups as well as from non-space companies seeking to enter the space sector.
- New solutions, including new products and services but also disruptive value propositions such as integrated solutions, lower prices, reduced lead times, lower complexity, better flexibility.
- New markets under exploration or development in both the upstream and downstream segments of the space value chain (e.g. in-orbit servicing, satellite broadband, satellite imaging, micro-launchers.)
- New industrial set-ups and implementation of new industrial methods and processes for the development and production of space systems as part of innovative business models.
- New private investment tools from various sources and involving various funding instruments (e.g. venture capital, private equity, loans, prizes, crowd funding.)

Asian economy has undergone remarkable transformation, from seeking technological assistance to providing state-of-the-art innovations to the world, journey of Asia is an exemplary case study. Since past three decades, driven by national strategic considerations, Asian countries such as India, China, Japan and South Korea have started to actively support the emergence of innovative space businesses, with an increasing number

35 NewSpace in Asia-Experts views on space policy and business trends in Asian countries; OECD (2016), Space and Innovation, OECD Publishing, Paris, available at < https://dx.doi.org/10.1787/9789264264014-en.>

36 Ibid.

of private start-ups now kick-starting space innovations and ventures to market end-to-end solutions in both the upstream and downstream segments.

Reportedly[37], more than hundred start-ups have come up in the space industry of India. Governments in these countries are also increasingly supporting the development of commercial services for tasks traditionally under government responsibility and therefore repositioning their agencies according to new mandates. Two key initiatives have been instrumental in shaping the transformation of India's space sector. First, the establishment of the Indian National Space Promotion and Authorization Centre (IN-SPACe) in 2020. This entity serves as a single-window agency, regulating all space activities in India and, most importantly, creating a level playing field for the space industry. Second, the Indian Space Policy - 2023 (ISP-23), released in April 2023.

WIPO states that, Asia is the most important research region for space exploration technologies. Between 2000 and 2023, there were 52,105 patent families published by inventors based in Asia.[38] Wherein, the work of China National Space Administration (CNSA), the government body that takes Chinese space ambitions to higher orbits, is a noteworthy case study from Asian region. This represents the trend by Chinese government that prioritizes space explorations and innovations as a core part of national development strategy. As per WIPO survey[39] , inventors from China have filed the highest number of patents, 38000 and these are related to space transportation technologies.

Challenges Before Space Technology Transfers

The space economy gallops ahead with private sector participation extending the earlier generation national space programs, the regulatory landscape that was aligned with the earlier sector construct, starts getting outdated and the need for the regulations to keep pace with the technological and economic developments seems both urgent and

37 "ESPI Report 77, NewSpace in Asia, Experts views on space policy and business trends in Asian countries, February, 2022.

38 WIPO, Technology Trends: Future of Transportation, available at< https://www.wipo.int/web-publications/wipo-technology- trends-future-of-transportation/en/index.html.>

39 WIPO ,based on patent data from Econ Sight/IFI Claims, October 2024 ,availabl eat: <https://www.wipo.int/web-publications/wipo-technology-trends-technical-annex-future-of-transportation-in-space/en/top-inventor-locations.html.>

important. The value, that this development of private sector participation brings, is demonstrated both with respect to technology disruption and socio-economic impact. The World Trade Organisation (WTO) Committee on Trade and Environment (CTE) recently conducted its first thematic session[40] dedicated to technology transfer, wherein key barriers to effective technology transfer were identified.

Challenges before space technology transfer are;

- High costs and technical requirements,
- Gaps in supply and demand,
- Lack of clarity and uniformity in intellectual property regulation,
- The need for adequate funding and innovative financing mechanisms,
- Limited stakeholder engagement and trust,
- Infrastructure constraints,
- Market size limitations for technology absorption.

In the light of this report, the analysis is, Asian economies are facing systemic issues like, inadequate infrastructure, financing gaps and uneven technical capacity, despite this, transformation of Asian market indicates its resilience and adaptability to embrace technological innovations as a means to overcome challenges. This brings us to the challenges faced by Asian region in technology transfers. The region-specific policy outlook is required from international forums like, UNCTAD, WIPO, WTO, etc.

Conclusion

The increasing investment in innovation and application of state-of-the-art space technology by private players in space economy across nations and specifically in Asian region has raised concerns about protection of intellectual property rights for activities performed in outer space region beyond earth's regulatory sphere. Application of Patent laws based on territorial principle is getting challenged as borders are diluted due to extra-terrestrial activities, like, in earth's orbit, aboard the international space

40 Jane Birch, Technology Transfer– a WTO thematic sessionvailabee at: <https://www.industrytransition.org/insights/technology-www.industrytransition.org/insights/technology-transfer-a-wto-thematic- session/#:~:text=On%20April%201st%2C%202025%2C%20the,Head%20of%20Secretariat%20at%20LeadIT.>

station, or activities performed by AI enabled machines on the surface of other planets. The frequent launching of a constellation of satellites by private player like SpaceX and sharing of services across continents also raises questions about licensing or technology transfer (sharing) modes and their regulation. The disruptive technology deployed in the space industry by private players with the regulatory support of national space agencies is ushering a NewSpace era; therefore, rules pertaining to patent, trademark, industrial design, copyright and other intellectual property under existing treaty frameworks shall be revisited and member States shall strive to bring clarity and uniformity on intellectual property rights in outer space. This is cardinal for the sustained future of space tech-revolution and its benefits for all.

Chapter 5

India's Space Liberalisation: A Need to Relook at India's Various Technological Regulations of Outer Space

-Lakshmi Haritha Nakka

Abstract

The era of Private Space Companies started recently in the Supreme States like the U.S. and the U.K. The desire to explore the celestial orbits by sovereign countries led to a curtain raise to public public-private partnerships tradition even in outer space for making space innovations. The government, to reduce its cost on developing space technologies, started allowing private space companies and entered into joint venture agreements with their strategic partners by framing their own regulations. For that, they are even coming out of International customary Treaties. The U.S. government recently announced it came out of the Moon Treaty and framed its own laws to explore celestial bodies. India is also a signatory of the U.S. Artemis Accord and is going to use SpaceX's Falcon 9 for launching a communication satellite.

Private Players support the State Mission for space exploration. They help space exploring countries to build infrastructure in outer space, provide functional services like communication, develop new technologies, provide space industrial space stations, etc. Primarily, PPP in outer space was introduced in US and UK for space transportation, for utilising mass scale 3D Printed rockets, logistic services, and deep space exploration and mining, space manufacturing, bio-production, space agriculture, satellite services and servicing satellite communications, navigation, and earth monitoring. This paved the way to commercialising outer space activities and valuable resources. For reducing the cost of space technologies, governments of developed States are collaborating with private players under public-private partnerships. Currently United States, the United Kingdom, Russia, India, Japan and China are exploring outer space activities on celestial bodies in collaborations with private space companies. PPP domestic regulations vary across countries. One fine example is the U.S. PPP contract with Elon Musk to use his SpaceX for docking U.S Space Station to bring Astronauts who had remained in the U.S. Space Station for a long time and accomplish its mission successfully. This furthermore enhanced privatising space contracts (at the cost of commons) globally. All six countries which are exploring space are coming out of the International common standards, its principles, treaties, and protocols.

Therefore, this chapter stressed the current outer space innovation technologies developed by States in collaboration with private space companies in recent decades, how India's Outer Space PPP Contracts are regulating under its various laws, how the Space Activities Bill, 2017, Indian Space Policy, 2023, intends to regulate space ecosystem were discussed in detail. In the Second Part, how common heritage of mankind principle is slowly being replaced by PPP Commercial contracts, the ill effects of outer space commercialisation when they are not properly regulated were discussed. Finally, in 3rd part, the author stressed the urgent need to re-examine Indian Intellectual property laws for regulating advanced space innovating technologies developed by private space companies, paper studied whether any redressal mechanism is established to resolve future outer space disputes that arise between the Indian government and domestic and foreign private space companies after its outer space liberalisation by signing to Artemis Accords are covered.

Keywords: Indian Space Policy, 2023, Public Private Partnership, Commercialisation, Common Heritage of Mankind, Technology Transfer.

Current Outer Space Technologies in Recent Decades

Introduction

The Government of India liberalised its territorial outer space to the private sector, which allows Non-Government Entities (NGEs) to engage in space activities without restrictions. For that Indian Government established Indian National Space Activities, otherwise known as (IN-SPACE) which promotes and supervises NGEs activities. NGEs Works on Earth

Observation (EO) System through Public Public-Private Partnership. The Government of India (GoI) also introduced the Indian Space Policy, 2023, formulated norms, Guidelines & Procedures (NGP) and FDI Policy. It also introduced various schemes like Technology Adoption Fund (TAF), Seed Fund, Pricing Support, Mentorship and Technical Labs to support space start-ups.

On 31 December 2024, India entered into a Memorandum of Understanding (MoU) and issued 72 authorisations to private space companies. On 18th November, 2022, IN-SPACE authorises India's first Private Launch Vehicle ***Vikram-S***, a suborbital rocket by ***Skyroot Aerospace,*** a domestic space start-up belongs to South India. It transferred technology of Small Satellite Launch Vehicle (SSLV) to Indian Companies. To boost up space activities, the Government of India proposed to set up Rs. 1000 crores venture capital fund. Nearly 330 industries are associated with IN-SPACE to initiate their private space activities.[1] GoI established a national committee for the adoption of space technology education in India under IN-SPACE.[2]

GoI has not newly liberalised its space activities to private sector. For many years onwards, it allowed the private sector, and now its number and scope is just enhancing. By 2023, private space start-ups reached to 189 in number. 124.7 million dollars of investments reached in India by private space Start-Ups. To promote foreign direct investment in Space sector, India collaborated with DPIIT, and reviewed FDI Policy guidelines of the space sector. It expected $44 billion profits from space activities from $ 8.4 billion by 2033. To reach its expectations, it depended purely on private sector participation. It allowed private space companies to manufacture satellites, ground systems and to launch vehicle manufacturing, allowed them to provide satellite services.[3]

ISRO has been engaging since 1976, but to commercialise its outer space, it established New Space India Limited (NSIL) on 6th March, 2019, a Public Sector Undertaking (PSU) under Company Act 2013, Department of Space & The Administrative Control of the Department of Space (DoS).

1 Parliament Question: Encouraging Private Participation in Space Sector, Department of Space, 20 March, 2025, New Delhi available at: <pib.gov.in/PressReleaseIframePage.aspx?PRID=1988864>

2 The Number of Space Start-Ups have gone-up, from just 1 in 2014 to 189 in 2023 as per DPIIT Start up India Portal, says Union Minister Dr. Jitendra Singh, Department of Space, 20th December 2023, PIB Delhi available at: <pib.gov.in/PressReleaseIframePage.aspx?PRID=1633892>

3 *ibid*

Its headquarters is situated at Bengaluru, Karnataka, India. Established with a main motive to scale up private sector participation in Indian space programmes. This company provides signals to satellite launch spacecraft and subsystems, it supports ground infrastructure for space-based needs etc.[4]

ISRO's Collaboration with Foreign Countries' Space Companies:

During 2015, Indian Space Research Organisation (ISRO) launched four Indian Satellites and 17 foreign satellites by collaborating with five countries. And proposes to launch a further eight Indian satellites (weighing about 12,000 Kg) and 19 foreign satellites (weighing about 850 Kg) by 2016. [5]

Space activities in collaboration with foreign private company:

From January 2013 to December 2015, Indian Space Research Organisation (ISRO) has launched 28 international customer satellites belonging to foreign companies/ Space agencies/ Universities from nine countries, namely Austria, Canada, Denmark, France, Germany, Indonesia, Singapore, the United Kingdom and the United States of America. These satellites were launched under a commercial arrangement entered into between Antrix Corporation Limited (Antrix) belongs to ISRO and the foreign customer. Antrix company brought 80.6 Million Euros profit through launching 28 foreign customer satellites. In 2013-2015 6.9,18.2 & 55.5 Million Euros were earned by Antrix respectively.[6]

Chandrayaan- l was an example of cooperation with different countries and discovered the presence of hydroxyl and water molecules on the lunar surface. It has renewed interest of the younger generation in scientific &

---

4 New Space India Limited. available at: <https://www.nsilindia.co.in/corporate-governance.>

5 Government of India, Department of Space, "Space in Parliament", Budget Session of Parliament 2016 (February-May 2016) Compilation of Replies Given in Parliament During 2016. p. 2, point a, pp 1-127. Availableat:<https://www.isro.gov.in/media_isro/pdf/docs/UsefulLinks/ParliamentQuestions/budget_session_in_parliament_2016_february_may_2016.pdf>. During the last 20 years i.e. from April 1996 to April 2016, Indian Space Research Organisation (ISRO) has launched 56 Indian satellites, which include (i) 24 Communication Satellites; (ii) 14 Earth Observation satellites; (iii) 7 Navigational Satellites; (iv) 3 Weather & Atmosphere satellites; (v) 4 Space science & Planetary exploration satellites and (vi) 4 satellites built by students of Indian Universities / Institutions.available at: < https://www.nsilindia.co.in/corporate-governance>

6 *Ibid* at 84.

space activities and enhanced India's prestige amongst the world scientific community. *Chandrayaan-2*, was also approved and succeeded, which helps in understanding the origin and evolution of the Moon.[7]

With Private Collaboration, India is initiating Solar Mission Aditya L1 Satellite

ISRO is also working towards launching its first Indian solar mission, Aditya L1 satellite which will be placed in a halo orbit around the Sun-Earth Lagrangian point-1 (L1), i.e. about 1.5 million kilometres from the Earth orbit. With prime objective to study the solar corona in different wavebands.[8]

By 2016, Indian Space Research Organisation (ISRO) had no plans to share satellite manufacturing technology with its own private Indian companies for tapping small commercial satellite market, but being in the line of supremacy race, India also moving its steps in commercial way to get many advantages from outerspace.[9]

Using Space Technology under NNRMS in Various Departments:

National Natural Resources Management System (NNRMS) collaborates with various Ministries/ Departments through nine theme-oriented Standing Committees for using space technology to carry out various national-level application projects, which include:

(i) Periodic mapping of land use/ land cover, land degradation, Geomorphology & Lineament

(ii) Space based Information Support for De-centralised Planning (SIS-DP) at Panchayat level.

(iii) Forest Cover Change Alert System.

(iv) Creation of GCP Library.

(v) Multi-tier/ Multi-theme capacity building programme for Ministries/Departments.

7 *Ibid* at 93-94.

8 *Ibid* at 2, Point C.

9 *Ibid* at 13.

In addition, under the umbrella of NNRMS, various. ISRO/DOS Centres are executing different application projects sponsored by various Ministries/ Departments.[10]

Recent space innovations:

- Test Vehicle mission (TV-D1) was innovated for escaping space crew in emergency and parachute deployment.
- Ground testing of propulsion stages solid, liquid and cryogenic engine.
- Design of environmental control and life support system. Sub-system realisation and Sub-system level tests are in progress.
- Gaganyaan First uncrewed mission (G-1) and Crew Module and Service Module structure realisation. Mechanical Interface generation and integration activities are in progress.
- Integrated Air Drop Tests, Crew module structural test and integration activities are in progress which are useful to test IAF Chinook helicopter.
- ISRO developed human spaceflight activities and planning to carry out crewed and uncrewed to induct various indigenous technologies such as flight suits, crew seat, viewport and advanced avionics systems.

Other undergoing Schemes

ISRO is formulating a proposal to develop and deploy Bharatiya Antariksh Station (BAS) in low Earth orbit for demonstrating Lunar landing by 2040.

To promote private sector participation in the space sector, the Indian Space Policy 2023 has been released by GoI, Various schemes are introduced to promote private sector participation in outer space under IN-SPACE, such as Seed Fund Scheme, Pricing Support Policy, Mentorship support, Design Lab for NGEs, Skill Development in Space Sector.

IN-SPACE has signed around 51 MoUs with Non-Government Entities (NGEs) to provide necessary support for the realization of space systems

10 *ibid* at 126, Point 2208.

and applications which helps in increasing manufacturing of launch vehicles and satellites.[11]

How India's Outer Space PPP Contracts are Regulating under Various Laws:

International Negotiations:

ISRO engaged in multilateral negotiation processes under various International and UN forums to protect India's interests in doing outer space activities. Such forums are:

- International Code of Conduct for Outer Space Activities led by the European Union.
- Formulated guidelines for Long Term Sustainability of Outer Space Activities under United Nations Committee on the Peaceful Uses of Outer Space (UNCOPUOS).[12]

In 2016, the Department of Space took initiative to draft ***National Space Act*** for enhancing private sector participation.[13] In the year 2017 a draft Space Activities Bill was introduced in parliament. The bill was introduced not as mere regulatory but to facilitate private sector participation in space activities under authorisation and supervision by the Government.[14]

How Space Activities Bill, 2017, Indian Space Policy, 2023 intends to regulate India's Space Ecosystem:

The Space Activities Bill, 2017: The bill was introduced to promote and regulate the space activities of India. It contains a total of six Chapters and 33 sections. The bill proposed to extend this Act to every citizen of India in and outside India or outside India and every legal or juridical person including Governmental and non-governmental or private sector agency, company, corporate body registered or incorporated in India and engaged in any space activity in India or outside India. This Act protects

11 Government of India, Department of Space, "Space in Parliament", Budget Session of Parliament 2024, p. 4-6, point 808.

12 Government of India, Department of Space, "Space in Parliament", Budget Session of Parliament 2016 (February-May 2016) Compilation of Replies Given in Parliament During 2016, *note* 5, p. 19.

13 *ibid* at 57.

14 Draft Space Activities Bill, 2017, pp 1-15, p 4, point 14 available at: <https://prsindia.org.>

any from violations in launching any space object, its use, and operations, against wrong guidance. It protects space entry objects. This act promotes commercial space activities which generates or is capable of generating revenue or profits. [15]

Under Chapter II, the proposed bill provided provisions regarding space activities regulatory mechanism by Central Government. The bill promotes central government to establish a regulatory mechanism to promote the growth of every matter relating to space activity including exploration and use of outer space and to promote scientific and technical knowhow. It was empowered to fame policies on outer space, to develop space activity plan for commercial and economic needs of the country, grant licence to any person, promotes technical support in launching and operating space object, authorises to launch or operate commercial space activity including corporate and other organisational structure either directly or through any agency. It regulates the procedure of space activities, monitors space activity with international space agreements, supervise every space activity, share access and benefits including pricing mechanism of products created by space activity and technology with any person or any agency, investigates space accidents in connection with the operation of a space activity.[16]

Under Chapter III, the Act provided authorisation and Licence for commercial space activity. Under section 6, the Act prohibited unauthorised space activity. It specified without obtaining licence, no person shall carry on any commercial space activity. At least such person must be an employee or agent of a licensed person. The Act further exempted any person to do any space any activity without licence if the requirement is not necessary to meet the international obligation of India. Whereas under Chapter IV, through section 12, the Act proposed to impose liability for causing damage on licensee. Licensee shall indemnify the central government against any claims brought against the Government in respect of any damage or loss arising out of a commercial space activity.[17]

Under Chapter V Act provided provisions for offences and penalties under sections 13-24. If any person without authorisation undertakes any commercial space activity shall be punished with imprisonment for

15 Draft Space Activities Bill, 2017, pp 1-15, sections 1(3), 2(f), p 4, point 14 available at: <https://prsindia.org.>

16 Draft Space Activities Bill, 2017, pp 1-15, section 4, p 4 available at: <https://prsindia.org>

17 Draft Space Activities Bill, 2017, pp 1-15, section 12(1), p 8 available at: <https://prsindia.org>

a term not less than 1 year but may extend to 3 years or with fine of one crore rupee, if offence continues additional fine which extend to 50 lakh rupees for every day will be imposed. Except section 13 all other penalties are very minimal. Section 16 provides punishment for causing damages or pollution to environment, earth, airspace, celestial bodies by any space activity shall be punished with 1 year imprisonment and with fine of 1 crore rupees. Section 23 provides offences by companies. But did not specified any term or cost of fine.

Indian Space Policy, 2023

Indian space policy 2023 was formulated to implement space reforms. This policy aimed to enhance participation of NGEs in space activities. This policy was introduced to encourage and develop commercial activities in space for socio-economic development. To encourage greater private sector participation in the entire value chain of the Space economy including in the creation of space and ground based assets. By liberalising outer space communication, remote sensing data services, launch services shall be directly available to Indian consumers.

According to this policy NGEs/private space companies whether domestic or foreign shall be allowed to undertake end-to-end outer space activities. NGEs are allowed to invite space-based communication services through self-owned or procured or leased GSO/NGSO communication satellites. They could establish and operate ground facilities for space objects operations, such as TT & C Earth Stations and Satellite Control Centres (SCCs). The private sector is allowed to use Indian orbital resources or non Indian orbital resources to establish space objects for communication services over India and outside India. Private Sector could make new ITU filings through WPC/DOT to acquire orbital Resources. NGEs are free to make ITU fillings through non Indian administration also.

Private Sector are allowed to establish and operate remote sensing satellite system within and outside India through self-owned or procured or leased satellites. They could be free to spread satellite-based remote sensing data anywhere. Develop and commercialise space technologies. They could freely manufacture and operate space transportation system including launch vehicles, shuttles. Establish and operate launch infrastructure. They are allowed to undertake research, innovation and technology for long-term sustainability of space activities. They could engage in the commercial recovery of an asteroid resource or a space resource. Any NGE engaged in such process shall be entitled to possess, own, transport, use and sell any such asteroid resource or space resource obtained in accordance with applicable law, including the international obligations of India. They are allowed to undertake any other IN-SPACE prescribed commercial space activity. But there is no appropriate mechanism to resolve any dispute arising out of space activity, as per the existing laws.[18]

Primarily, Permanent Court of Arbitration (PCA) resolves the Outer Space Disputes by adopting the Optimal Rules for Arbitration of Disputes Relating to Outer Space Activities (2011)[19] but these rules are not ultimately followed because the States which opt these rules for resolving their Outer Space disputes by 1976 UNICITRAL Arbitration Rules, 2010.[20] Currently, States are accepting their own outer space laws which facilitates title to space resources.[21] Supreme Countries are not willing to consider outer space as common mankind they see outer space resources as commercial products.

Based on the 2010 UNICITRAL Arbitration Rules PCA Resolves disputes which are having an outer space component involving the use of outer space by States, international organizations and private entities. PCA resolves the disputes in lines of public international law. PCA provides freedom to the parties to choose an arbitral tribunal with one, three or five persons as penal. To resolve the disputes between two or more States parties to a multilateral agreement relating to the use of or access to outer space. A model clause is inserted in its rule book for parties who may consider other treaties or other agreements like Artemis Accords for providing party states to resolve their future disputes through Permanent Court of arbitration.[22] Now to liberalise their outer space activities every country becoming signatory to Artemis Accord. U.S. declare is come out of the Moon Treaty. Though not officially declared by many countries out

18 Indian Space Policy - 2023, pp 1-11 available at: <https://www.isro.gov.in/media_isro/pdf/IndianSpacePolicy2023.pdf>

19 Mythili Srinivasamurthy, International Arbitration of the Quixotic Outer-Space Disputes Under PCA Optical Rules, I, (X), IJLRA, (2021),available at <https://papers.ssrn.com/sol3/papers.cfm?abstract_id=3865128.>

20 CC/Devas (Mauritius) Ltd., Devas Employees Mauritius Private Limited, and Telecom Devas Mauritius Limited v Republic of India, PCA Case No. 2013-09 (Ind)

21 Laura Yvonne Zielinski, Japan Authorises Space mining operation on the moon, (Jan, 18, 2023), available at <www.https://ibanet.org>

22 Permanent-court-of-Arbitration-Optional-Rules-for-Arbitration-of-Disputes-Relating-to-Outer-Space-Activities. 1 January, 2016, pp 1-24 available at: <https://docs.pca-cpa.org/2016/01/Permanent-Court-of-Arbitration-Optional-Rules-for-Arbitration-of-Disputes-Relating-to-Outer-Space-Activities.pdf>

of 55 countries till date still are parties to both Moon Treaty and Artemis Accords. For all these countries any disputes arise between them could resolve through PCA under 2010 UNICITRAL Arbitration Rules. But India wants to establish an appropriate mechanism to resolve any dispute arising out of doing outer space activities between it and other state(s). But till date it has not been established.

Hence it is clear that there is no dispute redressal mechanism to resolve any future outer space dispute arise out of PPP Contracts between India and foreign countries or domestic space companies after it become member to artemis accord. Either it has to establish its redressal mechanism or to accept PCA. Till date no law was finalised. If India Choose to follow its own national space law but other country opt for PCA or Its own national space law then conflict of laws might arise. Then theory of comity have to be make applicable to the Artemis Accords or new convention have to be formulated by G.A Assembly in lines of Private International Law. It completely depends upon parties to the disputes i.e. individual states to accept the forum and arbitrators. According to Article 35 of PCA Rules, The arbitral tribunal shall decide as *amiable compositeur* or *ex aequo et bono* only if the parties have expressly authorized the arbitral tribunal to resolve the dispute in accordance with terms and conditions of the agreement entered into between state parties. In case arbitral tribunal founds dispute un-resolvable, impossible etc. It terminates the proceedings as per Article 36.[23]

How Common Heritage of Mankind principle is slowly replaced by PPP outer space Commercial Contracts

Common Heritage of Mankind

Primarily common heritage of mankind is recognised and made applicable to oceans, seas. As per the UNCLOS, 1958 under Article 136 provides a definition of Common Heritage of Mankind. "The area and its resources are the common heritage of mankind". No state shall claim or exercise sovereignty or sovereign rights over any part of the area or its resources, nor shall any state or natural or juridical person appropriate any part thereof. No such claim or exercise of sovereignty or sovereign rights nor such appropriation, shall be recognised. All rights in the resources of the area are vested in mankind as a whole as per Article 137 (1) & (2). Whereas Article 140 provides that activities in the area shall be carried out for the

23 *Ibid* at 19.

benefit of mankind as a whole irrespective of the geographical location of States. Ocean, moon, sun, planets does not belongs to one nation. They are common resources to whole mankind. Then a question raised why could not UNCLOS principles which belongs to Sea could not be attributed to space.[24] But, in 1952 itself Scholar Schacht proposed common heritage of mankind principle to outer space and celestial bodies.[25] Legal subcommittee of UN General Assembly in 1979 adopted Moon Treaty under title "The agreement governing the activities of States on the moon and other celestial bodies" through resolution 34/68 but it came into force in the year 1984.[26]

Moon Treaty, 1979

Agreement governing the activities of States on the moon and other celestial bodies other wise known as Moon Treaty, 1979 provided protection to outer space resources. Moon and its natural resources are considered as Common Heritage of Mankind under Article 11, Para 1. Under para 2 it restricted states not to subject moon to national appropriation by claim of sovereignty, by means of use or occupation or by any other means. It strictly restricted States to explore exploit surface and subsurface of moon nor any part thereof or natural resources in place. Under para 3 treaty curtailed ownership rights on moon. "Moon shall not become property of any state, International intergovernmental or non-governmental organization, national organization or non-governmental entity i.e private space companies, or of any natural person." But with recent liberalization of outer space activities to private space companies against the provisions of article 11 of moon treaty by Artemis Accords. Common heritage of Mankind principle is totally kept aside.[27]

There can be no private or public appropriation of natural resources on celestial bodies, orbits etc. No one legally owns common heritage spaces.

24 United Nations Convention on the Law of the Sea-Part XI, Section 2 available at: <https://www.un.org/depts/los/convention_agreements/texts/unclos... >

25 G Wang, Xinyi huang, "on the common heritage of mankind principle in space", vol. 211, October.2023, pp 926-938 available at: < https://www.sciencedirect.com/science/article/abs/pil/S0094576523003521>

26 Moon Agreement. Available at: <https://www.unoosa.org/oosa/en/ourwork/spacelaw/treaties/intromoon-agreement.html >

27 United Nations Treaty Collection, No. 23002 Multilateral Agreement governing the activities of States on the moon and other celestial bodies. Adopted by the General Assembly of the United Nations, vol 1363, pp 22-86(5 December, 1979)available at: <https://treaties .un.org>

All nations must manage resources on behalf of all because they belong to all- sun, moon and planets belong to all. All nations must actively share with each other the benefits acquired from exploitation of the resources from the common heritage region, there should be restraint on the profit-making activities.[28]

The Outer Space Treaty and U.N. Office for Outer Space Affairs (UNOOSA) emphasise that the exploration and use of outer space shall be carried out for the benefit and in the interest of all countries and shall be the province of all mankind. Outer space is not subject to national appropriation by claim of sovereignty, by means of use or occupation, or by any other means. States shall be responsible for national space activities, whether carried out by government or non-governmental entities. Article VI of the Outer Space Treaty deals with international responsibility, stating at the activities of non-governmental entities in outer space, including the moon and other celestial bodies, shall require authorisation and continuing supervision by the appropriate state party to the treaty" and that states party shall bear international responsibility for national space activities whether carried out by governmental or non-governmental entities.[29]

But unfortunately, In 2020, America's president, Mr Donald Trump signed Artemis Accords and brought an executive order which Encourages States to recover and Use Space Resources through their NGEs. U.S. government Unanimously declared it is not going to considered outer space minerals as common heritage of mankind.[30]

28 Frakes, Jennifer, "The Common Heritage of Mankind Principle and the Deep Seabed, Outer Space, and Antarctica: Will Developed and Developing Nations Reach a Compromise?", *Wisconsin International law Journal*, vol. 21, issue 409 (2003).; see also G Wang, Xinyi huang, "on the common heritage of mankind principle in space", *Science Direct*, vol. 211, (October 2023), pp 926-938. Available at: <https://www.sciencedirect.com/science/article/abs/pil/S0094576523003521>

29 Treaty on Principles Governing the Activities of States in the Exploration and use of outer space, including the Moon and other Celestial Bodies, foreign and commonwealth office; See United Nations Office for Outer Space Affairs A Year of Transition Annual Report 2023, pp 1-36 at p 36 available at: <https://www.unoosa.org/documents/pdf / annualreport/UNOOSA_Annual_Report_2023.pdf> "UNOOSA is responsible for advancing international cooperation in the peaceful uses of outer space and helps all countries use space science and technology to achieve sustainable development."

30 Agreement Governing the Activities of States on the Moon and Other Celestial Bodies, (Dec. 5, 1979), 1363 U.N.T.S. 3,available at: <https://www.unoosa.org/oosa/en/ourwork/spacelaw/treaties/intromoon-agreement.html>

Under Artemis Accords Mission NASA sent its Orion spacecraft from its Kennedy Space Center in Florida. It broke the record of Apollo 13. It conducts deep space explorations. NASA planning to return humans to the moon's surface with Artemis 3 by 2025 for placing humans near the lunar south pole. NASA Planning to sent its first woman on the moon in 2024.[31] Though not ratified Moon treaty and Artemis accord, India is also a signatory to both these non binding arrangements, but in future, conflicts may arise between India and other countries because the moon treaty restricts commercial space activities whereas Artemis Accord is purely commercial agreement for exploiting outer space scarce common resources. Recently United States welcomes Bangladesh for signing on US Artemis Accords and became 54th signatory country.[32] States are not willing to be party to Moon Treaty. Only 17 States ratified. No State shown its willing to adopt Moon Treaty, Article 11 i.e. Outer space as common heritage of Mankind was not considered as customary international law.[33]

Ownership rights on advanced space innovation technologies belongs to whom

Space Activities Bill, 2017 proposed to Protect IPR

Under section 25 (1), (2) of the draft space activities Act, 2017 GoI intended to protect any invention or other form of intellectual property rights such as patents, copyrights, trademarks or such other rights, developed, generated

31 Robert Lea, "Artemis Accords: What are they & which countries are involved?" available at: <space.com/artemis-accords-explained>. Last visited on 17-05-2025; See also Brett Tingley, "The 10 greatest images from NASAs Artemis 1 moon mission", 11th December, 2022. available at <space.com/10-greatest-images-nasa-artemis-1-moon-mission>. Accessed on 17-05-2025.

32 Media Note, "United Stes Welcomes Bangladesh's Singing of the Artemis Accords", office of the spokesperson, 10th April, 2025, available at: <https://www.state.gov/united> -states-welcomes-bangladeshs-signing-of-the...> accessed on 16 May 2025.

33 Naman Khatwani, "Common Heritage of Mankind for Outer Space," *Taylor & Francis*, vol. 17, Issue 2, (25 July, 2019), pp 89-103 available at: <https://www.tandfonline.com/doi/abs/10.1080/14777622.2019.1638679.> Austria, Chile, Morocco, Netherlands, Peru, Phillipines, Uruguay are parties to the moon treaty. Uruguay though ratified moon treaty it signed on Artemis Accords and stood as 55th State. Whereas France, Guatemala, India and Romania were only signatories to moon treaty. India signed moon treaty on 18th January, 1982. And signed on Artemis Accords on 22nd June, 2023. Uruguay ratified moon treaty on 26th May 1981. The countries which are parties to the moon treaty namely Austria, Netherlands, Uruguay, Peru, Chile, France are currently signatories to Artemis Accords. France and Romania are also signatories to Artemis Accords. Saudi Arabia withdrawn moon agreement. Norway became 55th state to Artemis Accords.

or created during the course of any space activity shall be protected under any law for the time being in force, with the primary objective of safeguarding the national interest. Any form of intellectual property right developed, generated or created onboard a space object in outer space, shall be deemed to be the property of the Central Government of India.[34]

The 2023 policy nowhere mentioned about IPR protection to space innovations. No Space Act was currently in enforcement to resolve space disputes. No IP protection to domestic companies for their space innovation technologies. Though IPR laws are existing in India, they didn't protect domestic space companies. Ownership rights completely belongs to India.

Conclusion and Recommendations

Though India is recognised as fast developing country. It stood as developed country in outer space. It launched foreign satellites from 1967 onwards. With Chandrayaan mission it made every country to see India. By 2035 India is going to establish its space station alike America. Now it also initiated research on Solar Planet. Stood as 5th country in world in outer space research and development. Now it is ready to send human into space. India is the first country which successfully landed its rover on south pole on moon. Now to enhance its research and space technology it is liberalising its outer-space. It signed U.S Artemis accords (a non binding multilateral arrangements between US and other sovereign countries) on other side it is signatory to Moon treaty. Here conflicts arises when strategic parties in ppp contract belongs to party to moon treaty. i.e. commercialisation vs. Restrictions on outer space commercial activities i.e. Artemis Accord vs. Moon treaty). And between different national space laws and arbitration forums and selection of arbitrators. After observations from the study, author recommended below before liberalising India's outer space.

Recommendations

- The 2023 policy nowhere mentioned about IPR protection to space innovations. It must be relooked.
- Space Act has to be enforced soon for resolving IP space disputes if India do not intend to resolve its future disputes involving outer space element.

34 Draft "Space Activities Bill, 2017" pp 1-15, section 25, at p 12. available at: <https://prsindia.org>

- States party shall bear international responsibility for national space activities whether carried out by governmental or non-governmental entities in accordance with UNOOSA.
- Appropriate dispute redressal mechanism should be established for resolving any outer space dispute out of space activity to be.
- Penalties and Liabilities on NGEs for violations of Outer Space Activities under Space Activities Bill, 2017 are very minimal.
- Space Policy 2023 nowhere mentioned about IP Protection to space technology innovations, space technology IP ownership rights. Simply mentioned any form of intellectual property right developed, generated or created onboard a space object in outer space, shall be deemed to be the property of the Central Government of India. It raises conflicts of laws in case the strategic partner belongs to a foreign country.
- Section 23 of draft Space Activities Act, 2017 provides offences by space companies. But did not specify any term or cost of fine for its violations and breaches.
- There should be separate Outer Space IPR Laws or Indian IP Laws to be amended in accordance with the international outer space treaties.

Chapter 6

Outer Space, Intellectual Property and the Monopoly of Dominant Players: Legal and Strategic Challenges Ahead for India

Pawan Kumar and Simar Kumar

Abstract

Once the sole purview of independent nations and scientific aspirations, outer space has quickly transformed into a high-stakes arena of technological competition, commercial opportunity, and geopolitical significance. Intellectual Property Rights (hereinafter, IPR) have become increasingly important in regulating innovation, ownership, and control in space as a result of the quick commercialisation of space activities, which range from satellite deployment and space tourism to asteroid mining and lunar colonisation. Through exclusive data systems and proprietary technologies, companies like SpaceX, Blue Origin, and Amazon's Project Kuiper are redefining the boundaries of space governance as traditional state-centric exploration gives way to a thriving private sector propelled by billion-dollar investments.

A significant legal conundrum at the center of this change is whether intellectual property, which is by its very nature territorial, can coexist with the global commons nature of outer space. IPRs are crucial instruments for encouraging innovation and safeguarding high-risk investments in the space industry, but they also bring up challenging issues of equity, accessibility, and exclusivity—especially in light of the growing monopolisation of launch capabilities and orbital infrastructure by a small number of influential players.

The Outer Space Treaty of 1967, which is the cornerstone of international space law, forbids national appropriation of celestial bodies and emphasises that space is 'the province of all mankind.' However, it remains conspicuously silent on the treatment of intellectual property in extraterrestrial environments. In the absence of a dedicated global legal regime, space-faring nations have increasingly relied on domestic patent systems and bilateral arrangements to regulate IPRs in space, a fragmented approach that risks deepening the divide between technological haves and have-nots.

In this chapter, we seek to critically examine the intersection of intellectual property rights and monopolistic consolidation in the space domain. It explores the inadequacies of existing international legal frameworks, identifies the unique IPR challenges posed by the extraterrestrial context, and analyses how market concentration is reshaping the future of space law and governance, more so for India. Finally, the chapter proposes pathways for legal reform that balance innovation incentives with the need to preserve outer space as a shared domain for all humankind.

Introduction

The monopolistic inclinations of powerful space players further worsen this legal void. For example, SpaceX owns most of the operational commercial satellites and, through its Starlink constellation, has taken a major lead in reusable launch technology and worldwide internet access. These advancements create structural obstacles for new competitors, especially those from the Global South, in addition to solidifying market dominance through technological superiority. The space economy runs the risk of reflecting the disparities and exclusions that are already common on Earth as businesses utilise vast patent portfolios and proprietary data systems to achieve strategic dominance.

A set of multilateral agreements created under the direction of the United Nations Committee on the Peaceful Uses of Outer Space (UNCOPUOS) largely regulates human activity in space. The 1967 Outer Space Treaty (OST), which serves as the foundation for international space law, is the most important of these. The prohibition of putting nuclear weapons in orbit or on celestial bodies, the non-appropriation of celestial bodies by states, and the use of space for the benefit and interest of all nations are some of the fundamental principles that the OST outlines. Crucially, Article I of the Treaty declares that 'outer space, including the Moon and other celestial bodies, shall be free for exploration and use by all States without discrimination of any kind,' while Article II prohibits any claim of sovereignty over outer space or its constituents.[1]

Exclusive proprietary rights, like those provided by intellectual property law, are directly conceptually challenged by the res communis, or commons, principle. The ownership of intellectual outputs (such as software, designs, and inventions) created or utilised in space is not specifically addressed by the OST, despite the fact that it declares outer space a global commons. As a result, there is still a legal void that state and private actors are increasingly navigating through domestic laws and international trade instruments due to the under-regulation of IPR in the extraterrestrial realm.

The 1976 Convention on Registration of Objects Launched into Outer Space is another pertinent document that establishes a connection between a space object and its launching state for the purposes of control and jurisdiction.[2] When deciding which law applies to intellectual property produced or utilised on such a spacecraft, this principle becomes important. The laws of the country that registered the particular module in which the invention was developed, for instance, may apply to inventions developed aboard the International Space Station (ISS).[3]

The Moon Agreement of 1979, a lesser-ratified treaty, builds upon the OST by reiterating the 'common heritage of mankind' principle and advocating for an international regime to govern the exploitation of lunar resources.[4] Though only ratified by a handful of states and not by major space powers like the United States, Russia, or China, it offers a normative framework that could inform future discussions on equitable access and IP governance in space.

1 Treaty on Principles Governing the Activities of States in the Exploration and Use of Outer Space, including the Moon and Other Celestial Bodies, art. I-II, Jan. 27, 1967, 18 U.S.T. 2410, 610 U.N.T.S. 205 [hereinafter Outer Space Treaty].

2 Convention on Registration of Objects Launched into Outer Space, art. II, Jan. 14, 1975, 28 U.S.T. 695, 1023 U.N.T.S. 15.

3 See Agreement Among the Government of Canada, Governments of Member States of the European Space Agency, the Government of Japan, the Government of the Russian Federation, and the Government of the United States of America concerning Cooperation on the Civil International Space Station, art. 5, Jan. 29, 1998, T.I.A.S. No. 12927 [hereinafter IGA].

4 Agreement Governing the Activities of States on the Moon and Other Celestial Bodies, art. 11, Dec. 18, 1979, 1363 U.N.T.S. 3.

Intellectual Property in Space Activities

Unlike space law, intellectual property law is inherently territorial. Rights such as patents, copyrights, and trademarks are granted and enforced under national legal systems and typically do not extend beyond the jurisdiction of the granting country. This fundamental feature creates complex questions when applied to outer space, where sovereignty is expressly disallowed and territorial jurisdiction is fluid.

Some jurisdictions have passed legislation that expands their domestic IPR regimes into space in order to address some of these issues. For example, the US has made it clear in its patent law that inventions created, utilised, or sold in a space object that falls under US jurisdiction are considered to have been created in the US. Similar to this, each partner country maintains control over its own modules and staff under the Intergovernmental Agreement (IGA) that oversees the ISS.[5] This highlights the fragmentation of IPR enforcement in multinational contexts while also providing some clarity regarding patent rights in cooperative space missions.

International organizations such as the World Intellectual Property Organization (WIPO) have recognized the increasing importance of intellectual property rights (IPR) in space-related technologies.[6] Nonetheless, attempts to establish a unified IPR framework for space are still in their infancy. Although it is binding on WTO members, the Agreement on Trade-Related Aspects of Intellectual Property Rights (TRIPS) does not specifically address the extraterrestrial context. However, when national laws incorporate the TRIPS's general principles of patentability, licensing, and dispute resolution, they indirectly apply to inventions based in space.

This patchwork of treaties and national statutes results in a legal environment where innovators must navigate multiple, often conflicting, IPR regimes, increasing the risk of jurisdictional disputes and strategic monopolisation. In the absence of a dedicated international treaty on IPR in space, powerful nations and corporations enjoy disproportionate legal and commercial advantages, further entrenching monopolistic structures in the emerging space economy.

5 supra note 3, art. 5.

6 World Intellectual Property Organization, Intellectual Property and Space Activities, https://www.wipo.int/about-ip/en/ip-space/ (last visited July 13, 2025).

Unique IPR Challenges in Outer Space

The legal framework of intellectual property rights (IPR) is confronted with previously unheard-of conceptual and practical challenges as humanity expands further into space. These difficulties are caused by the distinct legal and physical features of the extraterrestrial environment in addition to the territorial boundaries of conventional IPR regimes. Space is a jurisdictionally ambiguous area governed by the principles of cooperation and non-appropriation, in contrast to Earth-based legal systems, where sovereign states exercise clearly defined jurisdiction. This raises difficult issues with respect to relevant legislation, patent ownership, enforcement strategies, and moral issues in space-based innovation.

Ambiguity in Jurisdiction

The ambiguity surrounding jurisdiction is arguably the most basic IPR issue in space. Intellectual works created outside of national borders raise challenging issues regarding which country's laws apply because space is a non-sovereign domain. For inventions developed on multinational platforms such as the International Space Station (ISS), which is subject to a network of bilateral and multilateral agreements that assign jurisdiction based on the nationalities of crew members and the ownership of particular modules, this issue is particularly severe.[7]

For example, depending on specific intergovernmental agreements and patent filings, an invention made by a French astronaut aboard the Japanese Experiment Module (JEM) may, in theory, be governed by French law due to the inventor's nationality, Japanese law due to module ownership, or another jurisdiction.[8] The protection of the invention and the enforceability of the resulting intellectual property rights are both made more difficult by this patchwork of overlapping jurisdictions.

Enforcement in an International Setting

IP rights enforcement in space is still very difficult, even if jurisdiction is made clear. Injunctions, administrative action, and civil litigation are

7 Agreement Among the Government of Canada, Governments of Member States of the European Space Agency, the Government of Japan, the Government of the Russian Federation, and the Government of the United States of America concerning Cooperation on the Civil International Space Station, art. 5, Jan. 29, 1998, T.I.A.S. No. 12927 [hereinafter IGA].

8 Tanja Masson-Zwaan & Mahulena Hofmann, Introduction to Space Law 84–87 (3rd ed. 2019).

examples of traditional enforcement methods that are territorially limited. There isn't a policing or judicial body in space that can decide cross-border IPR disputes, particularly when private actors or even non-state actors are involved.[9]

There are strategic issues with this disparity. For example, if a U.S. company illegally uses a U.S. company's patented propulsion system on a privately owned lunar rover, what options does an Indian satellite operator have? Particularly as commercial activity increases, the lack of an efficient enforcement mechanism encourages IP piracy, unauthorised use, and litigation deadlocks.

Ownership of Inventions in Space

Determining who owns intellectual property created in space presents an additional challenge, especially when those innovations are the consequence of cooperative experiments or joint missions involving several countries or businesses. Although many jurisdictions have a default legal principle that grants patent ownership to the inventor or their employer, this becomes ambiguous when facilities are located outside of the country and research is funded by several agencies or funding sources.

Furthermore, there may be new patentability issues because inventions made in microgravity settings might be viewed as essentially different from those made on Earth. Pharmaceuticals or biological tissues created in zero gravity, for example, might have characteristics that are impossible to duplicate in terrestrial environments. Are these inventions subject to the usual standards for novelty and non-obviousness, and can the inventiveness of such inventions be evaluated by patent offices located on Earth?

Multinational Platforms and Fragmented Norms

Despite being praised as an example of global collaboration, the ISS also serves as an example of the challenges associated with managing intellectual property rights across borders. Each partner state retains jurisdiction over its own modules and personnel under the Intergovernmental Agreement (IGA). Determining the legal and diplomatic rights to the inventions that result from experiments that span multiple modules or use data and equipment from multiple nations can be challenging.[10] The ownership,

9 Yanal Abul Failat & Anél Ferreira-Snyman, Outer Space Law: Legal Policy and Practice 310–12 (2d ed. 2022).

10 IGA, art. 5.

licensing, and exploitation of space-derived technologies may also be unclear due to contractual obligations that private companies involved in ISS projects may have that deviate from domestic IPR laws.[11]

Ethical Concerns and the Common Heritage Principle

IPR in space presents more general ethical issues than just practical ones. Space shouldn't be the sole focus of commercial appropriation, according to the "common heritage of mankind" principle, which was most forcefully stated in the Moon Agreement. However, it can be argued that this fundamental norm is being compromised when private actors are permitted to monopolise orbital slots, run proprietary satellite systems, and patent inventions derived from space.[12]

When it comes to data produced by navigation systems or Earth observation satellites, the problem is particularly obvious. Although businesses can claim ownership of such data through software protections or trade secrets, the data itself may have global environmental or humanitarian significance. Therefore, there is a conflict between the public interest and IPR exclusivity, particularly in fields like planetary science, disaster relief, and climate monitoring.[13]

Rise of Private Players and Market Consolidation: Privatisation and Commercialisation of Space

The 21st century has witnessed a profound transformation in space exploration—from a domain historically monopolised by national space agencies to one increasingly driven by private enterprise. The shift was catalysed by a combination of diminishing public space budgets, the need for technological innovation, and a favourable policy environment in countries like the United States, which opened the door to commercial actors through legislation such as the Commercial Space Launch Act of

11 Space Law and the Private Sector: The Need for Legal Innovation, 18 SMU Sci. & Tech. L. Rev. 235, 243–45 (2015).

12 Agreement Governing the Activities of States on the Moon and Other Celestial Bodies, art. 11, Dec. 18, 1979, 1363 U.N.T.S. 3.

13 Joanne Irene Gabrynowicz, One Half Century and Counting: The Evolution of U.S. National Space Law and Three Long-Term Emerging Issues, 36 J. Space L. 445, 452–54 (2010).

1984 and later the U.S. Commercial Space Launch Competitiveness Act of 2015.[14]

Private firms now play a critical role in every layer of the space economy—launch services, satellite constellations, Earth observation, orbital logistics, and data processing. Companies like SpaceX, Blue Origin, Amazon's Project Kuiper, and OneWeb are not only launching payloads but also building proprietary systems that control access to the near-Earth orbital environment and the flow of satellite-based information.[15]

These firms heavily rely on intellectual property portfolios, including patents on reusable launch systems, software algorithms, and sensor technologies, to protect their innovations and secure competitive advantages.[16] However, IPRs, when coupled with massive capital and first-mover advantages, can also become tools of market exclusion and monopolistic dominance—a trend that is increasingly visible in the space sector.

Case Study: SpaceX and Starlink

Among all private actors, Space Exploration Technologies Corp. (SpaceX) has emerged as the most dominant player in the modern space industry. Founded in 2002 by Elon Musk, SpaceX disrupted the aerospace market by developing reusable rocket technology, significantly lowering launch costs and creating new commercial possibilities.[17]

As of mid-2025, SpaceX operates more than 65% of all active satellites in Earth's orbit, a majority of which belong to its Starlink constellation—a low-Earth orbit (LEO) satellite internet service.[18] With over 6,000 satellites already deployed and permission to expand to more than 40,000, Starlink has quickly become the largest satellite network in human history.[19] These satellites provide broadband coverage to remote and underserved areas, but

14 Commercial Space Launch Act, 51 U.S.C. §§ 50901–50923 (1984); U.S. Commercial Space Launch Competitiveness Act, Pub. L. No. 114-90, 129 Stat. 704 (2015).

15 Malcolm Macdonald, The International Handbook of Space Technology 537–43 (Springer, 2014).

16 World Intellectual Property Organization, Patents and the Space Sector, https://www.wipo.int/about-ip/en/ip-space/ (last visited July 13, 2025).

17 Ashlee Vance, Elon Musk: Tesla, SpaceX, and the Quest for a Fantastic Future 197–214 (HarperCollins, 2015).

18 Union of Concerned Scientists Satellite Database (June 2025), available at https://www.ucsusa.org/resources/satellite-database.

19 European Space Agency, Large Constellations and Space Traffic Management, ESA Tech Report No. STM-2025-01 (2025), https://www.esa.int.

they also raise concerns of spectrum monopolization, orbital congestion, and strategic dependency on a private actor.

SpaceX has aggressively protected its technologies through a mix of patents, trade secrets, and proprietary data systems.[20] For example, the company's reusable Falcon 9 rocket system includes components and processes that are either patented or closely guarded as trade secrets.[21] Starlink's proprietary communication protocols, satellite control software, and ground-based user equipment create a vertically integrated ecosystem that is difficult for competitors to replicate without infringing on SpaceX's IP.

Furthermore, SpaceX's dominance over orbital real estate—particularly in the LEO band—has raised red flags in international circles.[22] Its mass satellite deployments have spurred fears of a "first-occupier advantage" that effectively bars smaller firms and countries from accessing desirable orbits, a concern exacerbated by the lack of a coordinated international regime governing orbital slot allocation.[23]

In effect, SpaceX exemplifies how intellectual property, when combined with technological supremacy and regulatory gaps, can be leveraged not just for innovation but for the consolidation of market power in outer space.

Antitrust and Monopoly Issues

The rise of vertically integrated space corporations raises fundamental competition law issues. Traditional antitrust frameworks struggle to apply in the context of space, where there are no established rules for market dominance in orbital infrastructure, data control, or launch services.[24] The absence of supranational competition enforcement mechanisms in outer space means that even clearly monopolistic behaviour can go unchecked if no terrestrial legal regime applies.

20 Jonathan McDowell, The Expansion of Starlink and Satellite IP Strategies, Space Policy, vol. 62 (2024), https://doi.org/10.1016/j.spacepol.2024.101547.

21 U.S. Patent No. 10,208,115 (filed by SpaceX, detailing reusable launch vehicle systems).

22 Brian Weeden, Crowded Orbits: Managing the Rapid Expansion of Satellite Constellations, Secure World Foundation Report (2023), https://swfound.org.

23 Tanja Masson-Zwaan & Mahulena Hofmann, Introduction to Space Law 134–37 (3rd ed. 2019).

24 Lucien Rapp & Arnaud de Nanteuil, Competition Law in Outer Space: A New Frontier, in Law and Regulation of Commercial Mining of Outer Space 239–58 (Springer, 2022).

Moreover, proprietary control over space-derived data (e.g., high-resolution Earth imagery or global broadband networks) allows private firms to influence downstream markets in agriculture, defence, logistics, and telecommunications.[25] As a result, technological dependency on a few dominant actors becomes a national security concern, not merely a market competition issue.

In addition, the patenting of foundational technologies, such as space-grade propulsion systems, docking mechanisms, or navigation software, may create "patent thickets" that inhibit new entrants. Licensing such technologies becomes expensive or strategically restricted, stifling innovation and reinforcing the dominance of early movers.

While competition law bodies like the U.S. Federal Trade Commission (FTC) and the European Commission have shown increasing interest in Big Tech monopolies, there has been little regulatory focus on the space-tech monopolies emerging in parallel.[26] Without international coordination, the space domain may become an economic extension of a few private empires, rather than a shared arena for scientific and societal advancement.

IPR and Monopoly: Legal and Ethical Tensions

Intellectual property rights (IPR), while crucial for innovation, have also evolved into tools for market control as the privatisation of space picks up speed. In space-based industries, dominant players have a quasi-monopolistic grip on access and infrastructure when they combine strategic exclusivity, vertical integration, and large IPR portfolios. This leads to ethical conflicts in the management of space in addition to legal difficulties.

The function of exclusive patents on core technologies is a major worry. Space-faring organisations may obtain patents in several jurisdictions for vital infrastructure, including propulsion systems, docking systems, satellite communication protocols, and AI-based space navigation, in the absence of a global regulatory framework.[27] Despite being legally justified under national systems, these patents frequently allow large corporations to erect

25 OECD, Space Economy for People, Planet and Prosperity (2024), https://www.oecd.org/sti/space-economy/.

26 European Commission, Antitrust: Overview, https://competition-policy.ec.europa.eu/antitrust_en (last visited July 13, 2025)

27 Gavin Clarkson and David Dekorte, The Problem of Patent Thickets in Convergent Technologies, University of Michigan, Ann Arbor, Michigan 48109-1107, USA.

intellectual property walls, or "patent thickets," that make it prohibitively expensive for smaller or emerging space actors to enter.[28] The intricacy of licensing agreements and the risk of legal action discourage competition and restrict cooperative innovation.

The fact that space-based patents usually cover dual-use technologies that are used for both military and civilian purposes furthers this monopolisation. Although legally sound, IPR protection of such technology may lead to a global strategic reliance on a small number of private companies. Countries that depend on satellite-based internet or Earth imaging services, for instance, might be left to rely on private enterprises whose proprietary systems are not bound by any legally binding commitments to neutrality, open access, or service continuity.[29]

Furthermore, this disparity is exacerbated by the absence of open-source substitutes or technology-sharing systems. Although R&D is frequently subsidised by public-private partnerships (PPPs), the resulting technologies are often privatised through intellectual property rights (IPR), which results in the privatisation of publicly funded space innovation. The idea that space should be available "for the benefit and in the interests of all countries," as stated in Article I of the Outer Space Treaty, is compromised by this.[30]

Data control is not exempt from the ethical conundrum. Many businesses, including satellite operators, monopolise access to data that could have wide-ranging societal value by using encryption protocols and proprietary software, such as environmental data, agricultural forecasting, or emergency management.[31] This type of IP protection, especially through trade secrets and contractual restrictions, creates asymmetries in access to space-derived knowledge and economic opportunity, especially for non-spacefaring and developing countries.

Furthermore, the Global South remains largely excluded from this ecosystem. The cost of filing and defending patents, limited domestic

28 Id.

29 Brian Weeden, Crowded Orbits: Managing the Rapid Expansion of Satellite Constellations, Secure World Found. Rep. (2023), https://swfound.org.

30 Treaty on Principles Governing the Activities of States in the Exploration and Use of Outer Space, Including the Moon and Other Celestial Bodies, art. I, Jan. 27, 1967, 18 U.S.T. 2410, 610 U.N.T.S. 205.

31 Joanne Irene Gabrynowicz, Data Access and Sharing Policies for Satellite Earth Observation, 14 Geo. Int'l Envtl. L. Rev. 739, 741–46 (2002).

launch capabilities, and a lack of reciprocal recognition of IP rights all conspire to keep developing countries outside the innovation circle. Even as they participate in collaborative missions, their capacity to generate or claim IPR is structurally constrained, reinforcing an unequal global space order.[32]

From a normative perspective, this dynamic is in direct conflict with the "common heritage of mankind" principle that underpins several space law instruments, including the Moon Agreement. While that principle is not universally accepted, it reflects a moral imperative that the benefits of outer space must not be monopolised by a few actors or nations.[33] The current trajectory, however, suggests a drift toward techno-feudalism, where powerful firms erect legal and technological fences around critical space domains.

Conclusion and Way Forward

The rapidly evolving landscape of space activities and IPR demands coordinated international reform. Given the insufficiency of current frameworks, it is necessary that there should be a separate IPR framework for space governance, given the rise of commercialisation of space activities by big tech companies. A multilateral treaty or model law under the joint auspices of WIPO and UNCOPUOS could standardise IPR enforcement and jurisdiction in outer space.[34]

We also suggest the creation of a Space Patent Registry. A centralised, transparent International Space Patent Register should be developed to record and monitor patents applicable in space, reducing duplicative claims and promoting fair access.[35] There should be a separate Dispute Resolution Mechanism for space activities where a specialised arbitration system (e.g., under the existing or a new space-specific tribunal) for cross-border IPR disputes in space can be channelised.[36]

32 Tanja Masson-Zwaan & Mahulena Hofmann, Introduction to Space Law 92–94 (3rd ed. 2019).

33 Agreement Governing the Activities of States on the Moon and Other Celestial Bodies, art. 11, Dec. 18, 1979, 1363 U.N.T.S. 3.

34 Yanal Abul Failat & Anél Ferreira-Snyman, Outer Space Law: Legal Policy and Practice 360–64 (2d ed. 2022).

35 Id. at 365–66.

36 Lucien Rapp & Arnaud de Nanteuil, Competition Law in Outer Space: A New Frontier, in Law and Regulation of Commercial Mining of Outer Space 239–58 (Springer, 2022).

As space is a common concern of mankind, there should be equitable licensing models applied, and this would help developing space markets like India in promoting open licensing, compulsory licensing, or technology pools for essential space technologies, especially for those developed with public funding.[37] Ensuring inclusion of developing nations will facilitate capacity building, patent access, and infrastructure development through global partnerships and tech-transfer programs.[38]

These reforms need not abandon innovation incentives but must balance them with access, transparency, and shared governance, lest the final frontier becomes the exclusive property of the few, more so when India is launching its very own Bharatiya Antariksh Station in this decade to make space more accessible for everyone, making it truly a common heritage of humankind.

37 Bart Custers & Eduard Fosch-Villaronga, Law and Artificial Intelligence 214–19 (Springer, 2022).

38 Organisation for Economic Co-operation and Development (OECD), Space Economy for People, Planet and Prosperity (2024), https://www.oecd.org/sti/space-economy/.

Part III

Patentability and Innovation Challenges

Chapter 7

Contested Ownership: Microgravity Inventions Aboard International Space Station

---

-Ancy P Anto and Abhishek Thommandru

Abstract

This article examines the complex legal dimensions governing intellectual property rights and technology transfer for inventions created aboard the International Space Station (ISS). The ISS's unique setup, with modules governed by different national laws, creates challenges for patenting and commercialising inventions made in space. Through comprehensive doctrinal analysis of international space treaties, the ISS Intergovernmental Agreement, and national implementing legislation, this research identifies critical gaps in the current legal framework. This chapter explores how territorial intellectual property rights fundamentally conflict with the extraterritorial nature of space activities, particularly when innovations emerge from collaborative research spanning multiple ISS modules.

The research further evaluates jurisdictional ambiguities through comparative analysis of European, American, Japanese, and Russian approaches to patent claims in orbit. Notable examples illustrating these challenges include protein crystallisation research by Merck and NASA's ZBLAN optical fibre production, which demonstrate practical difficulties in commercialising space-based innovations. The analysis extends to the 2001 controversy over BioDyn's peptide synthesis experiments conducted in both Russian and American modules, highlighting the legal complexities that arise from multi-jurisdictional research. Emerging commercial practices, international disputes, and proposed solutions are assessed using both legal and economic perspectives. The article concludes with policy recommendations for harmonising intellectual property protection in space to facilitate more effective technology transfer while balancing national interests with the common heritage principle that underpins space law, ultimately proposing a specialised international registry for space-based innovations.

Keywords: Microgravity, Patent, International Space Station, Technology Transfer

Introduction

The International Space Station (ISS), humanity's most ambitious cooperative venture in space, epitomises both the promise of international scientific collaboration and the intricate legal complexities that arise when terrestrial legal frameworks encounter the borderless realm of outer space. Since its inception, the ISS has served as a unique laboratory where the microgravity environment enables scientific discoveries and technological innovations impossible to achieve on Earth. Yet this revolutionary scientific platform has simultaneously generated unprecedented legal questions regarding intellectual property rights (IPRs) that challenge traditional territorial conceptions of patent law.

As commercial entities increasingly conduct research aboard the ISS, the question of who owns innovations developed in space has moved from theoretical legal discourse to pressing practical reality. The unique environment of space creates conditions where proteins crystallise with greater purity, alloys form without separation, and optical fibres develop without the structural flaws that occur under Earth's gravity.[1] These innovations potentially represent billions in commercial value, yet the legal framework governing their ownership remains frustratingly ambiguous. This ambiguity stems from the fundamental tension between space law's foundation in the principle of the common heritage of mankind and intellectual property law's inherently territorial nature.[2]

On Earth, legal jurisdiction typically aligns with clearly defined geographical boundaries. In space, however, these boundaries dissolve. The

1 Mark J. Sundahl, "Intellectual Property Rights and Space Activities", Journal of Space Law, vol. 42 (2018), pp. 201-225 at p. 210.

2 Francis Lyall and Paul B. Larsen, *Space Law: A Treatise*, 2nd Edition (Routledge, New York, 2018), p. 125.

ISS itself represents a patchwork of jurisdictions—each module technically falls under the registration and control of different partner nations. When a scientist conducts an experiment that spans multiple modules, or when international teams collaborate on innovations, the applicable legal regime becomes increasingly uncertain. Does jurisdiction follow the inventor's nationality? The module's registration? The funding nation? Or some complex interplay of these factors?[3]

This article delves into these questions through rigorous doctrinal analysis of the existing legal framework governing inventions aboard the ISS, with particular attention to the 1998 International Space Station Intergovernmental Agreement (IGA) and its treatment of intellectual property rights. Through examination of illustrative case studies and disputes, we identify critical gaps in the current regime that threaten to impede the commercialisation of space-based innovations. Subsequently, we evaluate emerging commercial practices and proposed solutions before offering policy recommendations to harmonise intellectual property protection in space while respecting the foundational principles of international space law.

The Legal Framework Governing Intellectual Property in Space

International Space Treaties and the Common Heritage Principle

The legal architecture governing outer space activities rests primarily upon five United Nations treaties developed during the space race era, with the 1967 Treaty on Principles Governing the Activities of States in the Exploration and Use of Outer Space, Including the Moon and Other Celestial Bodies (Outer Space Treaty or OST) forming the cornerstone.[4] Article I of this seminal treaty establishes that "the exploration and use of outer space... shall be carried out for the benefit and in the interests of all countries... and shall be the province of all mankind."[5] This language embodies what has come to be known as the "common heritage principle," emphasising that space and its resources belong to humanity collectively rather than individual nations or entities.

3 James E. Dunstan, "Towards an International Patent Registry for Space", Space Policy, vol. 25 (2009), pp. 40-47 at p. 42.

4 Treaty on Principles Governing the Activities of States in the Exploration and Use of Outer Space, Including the Moon and Other Celestial Bodies, 27 January 1967, 18 U.S.T. 2410, 610 U.N.T.S. 205.

5 Ibid., Article I.

The common heritage principle, while noble in its aspiration, creates immediate tension with intellectual property regimes that are inherently designed to grant exclusive rights. If space is the province of all mankind, how can innovations developed there be subject to exclusive ownership? This philosophical tension underlies many of the practical legal challenges discussed throughout this article.[6]

Notably, the OST does not directly address intellectual property rights. Article VIII merely establishes that objects launched into space remain under the jurisdiction and control of the state of registry.[7] This provision becomes the tenuous thread upon which the current intellectual property regime in space is constructed. As we shall see, this foundation may prove inadequate as commercial space activities accelerate.

The ISS Intergovernmental Agreement: A Pragmatic Compromise

Recognising the limitations of the general space treaty framework for governing a complex multinational facility like the ISS, partner nations (the United States, Russia, Japan, Canada, and participating European Space Agency member states) negotiated the 1998 International Space Station Intergovernmental Agreement. Article 21 of this agreement specifically addresses intellectual property rights, representing the most detailed treatment of space-based intellectual property in international law to date.[8]

The IGA adopts what might be called a "quasi-territorial" approach to intellectual property. Article 21(2) establishes that "for purposes of intellectual property law, an activity occurring in or on a Space Station flight element shall be deemed to have occurred only in the territory of the Partner State of that element's registry."[9] This provision effectively extends terrestrial intellectual property regimes into space by creating a legal fiction that activities in a particular module occurred within the territory of the registering nation.

---

6 Ram S. Jakhu, "Legal Issues Relating to the Global Public Interest in Outer Space", *Journal of Space Law*, vol. 32 (2006), pp. 31-110 at p. 45.

7 Treaty on Principles Governing the Activities of States in the Exploration and Use of Outer Space, Including the Moon and Other Celestial Bodies, note 4, Article VIII.

8 Agreement Among the Government of Canada, Governments of Member States of the European Space Agency, the Government of Japan, the Government of the Russian Federation, and the Government of the United States of America Concerning Cooperation on the Civil International Space Station, 29 January 1998, T.I.A.S. No. 12927.

9 Ibid., Article 21(2).

This approach, while providing some clarity, introduces its own complications. What happens when an invention results from activities conducted across multiple modules registered to different nations? The IGA attempts to address this through Article 21(2), which states that "for ESA-registered elements, European law with regard to intellectual property will apply." However, the term "European law" itself lacks precision, as intellectual property laws remain largely harmonized but not identical across ESA member states.

Furthermore, the IGA establishes a principle of non-interference in Article 21(3), stipulating that "the temporary presence in the territory of a Partner State of any articles, including the components of a flight element, in transit between any place on Earth and any flight element of the Space Station registered by another Partner State or ESA shall not in itself form the basis for any proceedings in the first Partner State for patent infringement."[10] This provision aims to facilitate the movement of equipment and materials to and from the ISS without triggering infringement claims, yet its scope remains untested in courts.

National Implementation and Divergences

The IGA framework requires implementation through national legislation, resulting in varied approaches that further complicate the intellectual property landscape in space. The United States has taken perhaps the most expansive approach through its 1990 Patents in Space Act, which amended U.S. patent law to establish that "any invention made, used or sold in outer space on a space object or component thereof under the jurisdiction or control of the United States shall be considered to be made, used or sold within the United States."[11]This broad assertion of jurisdiction contrasts with the more limited approaches taken by other ISS partners.

Japan's approach, codified in its Patent Act, creates a presumption that inventions made in space facilities registered by Japan are considered to be made in Japanese territory.[12] The European approach, complicated by the multilateral nature of ESA, generally follows the principle that inventions made in ESA-registered modules fall under European patent law, though questions remain about which specific national law applies in cases of dispute.

10 Ibid., Article 21(3).

11 Patents in Space Act, 35 U.S.C. § 105 (1990).

12 Japan Patent Act, Law No. 121 of 1959, as amended by Law No. 51 of 2006, Article 2(3).

Russia presents yet another variant, with its space law emphasising state interests in innovations while recognising private rights. According to Russian law, activities conducted in Russian modules are subject to Russian jurisdiction, including its intellectual property regime.[13] However, Russia maintains stronger state claims on resulting technologies than Western partners, particularly for innovations with potential defence applications.

These divergent national implementations create a maze of potentially conflicting jurisdictional claims that inventors and companies must navigate when conducting research aboard the ISS. The complexity only increases when considering collaborative research spanning multiple modules or involving multinational teams.

The Jurisdictional Paradox of Space-Based Inventions

Territorial Rights in an Extraterritorial Domain

Intellectual property rights, particularly patents, are inherently territorial in nature. A patent granted in the United States provides exclusionary rights only within U.S. territorial jurisdiction. This territorial limitation creates an immediate conceptual challenge when applied to outer space—a domain explicitly designated as beyond national appropriation by the Outer Space Treaty.[14]

The IGA attempts to resolve this paradox through its quasi-territorial approach, yet fundamental tensions remain. By creating legal fictions that activities in space modules occurred within national territories, the IGA superimposes terrestrial legal boundaries onto a realm where physical boundaries are meaningless. This approach raises profound questions about the appropriate legal framework for governing activities that are, by their nature, beyond territorial jurisdiction.[15]

Further complicating matters is the question of enforcement. Even if jurisdiction can be established under the IGA framework, enforcing intellectual property rights in space presents practical challenges unlike those on Earth. Traditional enforcement mechanisms rely on territorial

13 Law of the Russian Federation on Space Activities, No. 5663-1, 20 August 1993, Article 16.

14 Christopher J. Newman, "Seeking Tranquillity: Embedding Sustainability in Lunar Exploration Policy", Space Policy, vol. 33 (2015), pp. 29-37 at p. 32.

15 Melissa K. Force, "Intellectual Property Rights in Outer Space", *Journal of Space Law*, vol. 34 (2008), pp. 253-284 at p. 260.

control that simply doesn't exist in outer space. While activities aboard the ISS remain subject to significant ground control and oversight, future commercial space stations or lunar bases may operate with greater autonomy, further straining terrestrial enforcement mechanisms.[16]

Multi-Module Activities and Jurisdictional Ambiguity

Perhaps the most immediate practical challenge arises from research activities that span multiple ISS modules. Consider a scientific experiment that requires equipment housed in the U.S. Destiny laboratory, processing in the European Columbus module, and storage in the Japanese Kibo module. Under the IGA framework, different aspects of this single experimental process potentially fall under different legal regimes.[17]

The IGA fails to provide clear guidance for determining applicable law in such scenarios. Does jurisdiction follow the module where the "essential" part of the invention occurred? The nationality of the inventor? The source of funding? In the absence of clear rules, these questions must be resolved on a case-by-case basis, creating uncertainty that may discourage commercial investment.[18]

The case of BioDyn's peptide synthesis experiments in 2001 provides a telling illustration. The company conducted related experiments in both U.S. and Russian modules, leading to innovations that could potentially be claimed under either jurisdiction. When BioDyn sought patent protection, questions arose about which nation's laws should apply and whether filing in both jurisdictions was necessary to secure adequate protection.[19] While eventually resolved through negotiation, the case highlighted the need for clearer rules governing multi-module activities.

Collaborative Research and Competing Claims

International collaboration represents both the greatest strength of the ISS program and its most significant intellectual property challenge. When scientists from multiple partner nations collaborate on research, determining ownership of resulting innovations becomes exceedingly

16 Thomas Gangale, The Development of Outer Space: Sovereignty and Property Rights in International Space Law (Praeger, Santa Barbara, 2009), p. 78.

17 Sundahl, note 1, p. 215.

18 Theresa Hitchens, "Commercial Space and International Law", *Aerospace America*, vol. 57 (April 2019), pp. 45-50 at p. 47.

19 Case study based on confidential industry sources, with identifying details modified.

complex. Traditional terrestrial approaches to collaborative research typically rely on contractual arrangements that specify ownership rights in advance.[20] However, the uncertain jurisdictional framework of the ISS complicates the enforceability of such agreements.

The IGA does address inventor nationality in Article 21(2), stating that "in respect of an invention made in or on any Space Station flight element by a person who is not a national or resident of a Partner State, a Partner State shall not apply its laws concerning secrecy of inventions so as to prevent the filing of a patent application."[21] This provision aims to ensure that non-partner nationals can secure patent rights for their inventions, yet it leaves unresolved many questions about competing jurisdictional claims.

When inventors from different partner nations collaborate, each nation could potentially assert jurisdiction over the resulting innovation. This creates risks of inconsistent legal treatment, where an invention might be patentable in one jurisdiction but not another, or where different standards of novelty, inventive step, or industrial applicability might lead to protection in some jurisdictions but not others.[22]

Case Studies: Commercial Challenges in Practice

Protein Crystallisation: Merck's Pioneering Efforts

Among the earliest and most significant commercial research endeavours aboard the ISS was Merck Pharmaceutical's protein crystallisation experiments. The microgravity environment enables protein crystals to grow larger and with fewer defects than possible on Earth, allowing for more precise structural analysis critical to drug development.[23] Merck's experiments, conducted primarily in the U.S. Destiny laboratory, yielded insights into protein structures that proved valuable for drug development efforts.

20 Robert P. Merges, "Intellectual Property Rights and the New Institutional Economics", *Vanderbilt Law Review*, vol. 53 (2000), pp. 1857-1877, at p. 1860.

21 Agreement Among the Government of Canada, Governments of Member States of the European Space Agency, the Government of Japan, the Government of the Russian Federation, and the Government of the United States of America Concerning Cooperation on the Civil International Space Station, note 8, Article 21(2).

22 Michael Listner, "The Ownership and Exploitation of Outer Space: A Look at Foundational Law and Future Legal Challenges to Current Claims", *Regent Journal of International Law*, vol. 1 (2003), pp. 75-94 at p. 82.

23 Lawrence DeLucas, "Protein Crystal Growth in Microgravity", Reports on Progress in Physics, vol. 69 (2006), pp. 1103-1121 at p. 1110.

However, the commercialisation pathway for these innovations highlighted several intellectual property challenges. First, questions arose about the patentability of the process versus the resulting crystal structures. While Merck could clearly claim the novel processes developed for space-based crystallisation under U.S. patent law (as extended to the Destiny module), the status of the resulting crystals themselves proved more ambiguous.[24]

Furthermore, the necessity of ground-based analysis introduced additional jurisdictional complications. The actual scientific value emerged not from the crystals themselves, but from the structural insights gained through analysis conducted on Earth. This raised questions about where the "invention" truly occurred—in space where the crystals formed, or on Earth where their significance was determined.[25]

Despite these challenges, Merck successfully secured several patents related to its ISS research. However, the company's experience underscored the need for clearer rules governing the full innovation pathway from space-based experimentation to terrestrial commercialisation.

ZBLAN Optical Fibre Production: NASA's Commercial Challenge

The production of ZBLAN optical fibres represents one of the most promising commercial applications of microgravity manufacturing. These exotic fluoride-based fibres demonstrate theoretical transmission capabilities far exceeding conventional silica fibres, but their production on Earth is hampered by gravity-induced crystallisation defects.[26] Research aboard the ISS has demonstrated that ZBLAN fibres produced in microgravity exhibit dramatically improved performance, potentially revolutionising telecommunications if they can be manufactured at scale.

NASA's efforts to commercialise this technology have illuminated intellectual property challenges unique to space manufacturing. Unlike research that merely yields information (like protein crystallisation), ZBLAN production creates a physical product with direct commercial

24 Jennifer Isaacs, "Patent Protection for Space-Related Inventions: National Law and Policy in the ISS Era", *Journal of Air Law and Commerce*, vol. 70 (2005), pp. 519-554 at p. 540.

25 Ibid., p. 542.

26 Donald C. Johanson et al., "ZBLAN Processing in Reduced Gravity Environment", *Journal of Materials Processing Technology*, vol. 162-163 (2005), pp. 358-363 at p. 360.

value. This raises novel questions about the status of goods manufactured in space.[27]

Under the IGA framework, the intellectual property rights for the manufacturing process clearly fall under the jurisdiction of the module where production occurs (primarily U.S. modules in NASA's case). However, the status of the resulting fibres becomes more complex, particularly once they return to Earth. Are they subject to import regulations? Can they be considered "made in the USA" despite being manufactured in space? These questions have significant implications for commercialisation strategies.[28]

Furthermore, NASA's partnership with private companies for this research has required careful intellectual property arrangements. As a government agency, NASA operates under different imperatives than commercial entities, with a mandate to disseminate knowledge for public benefit while also facilitating commercial development. Balancing these objectives within the uncertain legal framework of space-based intellectual property has required novel contractual approaches.[29]

The BioDyn Controversy: Multi-Jurisdictional Research

The case of BioDyn's peptide synthesis experiments in 2001 provides perhaps the most illuminating example of jurisdictional complexity in space-based intellectual property. BioDyn, a multinational pharmaceutical company, conducted related experiments in both U.S. and Russian modules of the ISS, synthesising novel peptide compounds with potential applications in disease treatment.

When BioDyn sought patent protection for the resulting innovations, fundamental questions arose about jurisdiction. The company had deliberately structured its research program to span multiple modules, partly to explore the unique capabilities of different laboratory facilities but also as a strategic approach to intellectual property protection. By conducting related but distinct aspects of the research in different modules, BioDyn hoped to secure patent protection under multiple jurisdictions.

27 Sandra H. Magnus, "Commercialization of Space-Based Research: Confounding Factors", New Space, vol. 4 (2016), pp. 110-114 at p. 112.

28 Milton Smith, "Space Law and Space Resources", *Journal of Space Law*, vol. 33 (2007), pp. 289-316 at p. 300.

29 Commercial Space Act of 1998, Pub. L. 105-303, 112 Stat. 2843 (1998).

This strategy, however, encountered significant challenges. Patent applications filed in both the United States and Russia faced questions about priority and the extent to which the innovations constituted a single inventive concept versus separate inventions. Furthermore, differences in patentability standards between the two jurisdictions created uncertainty about the scope of protection available.[30]

The BioDyn case ultimately required diplomatic intervention, with representatives from NASA and Roscosmos negotiating an agreement on how the intellectual property rights would be allocated. This ad hoc approach, while eventually successful, highlighted the inadequacy of the existing framework for addressing multi-jurisdictional research and raised concerns about the scalability of such solutions as commercial activity aboard the ISS increases.[31]

Emerging Commercial Practices and Proposed Solutions

Contractual Approaches to Uncertainty

In the absence of clear international rules, commercial entities conducting research aboard the ISS have increasingly relied on elaborate contractual arrangements to manage intellectual property uncertainty. These contracts typically specify governing law, establish ownership rights in advance, and include provisions for dispute resolution outside traditional court systems.[32]

NASA's commercial partnership agreements, for instance, have evolved to include detailed intellectual property provisions that attempt to address the unique challenges of space-based innovation. These agreements typically specify that U.S. law will govern intellectual property rights, regardless of which modules research activities occur in, thus attempting to create certainty through private contractual choice of law.[33]

30 James D. Blumenthal, "Intellectual Property Rights in an Age of Electronic Commerce: Patents for Business Methods", IDEA: *The Journal of Law and Technology*, vol. 41 (2001), pp. 151-178 at p. 160.

31 Personal communication with NASA legal counsel, anonymized due to confidentiality requirements.

32 Sarah R. Langston, "Commercialization Challenges for ISS Research", New Space, vol. 6 (2018), pp. 245-251 at p. 248.

33 National Aeronautics and Space Administration, NASA Policy Directive 2091.1B: Inventions Made by Government Employees, 20 May 2015.

While effective for bilateral arrangements, these contractual approaches face significant limitations. They cannot resolve fundamental jurisdictional questions that might be raised by third parties not bound by the contracts. Furthermore, their enforceability across multiple jurisdictions remains untested in courts, creating lingering uncertainty, particularly for multinational collaborations.[34]

International Harmonisation Efforts

Recognising the limitations of purely contractual approaches, various stakeholders have proposed international harmonisation efforts to create greater certainty for space-based intellectual property. The World Intellectual Property Organisation (WIPO) has explored the possibility of developing specialised guidelines or agreements addressing intellectual property in outer space, though these efforts remain in preliminary stages.[35]

Some scholars have proposed more ambitious harmonisation through a specialised treaty on space-based intellectual property, potentially administered by WIPO in cooperation with the United Nations Office for Outer Space Affairs (UNOOSA). Such a treaty could establish uniform rules for determining applicable law, standards for patentability of space-based innovations, and mechanisms for resolving jurisdictional disputes.[36]

However, harmonisation efforts face significant challenges. Partner nations have divergent interests in the intellectual property realm, with some favouring stronger protection for commercial interests while others emphasise the common heritage principle and broader access to innovations. These philosophical differences complicate the development of consensus standards.[37]

---

34 Dan L. Burk, "Transborder Intellectual Property Issues on the Electronic Frontier", *Stanford Law and Policy Review*, vol. 10 (1999), pp. 9-16 at p. 12.

35 World Intellectual Property Organization, "WIPO Treaty on the Protection of Inventions in Outer Space: Working Draft", Document WIPO/IP/SPACE/05/1 (unpublished draft), 2005.

36 Leo B. Malagar and Marlo ApalisokMagdoza-Malagar, "International Law of Outer Space and the Protection of Intellectual Property Rights", *Boston University International Law Journal*, vol. 17 (1999), pp. 311-356 at p. 340.

37 Vilas K. Nair, "The Outer Space Treaty and States' Obligation to Remove Space Debris: A US Perspective", *Indian Journal of International Law*, vol. 58 (2018), pp. 487-506 at p. 490.

A Specialised Registry for Space-Based Innovations

Among the most promising proposed solutions is the creation of a specialised international registry for space-based innovations. Such a registry would function somewhat analogously to international systems like the Patent Cooperation Treaty (PCT), allowing inventors to file a single international application for innovations developed in space.[38]

The registry would not itself grant patents but would establish priority dates and provide a centralised examination process to determine whether innovations meet internationally agreed standards for novelty and inventive step. National patent offices would then have the option to grant protection within their jurisdictions based on this examination, potentially with expedited procedures.

Advocates argue that this approach would balance respect for national sovereignty in intellectual property matters with the need for greater certainty and efficiency in protecting space-based innovations. By providing a single entry point to the international patent system for space-based inventions, it would reduce transaction costs and jurisdictional uncertainty while preserving nations' ability to apply their own standards within their territories.[39]

Critics, however, raise concerns that such a system might disproportionately benefit advanced space-faring nations and their commercial entities while limiting benefits to developing countries. Any specialised registry would need to incorporate mechanisms to ensure technology transfer and benefit-sharing consistent with the common heritage principle.[40]

Conclusion and Policy Recommendations

As commercial activity aboard the International Space Station continues to expand, the need for greater legal certainty regarding intellectual property rights becomes increasingly urgent. The current framework, centred on the quasi-territorial approach of the ISS Intergovernmental Agreement,

38 Dunstan, note 3, p. 45.

39 Theodore U. Ro et al., "Patent Infringement in Outer Space in Light of 35 U.S.C. § 105: Following the White Rabbit Down the Rabbit Loophole", *Boston University Journal of Science and Technology Law*, vol. 17 (2011), pp. 202-226 at p. 220.

40 Ricky J. Lee, "Reconciling International Space Law with the Commercial Realities of the Twenty-First Century", *Singapore Journal of International and Comparative Law*, vol. 4 (2000), pp. 194-251 at p. 230.

provides a workable but imperfect solution that leaves significant gaps, particularly for multi-module activities and international collaborations.

Based on our analysis, we propose several policy recommendations to address these challenges:

First, ISS partner nations should develop detailed implementing protocols for Article 21 of the IGA, specifically addressing scenarios involving multi-module activities and multinational research teams. These protocols could establish clear rules for determining applicable law based on factors such as the primary location of innovative activity, the nationality of inventors, and the source of funding.[41]

Second, commercial entities conducting research aboard the ISS should adopt standardised contractual templates developed with input from all partner nations. These templates would provide consistent approaches to intellectual property allocation while respecting the jurisdictional framework of the IGA, thus reducing transaction costs and uncertainty.[42]

Third, the international community should pursue the development of a specialised registry for space-based innovations under the joint auspices of WIPO and UNOOSA. This registry would provide a single-entry point to the international patent system while respecting national sovereignty over ultimate grant decisions.[43]

Fourth, any solutions developed must incorporate mechanisms to ensure that benefits from space-based innovations are shared broadly, consistent with the common heritage principle embodied in the Outer Space Treaty. This could include requirements for reasonable licensing terms, technology transfer provisions for developing nations, and limitations on exclusive rights for certain categories of fundamental discoveries.[44]

Finally, as the commercial space sector continues to evolve beyond the ISS toward private space stations and potential lunar or Martian facilities, the international community must begin developing forward-looking legal frameworks that can accommodate innovation in these new environments. The lessons learned from addressing intellectual property challenges

41 Emmanuel Kayembe, "Innovations in Space: International Legal Implications", *Indian Journal of International Law*, vol. 56 (2016), pp. 329-350 at p. 342.

42 Sundahl, note 1, p. 218.

43 Bryon C. Brittingham, "Does the World Really Need New Space Law?", *Oregon Review of International Law*, vol. 12 (2010), pp. 31-54 at p. 45.

44 Jakhu, note 6, p. 90.

aboard the ISS should inform these efforts, with particular attention to balancing commercial incentives with the foundational principles of space as the province of all mankind.[45]

The microgravity environment of space offers unprecedented opportunities for scientific discovery and technological innovation. Realising this potential, however, requires legal frameworks that provide sufficient certainty to incentivise investment while respecting the unique legal status of outer space. By addressing the jurisdictional paradoxes of space-based intellectual property now, we can establish a foundation for sustainable commercial development of space resources that benefits humanity as a whole.

45 Steven Freeland, "For Better or for Worse? The Use of 'Soft Law' within the International Legal Regulation of Outer Space", Annals of Air and Space Law, vol. 36 (2011), pp. 409-446 at p. 425.

Chapter 8

Protecting Outer Space Innovations: A Comparative Study of Patent and Trade Law Regimes in the US, EU and India in the Age of NewSpace

-Animesh Pratap Singh and Anand Kumar Singh

Abstract

The NewSpace boom has shifted space competition from rockets to ideas: lighter structures, smarter software and proprietary manufacturing methods now define market advantage. Protecting those ideas, however, is complicated by national borders and orbital operations. This chapter compares the legal tools that guard satellite innovation in the United States, the European Union and India. It shows how US law pairs nationwide patents with strong trade-secret remedies and even extends patent reach to US-registered spacecraft. Europe, by contrast, offers continent-wide coverage through the Unitary Patent and harmonised secrecy rules, though orbital jurisdiction remains patchy. India's modern patent system and vibrant start-up scene contrast with its contract-based secrecy regime, which a pending bill aims to strengthen. The study concludes with policy options, statutory orbital clauses, prosecution highways and that could align the three systems, reduce enforcement gaps and foster cross-border collaboration in the rapidly growing satellite economy.

Keywords: NewSpace, satellite innovation, patents, trade secrets, comparative law

Introduction

Space is no longer a playground reserved for super-powered states. Private launch providers, miniaturised components, and low-cost ride-share missions have pushed thousands of new satellites into orbit and created what commentators call the "New-Space" economy.[1] In 2023 alone, operators placed roughly 2,900 spacecraft, up from a few hundred a decade earlier, raising the on-orbit population to about 12,600 and heightening both competition and congestion.[2] In this crowded arena, the decisive assets are seldom the aluminium tanks or solar wings bolted to a satellite; they are the ideas that could be lighter propulsion units or smarter signal-processing software, proprietary deployment mechanisms, among others, that make one platform outperform another.

Protecting such ideas is harder in space than on Earth. Patent rights stop at the border unless a statute extends them farther. The United States does so for craft under its registry, but most nations do not.[3] Even where patents apply, filing means publishing the invention, an approach some entrepreneur's distrust. Elon Musk, for instance, warned that if SpaceX patented its core designs "rivals would treat the documents as a recipe book," so the company relies instead on secrecy.[4] Yet pure secrecy has limits: it offers no defence against lawful reverse engineering, and once information leaks, the protection is gone forever. Balancing patents and trade secrets, therefore, becomes a strategic puzzle shaped by the legal tools available in each jurisdiction.

This paper attempts to examine how three key regions—the United States, the European Union and India protect satellite innovations through patent and trade-secret law and the paper proceeds in four parts. Part II sketches the New-Space economy and the twin IP tools available. Part III compares

1 Jeferson Zambrano, "What is the New Space Economy?" MIT Professional Education Blog (May 16, 2025), available at: <https://professionalprograms.mit.edu/blog/technology/what-is-new-space-economy/> accessed 8 May 2025.

2 Alison Snyder, "Congestion in Earth's Orbit Is Getting Even Worse," *Axios* (Washington DC) 5 May 2024 availabe at: <https://www.axios.com/2024/05/05/satellites-crowded-orbit-spacex> accessed 8 May 2025

3 35 United States Code § 105 (1990) (treating inventions made or used on a U.S-controlled space object as made or used within the United States).

4 Dave Mosher, "Elon Musk: 'If We Published Patents, It Would Be Farcical,'" Business Insider (New York, 9 Nov 2012) available at: <https://www.businessinsider.com/elon-musk-patents-2012-11> accessed 8 May 2025.

the mature U.S. and EU frameworks. Part IV analyses India's evolving system and its bid for harmonisation.

Background

Evolution of Space Technologies and the NewSpace Economy

Satellites today come in many shapes and sizes, but mostly are used for communications, earth-observation, navigation and for other scientific purposes. Their orbits differ by purpose. Low-Earth orbit, 160–2,000 km above the surface, is favoured by imaging constellations and broadband networks because the latency is low; medium Earth orbits are used by navigation systems; geostationary orbit at 35,786 km keeps television or weather spacecraft fixed over one point on the equator.[5]

Sixty years ago, a communications satellite was a school-bus-sized machine launched by a government rocket into the single ring of geostationary orbit. Today, spacecraft come in every scale from coffee-cup CubeSats to refrigerator-sized radar imagers and occupy three main altitude bands. Advances in micro-electronics, composite structures and electric propulsion have squeezed more capability into lighter frames, allowing a dozen small satellites to share one fairing and cut per-kilogram launch costs to a fraction of the price charged by expendable boosters a decade ago.[6] Reusable rockets multiply that saving: the first stage lands, is refurbished and flies again, pushing marginal costs even lower.

Cheaper access has produced an explosion of on-orbit hardware. Roughly 1,300 satellites were active in 2013; by mid-2024, the figure had passed 12,600, with close to 2,900 new craft launched in 2023 alone.[7] This surge, driven largely by private capital rather than public procurement, is what analysts now call the New-Space economy. Competition is no longer about who can reach orbit at all; it is about who can down-mass a star-tracker, stretch battery life or compress an imagery file more efficiently than rivals. The decisive assets have shifted from aluminium tanks and solar wings to novel propulsion nozzles, proprietary on-board software and tightly

5 European Space Agency, "Types of Orbits," ESA website (Paris, 2017) available at: <https://www.esa.int/Enabling_Support/Space_Transportation/Types_of_orbits> accessed 8 May 2025.

6 Satellite Industry Association, State of the Satellite Industry Report 2024 (Washington DC, 2024) available at: <https://sia.org/news-resources/state-of-the-satellite-industry-report/> accessed 8 May 2025.

7 Alison Snyder, *note 2.*

guarded production know-how. Because these intangible innovations create the real edge. They are also the most tempting targets for imitation or theft. As later parts of this paper show, the strengths and gaps in national patent and trade-secret laws often determine whether a start-up can defend that edge in a global, rapidly scaling market.

Intellectual Property Tools for Space Innovation: Patents vs Trade Secret

Inventors in the space sector depend mainly on two legal tools. A patent grants its owner a twenty-year right to stop others from making, using or selling the claimed invention inside the country of grant. To qualify, the invention must be new, non-obvious and useful. The TRIPS Agreement obliges every World Trade Organisation member, including the United States, the European Union and India, to make patents available in all fields of technology and to enforce them without discrimination.[8] The reward of exclusivity comes at a price: once the application is published, the technical details are open for all to read. Competitors anywhere can study the drawings and, after the term ends, copy the solution freely. For a satellite component that will be visible in orbit, such as a fold-out antenna or a heat-pipe arrangement, patenting is often the safest route because rivals could otherwise reverse-engineer the design.

A trade secret protects valuable information that remains confidential through reasonable measures such as non-disclosure agreements, restricted lab access and data encryption. Protection arises automatically and can last forever, yet vanishes the moment the secret becomes public or is lawfully reverse-engineered. In the United States, the Defend Trade Secrets Act of 2016 lets owners sue in federal court, obtain emergency seizure of stolen data and claim punitive damages for wilful theft.[9] The European Union harmonised similar civil remedies through Directive 2016/943, which requires courts to grant injunctions and preserve confidentiality during trial.[10] India still relies mainly on contract and equity, though a draft Trade Secrets Bill now before Parliament aims to fill that gap. Choosing between patents and secrecy, therefore, turns on several questions: Is the invention detectable once the satellite flies? Will publication help or hurt? Elon

8 Agreement on Trade-Related Aspects of Intellectual Property Rights 1994, arts 27, 39.

9 Defend Trade Secrets Act 2016, 18 USC § 1836.

10 Directive (EU) 2016/943 on the protection of undisclosed know-how and business information, 8 June 2016.

Musk's warning that patents can become "recipe books"[11] for rivals shows why some firms file sparingly and guard most of their know-how behind passwords and locked clean rooms.

Global Supply Chains and Cross-Border Missions

A modern satellite is rarely a single-nation project. A European prime contractor may bolt on star-trackers sourced from the United States, mount solar panels fabricated in Japan, load software written in India and then ship the finished bus to French Guiana for launch. At each hand-off, intellectual-property questions arise. A propulsion valve patented in California may pass through German and Indian factories before lift-off. Enforcement is complicated because the legal reach of patents and trade-secret rules stops at national borders unless a statute or treaty says otherwise. The United States, for instance, extends its patent law to "any invention made, used or sold in outer space on a space object under U.S. jurisdiction or control," giving owners a clear right to sue when a U.S.-registered craft carries infringing technology.[12] Most other jurisdictions rely on the 1967 Outer Space Treaty, which merely states that a launching State retains "jurisdiction and control" over its registered objects without spelling out whether domestic patent statutes follow a satellite once it crosses the Kármán line.[13]

Trade-secret coverage is just as uneven. In Munich, a leak of confidential test data triggers EU-wide civil remedies under Directive 2016/943;[14] the same disclosure in Karnataka may be addressed only through contract, because India still lacks a dedicated trade-secret statute, though a draft law is pending.[15] Meanwhile, the Indian Space Policy 2023 invites private launch ventures yet says little about how orbital activities will intersect with domestic IP rights.[16] Such gaps encourage "flags of convenience,"

11 Mosher, *note 4.*

12 35 United States Code § 105 (1990) (treating inventions made or used on a U.S-controlled space object as made or used within the United States).

13 Treaty on Principles Governing the Activities of States in the Exploration and Use of Outer Space 1967, art VIII, 610 UNTS 205.

14 Supra Note 10

15 Law Commission of India, Report 289 Trade Secrets and Economic Espionage (New Delhi, 17 Mar 2024).

16 Government of India, Indian Space Policy 2023 (New Delhi, 2023) available at: <https://www.isro.gov.in/media_isro/pdf/IndianSpacePolicy2023.pdf> accessed 8 May 2025.

where operators register satellites or form joint ventures in jurisdictions with the weakest rules. Understanding the inconsistencies of such laws and jurisdictions is thus important as it guides companies in structuring cross-border projects so that patents and secrets remain enforceable throughout the supply chain and even beyond Earth's atmosphere.

Outer Space Patent and Trade Secret Protection in the US and EU

The US

The United States uses a single, nationwide patent system administered by the Patent and Trademark Office. In the America Invents Act, priority is awarded to the first inventor to file, not the first to invent, which encourages early, well-documented applications.[17] The USPTO offers fast-track programmes for important technologies, a provisional filing route that secures an early date with minimal formality, and post-grant review procedures that let competitors challenge weak claims without going to court.[18] Patentable subject matter is defined broadly as "any new and useful process, machine, manufacture or composition of matter," yet courts exclude abstract ideas and natural laws, leaving satellite makers free to protect hardware, control algorithms embedded in a technical system and even orbital-debris-mitigation methods.[19]

University and contractor inventions developed with federal funding fall under the Bayh–Dole Act. The statute lets recipients elect ownership if they file timely, report government support in the patent, and grant the government a non-exclusive licence.[20] The rule has steered hundreds of NASA lab concept designs into private hands that can refine and market them for satellite constellations and deep-space probes.[21] If the public interest is threatened, the government may invoke "march-in" rights to

17 "First Inventor to File (FITF) Resources" USPTO (May 8, 2025), available at: https://www.uspto.gov/patents/first-inventor-file-fitf-resources accessed 8 May 2025.

18 United States Patent and Trademark Office, Performance and Accountability Report FY 2024 (Washington DC, 2024) available at:<https://www.uspto.gov/sites/default/files/documents/USPTOFY2024PAR.pdf> accessed 8 May 2025.

19 35 United States Code § 101 (1952).

20 35 United States Code §§ 200–212 (Bayh–Dole Act, 1980).

21 National Aeronautics and Space Administration, *Spinoff 2023* (Washington DC, 2023) avail;able at:<https://spinoff.nasa.gov/sites/default/files/2023-01/NASA-Spinoff-2023.pdf> accessed 8 May 2025.

license the technology to additional users, though no agency has yet done so for space hardware.[22]

Trade secrets receive federal civil protection under the Defend Trade Secrets Act of 2016.[23]Owners may sue in any U.S. district court, request ex parte seizure of stolen files, and seek enhanced damages for wilful or malicious conduct. Criminal prosecutions under the companion Economic Espionage Act, often involving aerospace data, show that unauthorised export or digital theft can also lead to prison sentences.[24] Because the statute does not pre-empt state law, companies can still rely on strong state-court remedies modelled on the Uniform Trade Secrets Act. This dual layer allows firms such as SpaceX and Blue Origin to pursue leakers wherever they reside, which is an important safeguard when employees move among California, Texas and Florida facilities.

Industry practice illustrates the mixed strategy. SpaceX keeps most core designs secret, arguing that patents would hand adversaries a "recipe book" for copying.[25] Blue Origin originally patented its sea-platform landing method, but later withdrew key claims after SpaceX unearthed prior art, demonstrating how disclosure can expose weaknesses.[26] Where visibility is unavoidable—an external grid-fin or a conspicuous inter-stageing—U.S. companies tend to patent. For hidden code, test data and manufacturing tolerances, they rely on the DTSA, layered NDAs and access controls. Further protection extends beyond Earth: 35 U.S.C. § 105 treats infringing use aboard any U.S.-registered spacecraft as if it occurred on U.S. soil, giving patentees a cause of action even when the act happens 400 km above the planet.[27] Taken together, robust patent examination, Bayh–Dole commercial pathways, and stringent trade-secret enforcement make the United States the most comprehensive jurisdiction for safeguarding satellite innovation.

22 Bayh–Dole Act, Supra 20 at § 203

23 Defend Trade Secrets Act 2016, 18 USC § 1836.

24 United States Department of Justice, "Former Raytheon Engineer Sentenced for Illegally Exporting Sensitive Missile Data" (Press Release, 18 Nov2020) available at: <https://www.justice.gov/archives/opa/pr/former-raytheon-engineer-sentenced-exporting-sensitive-military-related-technology-china>accessed 8 May 2025.

25 Dave Mosher, *note 3*.

26 Jeff Foust, "Blue Origin Withdraws Claims in Rocket-Landing Patent after SpaceX Challenge," *SpaceNews* (Washington DC, 1 Sept 2015) available at: <https://spacenews.com/patent-decision-may-not-spell-end-of-blue-origin-spacex-dispute/>

27 35 United States Code § 105, supra note 12.

EU

Europe protects satellite innovation through a blend of regional and national rules. At the centre stands the European Patent Office (EPO), which examines applications under the European Patent Convention. A single filing in Munich can, after grant, be validated country-by-country; the EPO's search report and written opinion give applicants early clarity on novelty and inventive step.[28] Like the United States, Europe operates a first-to-file system, so start-ups often lodge a quick, well-drafted application before disclosing designs at trade fairs or to potential investors. The substantive test is familiar—novelty, inventive step and industrial applicability yet Article 52 EPC excludes "programs for computers as such," forcing applicants who claim on-board software to frame it as part of a technical process.[29]

A major change arrived in 2012, when the Unitary Patent system entered into force. By filing a simple request within one month of the grant, an applicant can now obtain a single right covering seventeen EU states, administered centrally by the EPO and renewed through one annual fee.[30]Disputes go to the new Unified Patent Court (UPC), whose decisions apply across all participating countries.[31] For a satellite builder selling throughout Europe, this means one infringement suit or one revocation action replaces the old patchwork of national cases, cutting legal costs but raising strategic stakes.

National offices still matter. The United Kingdom, Switzerland and other non-participating EPC states continue to issue patents examined by the EPO but litigated at home. Germany goes a step further: its Patent Act expressly extends jurisdiction to inventions used "on a space object under German registry," giving patentees a clear cause against orbital infringement.[32] Most European countries rely only on Article VIII of the Outer Space Treaty to

28 European Patent Office, Annual Review 2024 (Munich, 2024) available at: <https://www.epo.org/en/news-events/press-centre/press-release/2024/1175755>accessed 8 May 2025.

29 European Patent Convention 1973, art 52 (as amended 2023).

30 Council Regulation (EU) 1257/2012 implementing enhanced cooperation in the area of unitary patent protection, 20 Dec 2012.

31 Agreement on a Unified Patent Court (UPC) 2013 (in force 1 June 2023).

32 Patentgesetz (Germany) § 9a (Use of patented inventions on space objects), Federal Law Gazette I 1981 294, as amended 2011.

link their law to registered spacecraft, leaving room for argument should a dispute reach court.

On secrecy, the EU harmonised rules through Directive 2016/943[33] . Member states must offer civil remedies such as injunctions, destruction of infringing goods and damages while allowing courts to shield confidential material during proceedings. Exceptions for whistle-blowers and reverse engineering balance protection with competition. Aero-space primes such as Airbus Defence and Space publicise a dual strategy: patent externally visible hardware, guard test data and production tolerances as trade secrets protected by non-disclosure agreements and the Directive's remedies.[34]

Taken together, the EPO's central search, the Unitary Patent pathway, the specialised UPC and Directive 2016/943 give innovators strong, predictable tools, provided they monitor national opt-outs and remain alert to software-patent nuances. For satellite ventures targeting the European market, a well-timed EPO filing plus disciplined internal secrecy now delivers continent-wide coverage that approaches the breadth and enforceability long associated with the United States.

The U.S. offers depth of remedy, Europe width of coverage. Companies operating worldwide therefore pursue dual portfolios, patenting and litigating in both regions, while policy-makers eye each other's strengths: the EU debates seizure powers, Washington studies unitary filing fees. Bridging these gaps, especially on orbital jurisdiction and emergency trade-secret relief, would give inventors clearer, more consistent protection in the borderless New-Space economy.

India and the Road to Harmonisation

India's Patent Landscape for Space Technologies and the Rise of Private Launch Start-up

India's patent law is anchored in the Patents Act 1970, overhauled in 2005 to meet TRIPS standards. Applications must show novelty, inventive step and industrial use, just as in the United States or Europe. One notable difference is Section 3(k), which bars "computer programs per se," forcing applicants who claim on-board software to draft it as part of a technical

33 Directive (EU) 2016/943,*note 10*

34 Airbus S.A.S., "Airbus Defence and Space: Intellectual Property" (Company Factsheet, 2024) available at: <https://www.airbus.com/sites/g/files/jlcbta136/files/2025-04/Airbus%20Annual%20Report%202024.pdf>accessed 8 May 2025.

system.[35] Despite that hurdle, hardware inventions central to space flight face no statutory block. The Indian Patent Office reports that filings grew by more than 56% percent between 2019 and 2023, with private applicants now out-numbering government research labs.[36] The office also runs an expedited track for start-ups that can cut the examination to under one year, crucial in a market where technology cycles move quickly.[37]

A policy shift rather than a statute triggered the sharpest change. The Indian Space Policy 2023[38] opened launch, satellite manufacture and downstream services to "non-government entities" and placed a single authorising body—IN-SPACe—between start-ups and the launch range. Within eighteen months, firms such as Skyroot Aerospace, Agnikul Cosmos and Pixxel had raised significant venture capital and filed domestic patent families on 3-D-printed engines, modular satellite buses and hyperspectral sensors. Skyroot's Vikram-S launch in November 2022, the first Indian rocket developed entirely by a private company, showcased indigenously patented technologies.[39]

Foreign investment rules have also been relaxed. A 2024 notice issued by IN-SPACe clarifies that up to 74 percent foreign direct investment is now automatic for satellite components, provided sensitive designs are patented through Indian-law non-disclosure agreements.[40] Investors view clear intellectual-property ownership as a precondition for funding, so founders increasingly file provisional specifications before pitching. The Indian government has also given strong backing to the sector and has approved a fund of 119 Million Dollars for space start-ups.[41]

---

35 The Patents Act 1970 (India), as amended 2005, s 3(k).

36 Office of the Controller General of Patents, Designs & Trade Marks, Annual Report 2023–24 (Mumbai, 2024) 78–79.

37 Expedited Patent Examination Procedure In India, <https://patentpanacea.com/expedited-patent-examination-procedure-in-india/>accessed 8 May 2025.

38 Space Policy, *note 16*

39 Press Information Bureau, "Skyroot Aerospace Successfully Launches India's First Private Rocket" (New Delhi, 17 Nov 2022) available at: <https://www.pib.gov.in/PressReleasePage.aspx?PRID=1876714>accessed 8 May 2025.

40 Indian National Space Promotion and Authorization Centre, Norms, Guidelines and Procedures for Implementation of Indian Space Policy-2023 in respect of Authorization of Space Activities (NGP)

41 "India Approves $119 Million Fund for Space Startups" Reuters (October 24, 2024), available at: <https://www.reuters.com/world/india/india-approves-119-mln-fund-space-startups-2024-10-24/>.

Yet challenges remain. Patent literacy is uneven; smaller firms sometimes skip prior-art searches and later discover blocking claims abroad. Enforcement, while faster in commercial courts, still delivers lower damages than U.S. awards. Finally, India has not copied the U.S. rule that treats use aboard a national spacecraft as domestic use, leaving orbital infringement an open question. Even so, India's strengthened patent pipeline, coupled with a vibrant launch ecosystem, marks a decisive break from its former state-monopoly model.

Trade-Secret Protection Without a Statute: Contract, Tort and Policy Limits

India does not yet have a dedicated trade-secrets statute. Instead, companies rely on a web of contracts, equitable duties and scattered statutory provisions to guard confidential know-how. The main pillar is the Non-Disclosure Agreement. Indian courts treat a well-drafted NDA as fully enforceable, even though Section 27 of the Contract Act voids broad restraints on trade.[42] Judges draw a line: a clause that merely prevents disclosure of valuable information is valid, whereas a clause that bars an employee from working for a competitor after leaving is usually struck down.

Where no written contract exists, litigants fall back on the common-law doctrine of breach of confidence. In John Richard Brady v Chemical Process Equipments, the court restrained a former employee from using proprietary drawings for a distillation column, holding that equity protects secrets disclosed in trust.[43] Similar orders have been issued for aerospace tooling data and customer lists. Remedies are mostly injunctive; damages awards remain modest by U.S. standards, limiting their deterrent value.

India's criminal statutes offer only indirect help. Sections 43 and 66 of the Information Technology Act punish unauthorised access to computer material, and the Penal Code addresses theft or breach of trust, but prosecutors rarely invoke these provisions for business secrets.[44] As cyber-intrusions rise, firms must therefore combine digital security with civil NDAs to plug gaps in policing.

42 Indian Contract Act 1872, s 27.

43 John Richard Brady v Chemical Process Equipments Pvt Ltd AIR 1987 Del 372 (Delhi High Court).

44 Information Technology Act 2000, ss 43, 66.

Recognising the patchwork, the Law Commission's Report 289 proposed a standalone Trade Secrets Bill that would define protectable information, spell out lawful reverse engineering and grant courts power to hold in-camera hearings to keep secrets sealed during trial.[45] The draft aligns with the U.S. Defend Trade Secrets Act and the EU Directive, promising clearer rules for foreign investors. While the Bill awaits Parliament, regulators have begun to act. IN-SPACe's guidelines require launch-license applicants to show "robust contractual mechanisms" for safeguarding third-party IP.[46] Venture capital term sheets now routinely demand evidence of NDAs with suppliers and staff before releasing funds.

Until the Bill passes, Indian space start-ups must weave a tight contract net: layered NDAs and employee-training programmes. The strategy works, but its success depends on quick injunctions and management discipline. A statutory framework would add the missing third leg: predictable damages, bringing India's secrecy regime in line with its modernised patent system and fast-growing launch sector.

Towards Global Alignment: Policy Options under ISRO, In-Space and WIPO

India's fast-growing launch scene will thrive only if its intellectual-property rules mesh smoothly with those of its partners. The forthcoming Space Activities Act should copy the U.S. model of 35 U.S.C. § 105[47] so that use of a patented invention on an Indian-registered spacecraft counts as use "within India." A clause to that effect already appears in the Draft Space Activities Bill and could be finalised without delay.[48]There should be licensing discipline. IN-SPACe prescribes vetting of every private mission; its licence checklist could require an IP due diligence certificate covering patent searches and trade-secret controls before launch clearance. ISRO, meanwhile, should publish standard technology-transfer terms that spell out ownership of improvements when agency know-how is adapted by start-ups.

Harmonisation through WIPO. India, the United States and the European Patent Office all belong to the Patent Cooperation Treaty. A Patent

45 Report 289, *note 15*

46 IN-SPACe, supra Note 40

47 USC,Supra Note 12

48 Draft Space Activities Bill, 2017 available at: https://prsindia.org/files/bills_acts/bills_parliament/1970/Draft%20Space%20Activities%20Bill%202017.pdf.

Prosecution Highway would let an applicant rely on a favourable search in one office to speed examination in the others, cutting costs for small satellite firms. WIPO's Arbitration and Mediation Centre, already popular for various forms of disputes, can also host bespoke clauses for satellite projects, offering neutral resolution when partners sit in different legal systems.[49]

Taken together, statutory precision at home, rigorous licensing, WIPO-facilitated shortcuts would give Indian innovators seamless protection from clean room to orbit, while offering foreign partners the confidence to share critical technology.

Conclusion

The New-Space boom has reshaped the rules of innovation. In little more than a decade, the active satellite fleet has grown almost tenfold, bringing fresh players and fresh risks. The comparative review shows that the United States offers deep remedies—nationwide patents, strict trade-secret law and even coverage in orbit—while Europe now delivers wide territorial reach through the Unitary Patent and harmonised secrecy rules. India, once a government-only arena, has modern patents and a vibrant start-up scene, but still relies on contracts to guard confidential know-how; its draft Trade Secrets Bill and forthcoming Space Activities Act can close that gap.

Every jurisdiction should make clear that its patent law follows the satellite it registers. Second, fast, low-cost prosecution highways among the jurisdictions would help start-ups secure protection before technology cycles turn over. If lawmakers act on these points, inventors from across jurisdictions will compete on ideas, not on loopholes. Strong yet balanced protection will encourage investment, speed technical progress and, in the end, deliver the benefits of space—better connectivity, sharper climate data, new scientific insight—to everyone on Earth.

49 WIPO's Arbitration, available at: <https://www.wipo.int/amc/en/>accessed 8 May 2025.

Chapter 9

Extraterrestrial Inventions: Patentability and Disclosure Dilemmas

-Lini Priya Vasavan

Introduction

The twenty-first century has brought an unprecedented shift in outer space from a realm of state-created exploration to a scene of private enterprise and commercial innovation. Not just the territory of NASA or Roscosmos missions, space venture increasingly involves a broader cross-section of private enterprise, from satellite communications companies to biotech start-ups testing products aboard the International Space Station (ISS).[1] With the burgeoning space race that seeks to lay its hands on lunar minerals, asteroids and project crewed missions to Mars, space is the next frontier of technology. Yet within this surge of growth arises a legal question that we must answer: How do we define and safeguard intellectual property (IP) rights for inventions conceptualised, produced, or used in extraterrestrial territory?

Ground-based patent systems are based on legal principles and administrative procedures that reflect terrestrial reality. Yet inventions that emerged in space in unique physical and jurisdictional contexts undermine those premises. Zero gravity, radiation, and closed-loop life support systems ensure conditions completely separate from those on Earth, which subsequently affect both invention as well as usefulness. Furthermore, the extraterritoriality of space whose sovereignty is constrained by the 1967 Outer Space Treaty presents significant challenges in terms of jurisdiction,

1 John Doe, *The New Space Race: The Rise of Private Enterprise in Outer Space* (Space Press, 2020).

enforcement and disclosure.[2] On a privately funded space station orbiting Earth, who controls your invention? Which law applies to a biotech process that has been jointly developed by scientists of different nationalities in the ISS? And how can we determine what is novel and what is prior art in a field where documentation and publication are often limited by reasons of national security or proprietary interests?

This chapter grapples with these challenges by focusing on the orthodox standards of patent-eligibility, novelty, utility, and non-obviousness, considering how they would apply to innovation originating beyond Earth's atmosphere. It also questions the disclosure and enablement premises that inform the transparency and replicability that are predicated by patent claims, which are tested by the secretive, multi-national, high-stakes qualities of space research. By comparing existing legal systems and global agreements, and by identifying existing gaps between the norm and practice, the present work aspires to pave the way for a place-based system of intellectual property. Now that human advancement in technology is actually ahead of its legal frameworks, a forward-looking IP regime that facilitates innovation based on the principles of human rights and international standards is not only timely but calls for urgent attention.

Basics of Patent Law- What Novelty, Utility and Non-obviousness Mean

At present, the international patent system is firmly based on three simple concepts, which establish when an invention can be patented: novelty, usefulness, and non-obviousness (or "inventive step" in some jurisdictions). These requirements operate as important filters to limit patent protection to inventions that actually make some meaningful contribution to technological advancement.[3] The applicability of these principles is relatively well-established in the context of terrestrial legal systems, but becomes much murkier when applied to inventions developed, tested and used in space.

The first element of patentability, novelty, means that an invention must be demonstrably new, in other words, not anticipated by prior art. The prior art is any piece of knowledge, documentation, or use of an invention that has been made available to the public before a patent application is filed.

2 United Nations, *The Outer Space Treaty* (United Nations, 1967).

3 World Intellectual Property Organization (WIPO), *Understanding Patents*, WIPO Publication No. 450(E), 2003, p. 6.

On Earth, novelty assessment is made by comparing the invention with the literature, patented technology and described use. But when it comes to alien innovation, all bets are off for what is proven and what is not. Inventions created in space could never be registered in public databases, or could be kept secret due to being classified or blocked on grounds of national security or business secrets.[4] Second, due to many space activities being temporary and experimental, it is not always possible to document or review every single activity; this results in a lack of evidence that can make it difficult to determine novelty. This has caused unease about accidental duplication of ideas and unfair monopolies on knowledge.

The second requirement, utility, requires a useful and practical application of an invention. Under the laws of many jurisdictions, such as the U.S, the elevation is low, in the sense that the invention just has to provide some objectively verifiable advantage.[5] But what counts as utility becomes a bit trickier when you're floating in space. Think of an IPR that could only work in microgravity or an increased radiation environment.[6] And while they may be useless on Earth, they could be a matter of life or death when in space. Do patent offices consider applying their utility limits consider or develop a new utility test to apply to extraterrestrial applications? Second, when inventions are directed to longer-term missions or planetary settlement, the claimed utility might not have been achieved at the time of patenting, calling into question timing and adequacy of utility disclosures.

The third, non-obviousness, is perhaps the most subjective and was hard enough to evaluate even before this crazy time. This standard necessitates that an invention to be patentable cannot simply be obvious to a person of ordinary skill in the art (PHOSITA).[7] However, inventions in the field of space are coming from the convergence of several advanced disciplines: astrobiology, space robotics, materials science and zero-gravity engineering and increasingly new ideas are taken out of context from their original source and find homes in unforeseen indigenous surroundings. The

4 Kuan-Wei Chen, "Intellectual Property Rights in Outer Space: New Frontiers," *McGill Institute of Air and Space Law Occasional Paper Series*, No. 7, 2020, pp. 9–11.

5 United States Patent and Trademark Office (USPTO), *Manual of Patent Examining Procedure* (MPEP), 9th ed., Rev. 10.2019, § 2107 – Utility Requirement.

6 Ariane Flightney, "Utility and the Final Frontier: Assessing Patent Usefulness Beyond Earth," in Katarina Eriksson & Philip de Man (eds.), *Space Law and Intellectual Property: Legal Challenges in Orbit*, Springer, 2021, pp. 112–114.

7 Robert P. Merges, Peter S. Menell & Mark A. Lemley, *Intellectual Property in the New Technological Age*, Aspen Publishers, 6th ed., 2012, pp. 137–141.

identity of the "person skilled in the art" gets foggy, especially when the invention gleans teachings from a field that is still evolving or that has few experts. That could mean non-obviousness has a much higher bar in space than it does here on Earth.

The intersection of these three criteria in the extraterrestrial context reveals the inherent Earth-biased presuppositions of modern patent law. As it happens, our existing environments were constructed to accommodate innovation within established physical, legal, and industrial ecosystems, and there isn't much precedent for the fact that the math could fail outside the immediately ending physical and jurisdictional sense space is an entirely different environment, marked by isolation, constrained access, and jurisdictional murk.[8] Thus, transferring these fundamental criteria to the case of space-originating inventions would require re-evaluating patent examination standards, re-setting evidentiary standards, and potentially, creating a specialised evaluative norm which acknowledges the very different realities of off-Earth invention.

In practice, this discovery does not diminish novelty, utility, and non-obviousness as ethical foci of the patent system. I instead take it to mean that as innovation reaches new frontiers, the way that these criteria are understood and applied must change as well. The need for such a flexible system is not just needed to maintain the integrity of the intellectual property systems themselves, but also to ensure that space-based innovation is promoted and fairly and appropriately acknowledged and protected.[9]

Novelty Challenges in Outer Space

Unfamiliarity in Space

One of the most significant challenges in extending earthbound patent law to inventions made in outer space is proving that the invention is new. This is so because the doctrine of novelty is a cornerstone of the patent system - an invention must not have been made available to the public in any prior art reference before the date of filing. But outer space is a particularly novel and insufficiently mapped territory in which the conventional means

8 Tanja Masson-Zwaan & Mahulena Hofmann (eds.), *The Law of Outer Space: An Experience in Contemporary Law-Making*, Brill Nijhoff, 2016, pp. 162–165.

9 Rachael L. Johnstone, "Intellectual Property and Space Innovation: Adapting Terrestrial Principles for Extraterrestrial Inventions," *Journal of Space Law*, Vol. 43, No. 2, 2020, pp. 225–230.

for documenting, accessing, and confirming evidence of previous art can be highly inadequate.[10]

A Definition of Space Prior Art if Pluto Is in It

On Earth, prior art is described as patents, academic publications, public demonstrations, and uses available to the public or those "skilled in the art". On the other hand, innovations created on a spacecraft, space station, or lunar or Martian surface tend to emerge from confined, mission-specific settings with limited observational transparency.[11] Many of its advancements are generated through experiments or improvised solutions for the highly unusual experiences one might encounter on long-duration missions, where microgravity, radiation, or atmospheric dissimilarities provide contexts completely alien to laboratories on Earth. But lots of those exchanges never make it into journals or patent applications, especially the mission-specific, experimental or in-review ones. Thus, the question of whether an invention is truly novel becomes highly controversial. The lack of a single, easy-to-use collection of space technology-developed innovations only adds to this confusion.

Gaps in Jurisdiction

But it's not that straightforward, because national patent offices are subject to territorial restrictions. The vast majority of national IP systems use either national or supra-national databases to perform the search for prior art. These systems generally do not consist of classified research, business proprietary information from space companies, or results from space-based experiments never been made public. For example, the novelty of an invention that international partners on the ISS jointly create might not be publicly disclosed through any one national stream, and the new subject matter might fall through the gaps created by traditional patent searches.[12] In addition, inventions originating from private space ventures can be protected by trade secrets or non-disclosure agreements, leading to knowledge silos complicating the necessary transparency needed for a substantial decision. Such blind spots, however, hinder the integrity of

10 Rika Katsuno, "Patenting in Outer Space: Addressing Novelty and Prior Art Challenges Beyond Earth," *Annals of Air and Space Law*, Vol. 45, 2020, pp. 301–305.

11 Philip De Man, *Exclusive Use in an Inclusive Environment: The Meaning of Non-Appropriation of Outer Space for Space Resource Exploitation*, Springer, 2016, pp. 198–200.

12 Merges, Robert P., *Justifying Intellectual Property*, Harvard University Press, 2011, pp. 189–192.

novelty screenings, and can potentially cause duplication of patent rights, infringement conflicts and issues concerning the correct attribution of inventorship.

Time Lag in Publication

Another difficulty continues to be related to the time gap between invention and disclosure. This could certainly be delayed in the case of space research, which usually requires extensive validation, mission debrief, and occasionally some kind of clearance by the defence or governmental authorities. And when the results are eventually published, those no longer can be used as prior art for a contemporaneous patent application, even if the inventions for those patents were developed first. This leads to an artificial novelty gap, in which later commanding applicants can obtain patents for already existing, but undisclosed, inventions. However, such time delays may result in warping the timeline of invention, with the loss of the advantage accruing to the actual inventor on the basis that the first to file should be the first to receive a patent policy that is difficult to justify absent the possibility of contemporaneous innovation and publication.[13]

Utility in Microgravity and Non-Earth Environments

Utility or industrial applicability is a central aspect of a patent in most major patent law systems. To be eligible for a patent, an invention must be utilised for a useful purpose or have a consequence that is concrete and automatically or causally related to the result. Simple on Earth, this standard creates quite a maze when it is applied to inventions simulated or developed in space. Microgravity, exposure to cosmic radiation and other extraterrestrial conditions can also cause functionality to develop that does not work well when it is brought back to Earth. It begs the question: Should utility be measured by earth-bound standards, or do we need to create new paradigms to make sense of a new environment?

The Problem of Contextually Appropriate Utility

In space, the laws of physics work differently on materials and biological systems, producing inventions each with no Earthly counterpart. For instance, pharmaceutical crystallisation under these conditions in microgravity can result in purer and potentially more effective compounds due to reduced sedimentation and more uniform crystal growth. In the

13 Margo A. Bagley, "Patent Law's Policy Dilemma: The First-to-File vs. First-to-Invent," *University of Virginia Law Review*, Vol. 88, No. 4, 2019, pp. 637–640.

same fashion, fluid dynamics systems exhibit unique behaviours in the absence of gravity, which could inspire new engineering concepts for propulsion and life support systems. These innovations are worth a lot in space but may have little, if any, value down here.[14] So long as space activity is exclusively viewed from a terrestrial perspective, such advances may be dismissed as "non-useful" even if they are vital for space missions. This gap provides a disincentive to investment in space-based research, and undermines the incentive system that is intended to be supported by the patent laws.

Further, the utility standard, how it is currently applied, frequently demands that an invention be both operable and reproducible in the appropriate setting. In space, these functional conditions are not always available for continuous assessment or demonstration, which leads to further uncertainty in utility. It's this gap that requires a rethinking of what "useful" means in a medium that is, inherently, both experimental and restrictive.

Customised Utility Standards

One way to bridge this gap is for the patent systems of the world to develop adjustable (bifurcated) standards of utility, a standard for potential utility in terrestrial environments, and another for potential utility in extraterrestrial environments. Such a twin approach would preserve space-specific utility and not compromise. For example, any invention that is operationally significant for lunar habitation or interplanetary travel should be eligible for a patent due to its contribution to space science, even if the utility of the invention is limited to space and the invention provides no practical use on Earth.

Creating adaptive standards would also benefit the expanding commercial space sector by approving innovations for use in orbit, on the moon or on Mars. Patent offices could develop expert committees or standards dedicated to assessing utility in a non-Earth environment, consulting with astrobiology, aerospace engineering, and space medicine. This approach would lead to more informed (more intelligent) conclusions, stimulate innovation in a rapidly evolving area for which terrestrial relevance will no longer be all that significant.

14 Stephen D. H. Houghton, *Innovations in Space Engineering: Fluid Dynamics and Microgravity Effects on Propulsion and Life Support*, Springer, 2018, pp. 72–75.

The Non-Obviousness Standard and Space Science

The standard of non-obviousness and space science

The non-obviousness (or inventive step) requirement is there to help ensure that patents issue only for true inventions, rather than simple variations available to be discovered by routine experimentation. But employing this criterion in the context of space inventions presents both theoretical and practical difficulties. Most typically, this determination asks whether the invention was obvious to a person having ordinary skill in the art (PHOSITA) at the time of the invention. But here's the thing: When it comes to outer space, the very nature and knowledge base of this hypothetical figure is a bit up in the air.

If the Skilled Person is redefined

Ideas generated in microgravity or the extreme environment of space tend to be cross-disciplinary, combining space robotics, astrobiology, materials science and propulsion engineering. Thus, the traditional PHOSITA career pursuit, based on earthly technology, might not be enough anymore. So are we to now act as if this imaginary character has just gained an understanding of the politics of spaceflight or what interplanetary missions involve? Rebalancing of this legal make-believe is needed in order to test for a realistic amount of space between steps for patentable space inventions.[15]

Rapid Knowledge Evolution

The field is changing fast, with each mission delivering propulsion, life-support, and planetary systems breakthroughs. This rapidly moving frontier reflects the idea that you never know what will become commonplace tomorrow, because short experiences have long-term impacts. Static interpretations of the non-obviousness requirement will tend either to unduly enforce valid patents or to issue patents too hastily in a fast-moving area. Patent regimes need to write into their rules systems for periodically reassessing (and adjusting) the inventive step threshold in the context of space technology.

15 Keith H. G. Baumeister, "Redefining PHOSITA: The Challenges of Cross-Disciplinary Innovation in Space," *Journal of Space Law and Technology*, Vol. 31, No. 2, 2022, pp. 118–123

Disclosure, Enablement, and Confidentiality Dilemmas

The patent laws require the inventor to disclose his invention in a full, clear and enabling manner whereby others skilled in the art can make and use the invention after the patent expires. In the world of space innovation, however, satisfying these needs is especially challenging. Most inventions in space are made as part of international deals, or are hidden from public view in top-secret defence projects. In those instances, as illustrated in considerations of national security or concerns that valuable technology will be appropriated by others, typically trump the requirement of disclosure, leaving the inventor with a tension between patent law's transparency mandates and those of its secrecy dictates. Territorial Disclosure Battles, even where relations between patent holders and generics are harmonised across jurisdictions, different jurisdictions have different standards for sufficiency of disclosure. For instance, a joint experiment between NASA and ESA might need to satisfy both U.S. and EU patent laws, which could disagree on what constitutes sufficient disclosure. The broken nature of this landscape also raises the prospect of a patent being invalidated in one jurisdiction as a result of non-compliance in a separate jurisdiction.

Additionally. In-Orbit Experiments and Data Limitations point to a more general structural speed bump in space-based experiments, many of which are conducted under tight schedules with little chance for repetition. Accordingly, the evidence necessary to prove enablement, the showing that the invention works effectively and as claimed, might be missing or preliminary, failing to meet legal standards for patent protection.

Jurisdictional and Regulatory Gaps

Regulation and Sovereignty Gaps

Space commercialisation progress is so fast that it surpasses the legal framework for IP (intellectual property) in outer space. At the root of this confusion is the Outer Space Treaty of 1967 (OST), a landmark in international space law that is notably quiet on matters of IP ownership. By making space the "province of all mankind" and prohibiting appropriation by any nation, the OST has left patent enforcement up in the air.[16] But without explicit guidelines for ownership and jurisdiction, inventors and nations lack a firm legal stance to assert patent rights off-planet.

16 Samantha L. Smith, *Space Law: The Interplay of International Treaties and Intellectual Property*, Cambridge University Press, 2020, pp. 57–61.

Some countries have tried to do this through national extensions of jurisdiction, like that of the United States over its modules on the International Space Station (ISS). On the one hand, the principle does allow crude enforcement over distinct regional patches, but on the other hand, it does not address problems arising from a general conflict involving multinational missions, private entities and shared platforms for which no single country can lay exclusive claim. Then, enforcement is piecemeal and largely unenforceable in the field.[17]

"Most importantly, though, there is still not a harmonious worldwide patent system to cater for space-related inventions." Indeed, existing legal mechanisms such as the PCT do not provide a way of dealing with patent applications resulting from innovations invented in space or produced in space. This Earth focus would expose inventors whose rights might not be acknowledged or enforceable, within the peculiar, extraterritorial scope of future activities in space.[18]

Policy Recommendations and Way Forward

Recommendations and Policy Implications

As the human race pushes towards a more aggressive human presence and commercial activities in outer space, an international legal regime covering intellectual property rights (IPRs) in space has become more pressing. Although national laws and established treaties already offer some basic protection, they are inadequate to meet the challenges of inventions in space. The following is a set of policy recommendations that suggests some possible ways for a more integrated and uniform approach to space IP.

Defining a Space IP Protocol

The first step is the development of a space domain-related IP protocol standard for the international community. The development of such a protocol could be undertaken within a framework developed under the aegis of a UN COPUOS, considering the principles of international

17 Miriam C. A. Klein, *Space Law and Policy: Jurisdictional Challenges in the Age of Multinational Space Exploration*, Oxford University Press, 2021, pp. 102–105.

18 Josefina J. Thomas, *Global Patent Law and Space Innovation: The Gaps in the PCT System*, Journal of International Law and Technology, Vol. 37, No. 3, 2023, pp. 215–218.

cooperation and the collective use of space for peaceful purposes.[19] Perhaps this framework could resemble the Antarctic Treaty System, a broad governance agreement for international collaboration and a perceived sensitive habitat in the form of the continent. A Space IP Protocol could establish clear rules on who owns patents and how these would be enforced and settled in disputes in space, as per the common format agreed by all space-faring countries.

Establishment of a Space Patent Database

A central public space patent repository may alleviate the novelty issue and help in avoiding patent infringement. This repository would contain all inventions created in space, making it easier to check prior art and minimising the chances of granting the same patent twice. They would also encourage transparency and collaboration between public and private actors by offering space technologies to the world. Centralising these records will help space agencies, private companies, and researchers to avoid expensive patent fights by offering a wealth of information about what kinds of innovations are already being worked on. It would also contribute to the overall development of space technologies.

Establishing Context-Specific Patentability Threshold

Global patent offices will need to form space-specific patentability criteria. These regulations would account for the special challenges of microgravity, space environments, and cooperation in space research. For instance, patent law should consider the possibility that some space inventions may not have any utility on Earth or may only be practical for extremely limited operations that may fall outside ordinary utility requirements on Earth. It should also be clear about the reality of multi-national co-operation in space missions and offer explicit guidance on how to deal with inventions emerging from such co-operation.[20] Last but not least, a cautious attitude towards the praxis of patents on data in the light of the lack of empirical wealth of experimental findings in the context of time restrictions, no access and resources in space should find its way into patentability criteria.

19 Philip G. Duffy, "Towards a Space Domain IP Protocol: The Role of UN COPUOS in Shaping Global Space Law," in Sarah D. Johnson (ed.), *Space Law and International Cooperation: Frameworks for the Future*, Routledge, 2022, pp. 128–132.

20 David J. D. West, "Reforming Patentability: Crafting Space-Specific Criteria for Space Innovations," *Journal of Space Law*, Vol. 39, No. 1, 2024, pp. 141–145.

Promoting Multilateral Treaties

We need more multilateral instruments to shield IP in space for greater certainty and effective safeguard of IP in space. We must stimulate multilateral treaties to unify patent rights between jurisdictions. An international treaty tailored to regulate IP matters in space shall facilitate cooperation on the patent-granting procedure, enforcement means and dispute settlement at the global level.[21] The government-sponsored WIPO, which is behind the new treaty, would like to see a level legal line drawn in the sand so inventors, from the public or private sector, receive the same treatment for their inventions worldwide. Moreover, such a treaty might help to resolve the existing vacuum in patent enforcement by codifying internationally recognised jurisdiction and extra-terrestrial patent protection standards, providing standards to resolve IP disputes, as well as to clarify enforcement.

Conclusion

With the increasing exploration of space by mankind, a legal regime to protect intellectual property on other celestial bodies is becoming a major issue. The old patent regime, which was designed for innovations on Earth, needs a relook to adapt to the realm of space. This involves grappling with novelty, utility and non-obviousness under circumstances where prior art is frequently unavailable, practical applications of an invention may be dramatically different, and advances in technology have been occurring at an ever-increasing pace.

In addition, disclosure of the private space research should be reconsidered so that space research is not classified to obstruct the establishment of a transparent innovation ecosystem. Furthermore, the ambiguous territoriality of space activities requires international collaboration, respect for other nations' interests and adaptability to play a major role in developing IP laws in the field of space exploration.

A forward-looking and flexible view of space IP will safeguard not only the interests of individual inventors and organisations, but also the continued development of space as an area where the benefits of technological development can be claimed for the whole of humanity. To really realise the vast potential of outer space, we will need to build a legal regime that

21 Luca L. Z. Becchetti, "Strengthening Intellectual Property in Space: The Case for Multilateral Treaties," in Timothy D. Meyers (ed.), *International Space Law and Policy: Protecting IP in the New Frontier*, Springer, 2023, pp. 98–101.

encourages cooperation, respects the limitations of territorialism, and is rooted in the deeper principles of equity and sustainability in the final frontier.

Chapter 10

A Spaceborne Crucible: Re-evaluating India's Patents Act, 1970 for Innovations in Outer Space

-Saumya

Abstract

By the ISRO's landmark achievement and through the rapid growth of private Space-Tech start-ups, India is steadily solidifying its place as a leading space-faring nation, as its territorial-bound intellectual property framework faces an unprecedented challenge. The article argues that the Indian Patents Act, 1970, in its present form, contains significant ambiguities regarding the jurisdiction, patentable subject matter, and the standard of inventive step for inventions created or applied in outer space. Situating these issues within the key provisions through the lens of the Outer Space Treaty and the fast-evolving dynamics of commercial space activity, the paper further highlights critical issues that risk impeding innovation. It concludes with the targeted policy recommendations and a framework for the judicial interpretation to ensure India's Patent regime acts as a catalyst, not as an obstacle for the nation's "Atmanirbhar" space aspirations.

Keywords: Indian Patents Act 1970, Space Law, Jurisdiction, ISRO, Inventive Step, Patentable Subject Matter, Outer Space Treaty

Introduction

The historic landing of Chandrayaan-3 in 2023 was a successful touchdown at the moon's south pole, a milestone for India, which secured its position as a preeminent space-faring nation[1]. With companies like Skyroot Aerospace as well as Agnikul Cosmos at the cutting-edge of creating new launch technologies, the accomplishment that resulted from decades of ISRO's hard work has now served as the impulsion for a very vibrant commercial space industry[2]. Based on a state-led exploratory model of an increasingly dynamic, multi-actor industry, Indian innovation enters a new era. A well-built legal and regulatory framework is necessary to control activities that take place outside of our planet if we want to have a bright future[3]. The Indian Patents Act of 1970, in particular, which was created to protect and encourage domestic business, is currently being put to the final extraterritorial test[4].

The case brought about by the current progress raises significant legal issues that require immediate attention. If a public or private Indian entity develops a new technology for resource extraction on the Moon or on an asteroid, which regime of law would they be able to use for protection? How would the Indian Patent Office, under the configured parameters of the Earth, determine the non-obviousness or "inventive step" of a crystallisation process of a pharmaceutical product that can be done only in a microgravity environment? The current silence of Indian law regarding this particular question poses a legal vacuum. This vacuum would mean discouraging the almost crucial private investment and risk that would be needed for the next step in India's space development, which undermines the national goal of "Atmanirbhar" (self-reliance) strategically in space[5].

This article reports that India may no longer put forth a passive response to the intellectual property issues of outer space. Proactive rethinking of the Patents Act of 1970 is required. The Act's present focus on territory is at odds with that of outer space, which international law designates as

1 Jayati Datta and S.C. Chakravarti, Chandrayan–I booklet, *ISRO*, *available at*: http://www.isro.org/publications/pdf/Chandrayaan-1-booklet.pdf, (last visited on Sept. 02, 2025).

2 Monika Shailesh, Artificial Intelligence: Facets & Its Tussle with IPR, *MONDAQ*, *available at:* https://www.mondaq.com/india/new-technology/740638/artificialintelligence-facets-its-tussle-with-ipr. (last visited on Sept. 02, 2025).

3 Henry R. Hertzfeld and others, "Bringing Space Law into the Commercial World: Property Rights Without Sovereignty," *Chicago Journal of International Law*, vol. 6, no.1, 2005, pp. 81-99.

4 *Ibid.*

5 Christopher Miles, "Assessing the Need for an International Patent Regime for Inventions in Outer Space," *Tulane Journal of Technology & Intellectual Property*, vol.11, 2008, p. 62

a global common, the "province of all mankind". We will put forth that which is required is a mix of what purpose the Act was meant to serve, how admin may interpret it, and also targeted legislative changes which will in turn create a predictable and effective IP framework for space-related inventions. The paper will first demonstrate the underlying contradiction between the international space legislation and local patent legislation, and will then break down the individual issues of jurisdiction, inventive step and patentable subject matter and then suggest a forward-looking policy framework aimed at ensuring that the Indian legal system catapults its space aspirations into outer space.

The Dual Regime: Indian Patent Law and The Global Space

The intellectual property governance of space activities is at the intersection of two systems of law: the internationally binding body of treaties that outlines the legal status regarding outer space, and the national system of laws that provides and implements the grant of patents. For India, this would entail striking a balance between the Outer Space Treaty's universalist ideas and the Patents Act of 1970's territoriality and sovereignty tenets[6].

The Global Structure: Outer Space Treaty (OST) Principles

As a signatory and ratifying state, India is bound by the Outer Space Treaty of 1967's tenets, which serve as the foundation for international space law. Regarding the topic of intellectual property, many of its articles are important in this aspect.

- Article I and II: The Principles of the Commons versus Exclusionary Rights: Article I says that everyone has the right to explore and use outer space, and that this issue will be done for the good of all nations. Article II strengthens this by saying that outer space does not constitute an area of national assertion through sovereignty, use, occupation, or any other means. This, as the investigation by Md Jewel Ali shows, is a fundamental contradiction with the nature of patents, which serve as temporary monopolies that exclude others. While the articles do not explicitly prohibit intellectual property, they caution against any of intellectual property claim that would imply a de facto expropriation of a celestial body or its resources[7].

6 The United Nations Convention on the Law of the Sea, 2002

7 *Id.*, art.1, 2.

- Article VI: State Obligation: This article says that states are responsible for all of their national outer space activities, whether they are done by government agencies or non-governmental organisations. This puts the Government of the country on the record as being responsible for licensing and constantly regulating the operations within the domestic space industry. This also means that it is responsible for creating a consistent set of rules for how the industry works, including IP[8].
- Article VIII: The Anchor of Jurisdiction: The most practical legal tool for implementing local laws in space is presented in this article. It grants the state of authorisation legitimate authority and control over its registered personnel and space objects. This quasi-territoriality principle would essentially treat a spacecraft, satellite, and space station as belonging to the registering state's sovereign territory. In the case of India, this suggests that Indian law supersedes the laws of the nation in which the invention occurred. In particular, when an ISRO-launched vehicle has an Indian address and is therefore weakly rooted in the nation, the invention is presumed to be under Indian law and can therefore act as the necessary jurisdictional hook with regard to the Patents Act.

The Domestic Framework: The Indian Patents Act, 1970

Although their patent law, consistently strong and TRIPS-consistent, is ancient mariner-friendly, India's invention law was originally designed to serve the world of land-based invention[9]. Space use inherently shows the structural constraints of its use.

- Territorial Scope: The Act does not make any reference to its extraterritoriality. India lacks a similar provision, as does the United States, where the nation enacted a statute (Patents in Space Act (35 U.S.C. SS 105)) to expressly apply its patent protection to space objects under U.S. control. This creates a statutory ambiguity so as to leave the application of the Patents Act to space activity dependent entirely on the interpretation of the obligations of India under Article VIII of the OST, a resolution that is deprived of the

8 *Id.*, art. 6.

9 HR 2946, 101st Cong., 1st Session (1989). Please see Glenn H. Reynolds, "Legislative Comment: Patents in Space Act," 3 *Harv. J. L. & Tech.* 13 (1990); *See also* Journal of Space Law, vol. 18, No.2; the Regulation will appear as Section 105 of 35 U.S.C (1982).

certainty of express domestic law.

- The patentability Requirements: An invention needs to meet three requirements, namely: novelty, inventive step (Section 2(1)(ja)) and industry applicability. The notion of inventive step, which is a characteristic not apparent to a man skilled in the art, is highly problematic when such art is being practised in a world which is governed by different physical laws, which is itself what this article will break down even further.
- Exclusionary Provisions: Section 3 of the Act enumerates what may not be patented. In particular, as the analysis by K.D. Raju shows, the line between a non-patentable discovery and an invention is especially subject to attack[10]. The location and discovery of a new mineral on the Moon would not be patentable, but a new process to retrieve it would be. Moreover, the situation of computer programs per se and algorithms is a real disadvantage to the space industry of modernity, which depends heavily on AI, autonomous navigation modelled by machine learning and advanced software in information processing. On the one hand, as in *Ferid Allani v. Union of India*[11], which has now allowed patents based on software showing a technical effect, the ambiguity has remained an issue of concern for space robotics and autonomous systems innovators[12].

Critical Challenges Facing the Indian Patent System in Space

Projecting the terrestrial framework of the Patents Act into the extra-terrestrial domain raises significant legal and, in practice, critical problems that have the potential to introduce uncertainty and risk to innovators.

The Jurisdictional Void: Made in Space, Protected in India?

The most basic issue is the absence of clarity of jurisdiction. On the one hand, Article VIII of the OST hints at a solution; on the other hand, in India, it does not have implementation at all. This gap gives rise to several problems:

10 Christian Mammen & Carrie Richey, "AI and IP: Are Creativity and Inventorship Inherently Human Activities?", 14 *Florida International University Law Review* 275 (2020).

11 W.P.(C) 7/2014 & CM APPL. 40736/2019

12 Annemarie Bridy, Coding Creativity: Copyright and the Artificially Intelligent Author, *Stanford Technology Law Review* 5, 21, (2012).

- Legal Uncertainty to the private players: a private Indian company that invests billions in the creation of a space-based manufacturing process must be certain that its invention will be accepted and protected in Indian law. Based on an interpretation of an international convention, where there is no obvious domestic law, on such a risky investment is a very unsound basis.
- International Cooperation Issues: Space exploration is becoming more of a team effort. And what happens should an Indian astronaut join with a European astronaut on an international lunar base in developing an invention, which country's patent law holds? In the absence of explicit bilateral or multilateral arrangements, or of an explicit domestic legislative provision affirming jurisdiction on the basis of the nationality of the astronaut or the registry of the module, ownership questions cannot help but arise.
- The Enforcement Gap: even a patent issued in India can only be enforced locally. The Indian patent holder has no practical legal recourse if an international company using its own globally registered satellite violates an Indian-registered technology. In order to prevent infringement lawsuits that would diminish the value of Indian patents, this encourages the flag of convenience strategy, which allows players to actually establish their space objects in countries with lax IP laws.

The Ordinarily Skilled Astronaut: Re-evaluating Inventive Step

The forfeiture of the patent regime is what sets inventiveness, or non-obviousness, apart: truly inventive acts can be considered inventions, while insignificant improvements cannot. The person of common proficiency in the art (PHOSITA), a legal fictive of a person of ordinary understanding and creativity in a field, serves as its standard. In the environment of outer space, such a norm is deeply distorted[13]. The state of the art is being radically altered by the unusual physical conditions, such as microgravity, vacuum, extremely high and low temperatures, and unfiltered radiation. In space, something that seems brilliant on Earth might be obviously incorrect, and vice versa. For example:

- A device to make balls of metal fall in free-fall would be very inventive on a planet and demand complicated equipment to

13 Gyandeep Chaudhary, Artificial Intelligence: The Liability Paradox, *Summer ILI Law Review* 144 (2020).

produce the perfect round ball bearing merely by cooling the metal. Microgravity has a well-known and evident effect on Surface Tension.

- However, to overcome the lack of gravity in space, even a simple terrestrial technique like decanting a liquid requires a complex and highly inventive centrifugal or bladder-based mechanism. It would be challenging for an Indian Patent Office patent officer without specialised training or clear instructions to correctly apply the PHOSITA standard. For example, they might create an invalid patent on a process that is widely known among aerospace engineers, or they might mistakenly dismiss a patent claim on an actually innovative approach to a microgravity problem because it is thought to be obvious in a terrestrial context. The process of patented space-tech inventions is one of the most uncertain due to this subjectivity.

In-Situ Resource Utilisation (ISRU): Patentable Subject Matter

Commercial viability of a long-term space economy is based on the principle of ISRU, the possibility of living off the land using resources such as lunar water-ice or asteroid metals. This brings controversial issues of patentable subject matter in Section 3 of the Patents Act, 1970. Indian law, as K.D. Raju highlights and makes a very sharp distinction between discovery and invention. The discovery of helium-3 in the lunar regolith cannot be patented. But a new extraction and processing technique of that helium-3 would be a patentable production[14]. This imposes a burden of responsibility on Indian innovators to concentrate their IP strategy on processes and technologies, rather than on the raw materials themselves. This jurisprudential philosophy is highly comparable to that of the jurisprudence of Section 3(d) of the Act. In the case law case, *Novartis AG v. Union of India* [15] established a very high standard of patenting of new forms of already known substances, and the claimant needs to demonstrate substantially increased efficacy. This ruling represents part of a more general judicial trend in India to limit the evergreening of patents and a narrower interpretation of the meaning of a patentable discovery versus a

14 Ty S. Twibell, "Space Law: Legal Restraints on Commercialization and Development of Outer Space," *UMKC Law Review*, vol. 65, 1997, p.609.

15 AIR 2013 SC 1311

non-patentable discovery[16]. Very likely, Indian courts would use an equally restrictive test on inventions relating to extraterrestrial resources and would require a truly transformative and non-obvious test before awarding a patent. This presents a greater barrier to Indian space-mining firms than their alter-egos in jurisdictions with somewhat more lenient doctrines of the product of nature.

Proactive IP approach to a new Space India

India needs to create a purposeful and future-oriented IP strategy to counter these challenges to give confidence to the world in the prospect of realising a great space industry in India. Such a plan demands a coordinated effort at legislative, administrative and judicial levels[17].

Legislation: Space Activities Bill

A Space Activities Bill will best help to bring the matter of legalization to light. The next incarnation of this bill should not be focused on regulation and liability as it is now, but should incorporate a strong Intellectual Property chapter. This chapter should:

- Create Explicit Extraterritorial Jurisdiction: A clear provision, following the lead of the US Patents in Space Act, should be passed to the effect that, under the Patents Act 1970, any invention or use of a space object that transpires or is transacted under the jurisdiction and control of India shall be treated as having occurred within the territory of India.

- Intellectual Property ownership should be defined within a clearly articulated public-private partnership: The proposed bill must include default rules regarding who owns IP developed during an ISRO-company collaboration. They could include clearly demarcated arrangements, such as recognising the originator's rights by acquiring background IP, establishing joint ownership or granting foreground IP field-of-use rights, even though these rules might be freely modified by the parties under the contract.

- Establish a Sui Generis Data Protection Right: While the bill may not meet the creative test of copyright, it could instead establish a comprehensive sui generis right to safeguard the considerable

16 James Boyle, Endowed by their Creator? The Future of Constitutional Personhood, The Brookings Institution Future of the Constitution Series, 70 *NCLREV* 1231 (1992).

17 Anna Comer, "AI: Artificial Inventor or the Real Deal", 22 *North Carolina Journal of Law and Technology* 447 (2021).

resources with large investments made in producing such data, since data makes up a major portion of the value created in space endeavours (e.g., scientific measurements, remote sensing images).

Administrative and Judicial Frameworks

In the short run, other channels can be used, but in the long run, Legislation is perfect.

- **Guidelines for Specialised Examination**: The Controller General of Patents, Designs and Trade Marks (CGPDTM), in collaboration with ISRO, the Department of Space, and industry participants, will establish a set of guidelines to be followed when reviewing space-related patent applications[18]. These guidelines are meant to serve as a guide for examiners on how to:
    - Define "person skilled in the art" in relation to the space environment; this may entail using expert testimony.
    - Evaluate novelty and inventive step where the aerospace technologies covered by the prior art base are classified or export-controlled.
    - Process a more complex case of Section 3(k) of autonomous systems and AI in space.
- **Purposive Judicial Interpretation**: The Indian judiciary has a track record of interpreting the statutes in a way that would meet the constitutionally aimed objective and national development. With reference to space law, the courts are counselled to interpret the Patents Act in a purposive manner, keeping an eye on the national interests of India as a future space power[19]. This would include establishing that an object registered in India is within the boundaries of the Act, and that the inventive step test is applied on a highly sophisticated interpretation of the technological specifics of the space environment.

18 Jeanne C Fromer, An Information Theory of Copyright Law (2014) 64 *EMORY LAW JOURNAL* 71, 74-75, (2014) *see also*, Alina Ng, The Author' s Rights in Literary and Artistic Works, 9 J. *MARSHALL REV. INTELL. PROP. L.* 453, 453 (2009); Symposium, The Constitutionality of Copyright Term Extension: How Long Is Too Long?, 18 CARDOZO ARTS & ENT. L.J. 651, 676 (2000).

19 Lucy Rana, Artificial Intelligence and Copyright – The Authorship, *MONDAQ* (December 18, 2019), *available at*: https://www.mondaq.com/india/copyright/876800/artificialintelligence-and-copyright-the-authorship. (last visited on: Sept. 02, 2025).

Conclusion: Indian Civilisation to the Cosmos

An extremely powerful piece of statute designed for the terrestrial realm, the Indian Patents Act of 1970, is currently on the verge of becoming redundant. Its applicability in the distinct field of space is hampered by significant issues with jurisdiction, inventive step, and the scope of patentable subject matter, as this analysis indicates. These limitations pose tangible risks to the flow of money, talent, and innovations into India's rapidly growing commercial space sector, in addition to theoretical legal conundrums. A merely proactive legal covering stance cannot be the bedrock of an Indian nation's nationalism. The future also demands a multifaceted strategy that includes an ambitious and proactive judiciary solution, a pragmatic administrative framework, and a proactive legislative measure, illustrated by an inventive Space Activities Bill. The pathway to achieving the goals of Atmanirbhar Bharat and Made in India in the advanced aerospace sector is integrating a sophisticated intellectual property policy into our broader national space policy. By addressing these legal challenges, India can create a predictable, consistent, as well as favourable legal ecosystem that will support the growth of its scientists and entrepreneurs by tackling these legal issues with a long-term strategy and resolve. The moment is ripe for India's legal and policy communities to engage conversation about creating this framework that will ensure our laws, like our rockets, are capable of reaching for the stars.

Chapter 11

Satellite Technology, Patents and Trade Secrets

-Shreeni Jaiswal and Shivangi Trivedi

Abstract

When it comes to Satellite Technologies and Outer space functionality, Trade Secrets and Patents echo the sentiments, "I am there waiting, watching, keeping to the shadows. But when you need me, I'll step out of the shadows and protect what's mine." Patents and Trade Secrets play distinct yet crucial roles in providing protection to satellite technologies and innovations, each addressing the varying needs for protection. Together, they provide a strategic shield for those formulating and developing these advanced technologies. As humanity's reach has extended beyond the earth's surface, advanced satellite technologies have emerged as a cornerstone of how we connect with one another, navigate around the world, protect the country and explore the mysteries of science and space. Satellite technology, similar to any other technology, is a creation of mind, thus attracting the protection of Intellectual Property Laws which leads our way towards this research paper and its major findings.

Through this chapter, we aim to highlight the aspects of space exploration which are performed smoothly because of the protection provided by the Intellectual Property Rights, along with the dual spectrum protection provided by Patent and Trade Secrets. The chapter also examines how international organisations, private sectors and governments navigate these intellectual property frameworks to protect and safeguard their knowledge, amplify competitiveness and drive technological growth. Through case studies and legal analysis, the research focuses on the challenges of enforcing Intellectual Property Laws in outer space and creates a balanced approach towards transparency and secrecy for sustainable innovation in satellite industries.

Keywords- Intellectual Property; Satellite Technology: Protection; Challenges; IP Rights.

Satellite Technology: An Overview

Satellite technology refers to the use of artificial satellites or man-made satellites to perform various tasks in space which serve purposes on Earth or in space itself. These Satellites are the objects that are placed into orbit around the Earth and other celestial bodies for various applications such as navigation, communication, weather observation, research, and military operations. These are operated through onboard systems and communicate with stations on Earth, where they transfer data and receive operational commands.

The evolution of satellite communications is a remarkable journey from just mere analog transmission to today's high-speed technology and networks that power global connectivity. As technology continues to grow and advance, satellite systems are enhancing a solid global communication framework that enables intelligent technologies, drives digital innovations and last but not the least fosters international collaboration.

However, there are various kinds of satellites, that include:

1. **Communication Satellites**: these are used to amplify radio and connect telephone, television and internet signals across the world. They act as signal repeaters, receiving signals from one location and then amplifying them, and then transmitting them to another location.
2. **Navigation Satellites**: These satellites give accurate timing, positioning and velocity data to the people around the globe and are essential to support navigation to military, civilian and commercial use.
3. **Scientific Satellites**: These satellites are made to conduct astronomy research and space science. They are essential to study planetary systems, solar activity, cosmic phenomena, and the fundamental nature of the universe.
4. **Earth observation satellites**: These satellites are designed to

monitor and collect data regarding Earth's surface and atmosphere. Essential for understanding agriculture, urban planning, disaster management, meteorology and climate science.

5. **Weather Satellites**: These satellites are very specialised that track the atmospheric conditions to provide weather forecasts, climate changes and monitor cyclones.
6. **Military Satellites**: These are used for military or intelligence purposes. They perform reconnaissance, conduct surveillance and missile tracking.

Each type of Satellite plays a major role in today's modern era. Their continuous development and advancement contribute significantly to international and national development, technological advancement and global cooperation.

Patents in Satellite Technology

Before moving forward with the specifics of Satellite Technology Patents let us understand what Patent is and what purpose it serves in granting protection to Intellectual Property.

As per the WIPO (World Intellectual Property Organisation), a Patent is an exclusive right granted to an invention, which allows the patentee to exercise a variety of exclusive and time-bound rights. A patent aims to protect those creations of the mind which deal with providing novelty in either the product or the process. In simple terms, a patent protects an invention which is novel, involves an inventive step and has industrial utility. Patent as a tool for IP protection has evolved over time all around the globe, while it seems important to understand this evolution, it is safe to say that it has evolved for the good and for providing at most security to the inventions around the globe.

With regard to the basic understanding of patents let us now move forward with understanding various aspects related to patents of satellite technology, we will be dealing with this broad section by way of answering questions which are bound to arise when it comes to patenting of satellite technology, which can be categorised into the following sub-heads:

Patentability of Satellite Technology

One of the most common questions that arises while seeking protection for satellite technology is regarding its patentability i.e., its ability to satisfy the criteria for acquiring a patent. To answer this question, we can divide any satellite technology in the following heads:

- Technological Innovations: this head deals with the Hardware of Satellite Technology, its design and those other physical features which have the ability to either enhance the functioning of existing technology or bring about a novel one. Once the novelty and inventive step is proved, the Hardware of any Satellite Technology becomes ready to be protected.

- Software and Algorithms: as the name suggests, this head deals with the Software of the Satellite Technology, inclusive of optimised signal processing algorithms or satellite trajectory calculations, which are able to emphasise the novelty in functioning and are Patentable.

- Systems and Methods: sometimes, a Satellite Technology may not necessarily be seen as one having novel hardware or software but, can be novel as a whole for instance, a new technology of 3D weather forecasting satellite, these kinds are patentable under this head.

Multijurisdictional applications for Satellite Technology

As much as it sounds fascinating, it is not easy to claim Patent head over the outer space around the globe; to achieve this protection both around and above the globe it is essential for the applicant to dodge the balls which Multijurisdictional applications throw at them. To do so, one must be consistent and clear in the following terms,

- Consistency: in terms of technical description in filing any application, failing to do so might lead to confusion and non-patentability due to lack of novelty.

- Clarity: in terms of translation, with each region, the requirements change and thus, one must maintain clear translation to avoid ambiguity and unintended interpretations.[1]

Once Patentability is achieved and multijurisdictional challenges are dealt with the Satellite Technology can be protected under the IP protection of a Patent. This protection is suitable for those technologies which are useful

1 For details pertaining intellectual property strategies see, https://spaceeast.co.uk/intellectual-property-strategies-for-space-technologies-patent-or-trade-secret/

for mankind but the developer looks forward to having a time-bound monopoly over the invention. Similar to Patent there is yet another IP Right, namely, Trade Secret whose protection can be used as a shield to preserve Satellite Technology beyond a specified period. We will be dealing with Trade Secrets & Satellite technology in the next section of the paper.

Trade Secret in Satellite Technology

Similar to Patent, Trade Secret is another type of IP Right which typically involves a variety of agreements like that of non-disclosure and aims towards providing a lifelong monopoly over any process, product or service. As per WIPO (World Intellectual Property Organisation), Trade secrets IP rights on confidential information which may be sold or licensed. In simpler terms, a Trade Secret involves agreements not to disclose secrets or essentials, which serve as a means to gain a competitive edge in the market. Though Trade Secret may appear to be a sorted and more advantageous aspect, the protection of Satellite Technology via Trade Secrets does raise concerning issues which may be dealt under the following sub-heads:

Does Satellite Technology qualify to be protected via Trade Secret?

While, dealing with this issue, we must look at the elements which are essential to attract the protection of trade secrets and analyse them in the context of Satellite Technology:

Blend of advantageous information: Trade Secret provide protection to that information, which might give a competitive advantage to businesses. Looking at satellite technology, it is by way of the Outer Space Treaty of 1967 that it was agreed that space and celestial bodies are not subjects of any nation. However, objects launched into space remain under the jurisdiction of the country where they are registered making Satellites, Space shuttles and Space Stations a means of livelihood and profit. Thus, any piece of information which might lead to monopoly of any inventor is subject of Trade Secret and can use it to protect the same.

Inclusive of valuable information: Trade Secrets provide protection to any valuable information which may either be Technical or Commercial in nature, its purpose is to protect that information which is valuable and has utility. When it comes to Satellite Technology, it is generally Technical in nature but, as discussed above, Satellite Technology may not always consist of hardware and software information, but can also include those aspects that describe its utility and have a commercial value capable of being protected.

Element of Confidentiality: everything which is looked forward to be protected by way of agreements under Trade Secret is aimed to be protected solely because it involves preservation and conservation aspects, in lieu of this confidentiality we can clearly identify that Satellite Technologies are developed to bring about advancement in outer space functionality and thus, without any doubt it consists of certain elements which must be kept preserved and limited to knowledge of those concern.

What amounts to Trade Secret misappropriation & available Legal remedies?

Trade Secret Misappropriation refers to breach of the trade secret by unauthorised acquisition of protected information or going beyond the Nondisclosure agreement. It typically refers to the infringement of the Right of the Trade Secret holder by breaching the agreement or wrongfully transferring the information so protected.

Misappropriation of a Trade Secret does not necessarily refer to a malafide intention to infringe the holder's right but is composed of the following key elements:

- Use of Improper Means: This implies to performance of actions like theft, fraud, bribery, inducing those in possession of information to breach confidential duties or contractual obligations and release the protected information. These means are used to gain unfair advantage in the market.
- Disclosure without Consent: Disclosing of trade secret and its utilisation without the express or implied consent of the owner constitutes misappropriation. The very purpose of this and any other form of misappropriation is to simply gain a competitive edge.

Trade Secret misappropriation is subject to the exception of *"Reverse engineering"*, which implies to gain or acquisition of a Trade secret as a part of the information supply chain and regaining it via once intellect. This does not amount to misappropriation as held in the case of *Kewanee Oil Co. V. Bicron Corp.*[2], where the US Supreme Court gave judgment that reverse engineering, which involves starting with the known product and working backwards to divine the process which aided in its development or manufacture, cannot be considered as a misappropriation of a trade secret.

2 Kewanee Oil Co. V. Bicron Corp, 416 U.S. 470 (1974)

Now that we have understood the malpractice of Trade secret misappropriation, let us now look at the Legal Remedies which are available for this wrong. In light of several National and International Legislations like, Uniform Trade Secrets Act (UTSA); Defend Trade Secrets Act (DTSA); the Economic Espionage Act (EEA) & Indian Contract Act 1872 following are some Legal remedies available for breach of Trade Secret and agreements of Nondisclosure:

1. Injunctions: often used as a preventive remedy at the initial stage of the cases of Trade Secret Misappropriation.
2. Monetary Damages: are provided in the form of compensation, Account of profit and development costs.
3. Return of Trade Secrets: by way of returning misappropriated documents, materials, or digital files containing trade secrets.
4. Other orders: inclusive of Search and seizure orders and order for the confiscation of misappropriation technologies.

Thus, Trade Secrets can be used a protection for satellite Technology but are subject to risks of misappropriation and breach, this protection is suitable for those technologies which look forward for a lifelong monopoly and are based on the information necessary to protect the core of the technology. Qualifying the parameters of trade secret information, it is essential for technology developers to be clear with the terms of the contract and ensure transparency yet encryption in this process of technological development.[3]

International Legal Framework

It is only in recent years that the intellectual property rights in regard to outer space activities have raised wider attention. The reason is that these activities are shifting rapidly from state-controlled activities to private and commercial activities. So, the need to establish a legal framework for the enforcement and protection of intellectual property becomes critical. While no treaty or convention specifically governs these in outer space, a combination of international agreements, legal principles and conventions contributes to a functional framework to some extent.;

3 For details pertaining to Trade secrets in space technology see, https://www.esa.int/About_Us/Law_at_ESA/Intellectual_Property_Rights/Trade_secrets_and_other_IPRs#:~:text=A%20trade%20secret%20requires%20you,an%20action%20before%20the%20courts.

1. **TRIPS and its Application to Space Technology**: The agreement on Trade-Related Aspects of Intellectual Property Rights was adopted in 1994 under the framework of the World Trade Organisation. It is a key instrument that sets standards for the protection of intellectual property rights within the member states. Although it is not space specific, it governs patent protection, technology transfer and licensing, which are highly relevant to space technologies. Satellite components and its software can be qualified for patent protection under the agreement, also complying with national laws. It promotes licensing and intellectual property-based technology transfer, which is essential for international cooperation and collaboration in outer space missions. It also protects the sensitive and confidential operational protocols and software codes used in space technologies.

2. **The Outer Space Treaty, 1967**: This treaty does not specifically discuss Intellectual Property rights; however, its principles affect the enforceability and scope of Intellectual property in space. Article 1 and 2 of the same contain rules regarding the exploration and use of outer space, including the moon and other celestial bodies. It further states that entities must be used for the interest and benefit of all the countries.

3. **World Intellectual Property Organisation**: it is one of the 16 specialised agencies of the United Nations who plays an epic role in the administration, protection and promotion of Intellectual Property Rights throughout the world. The organisation also does not expressly or directly regulate outer space activities, its objectives to promote and protect the intellectual property has increasing relevance in regard to space technology where collaboration between countries and commercialisation are rapidly expanding.

4. **Paris Convention for the Protection of Industrial Property**: also known as the Paris Convention, is an international treaty in the field of industrial property. Although it does not expressly mention the inventions in outer space. However, it talks about the establishment of the national treatment principle under Article 2 and the right of priority under Article 4. In regard to the Patent, as per Article 4bis, a patent granted for an invention in one member state does not require other member states to grant a patent for that same invention.

5. **Registration Convention**: Article II of the Registration Convention states that the launching state shall register the state object through an entry in an appropriate registry maintained. If there are two or more launching states, they should jointly decide which one they will register, keeping in mind Article VIII of the Outer Space Treaty.

In light of the above-mentioned international treaties, let us now look at the Indian perspective and what take India has while granting IP protection to Satellite Technology.[4]

India's National Legal Framework Related to IPR in Outer Space Activities

As India continues to grow rapidly as one of the major spacefaring nations through the Indian Space Research Organisation (ISRO) and other private companies in space technologies, the importance of a legal framework for safeguarding the intellectual property rights has grown significantly.

In November 2017, the Indian government's Department of Space came up and introduced the Draft Space Activity Bill aimed at providing a legal framework for outer space activities and defining the major role of private players. Due to various constraints, it is yet to be enacted.

India, while being a signatory to the Outer Space Treaty, finds difficulty in enforcing IPR in space, since the treaty prohibits territorial claims in space making it difficult for the countries to apply traditional intellectual property right laws.

Despite a strong intellectual property foundation, there are some challenges and gaps in the application of IPR laws:

1. Lack of a specific legal framework for space IPR: While India has signed several International treaties, there is no single legislation in its own country that addresses intellectual property ownership in space-related activities.

2. Absence of a Cohesive Legal Framework for Private Sector Involvement: India's space sector has been state-dominated with very little involvement of private companies in satellite design, launch services and remote sensing. This has accelerated, but

4 For details pertaining to international legal framework see https://www.wipo.int/export/sites/www/patent-law/en/pdf/developments/ip_space.pdf

without a clear legislative backing, these actors face uncertainty in terms of ownership of IP developed through public-private partnerships, dispute resolution, and licensing procedures.

3. National Security and Strategic Autonomy Concerns: As space activities or satellites play a major role in defence communications, navigation, surveillance and cyber intelligence, securing the intellectual property rights becomes a matter of national interest. The dual use for both civilian and military functions means that IP is essential for safeguarding not only commercial competitiveness but also for security of the nation from external forces.

Thus, India should look forward to resolving all the ambiguities around IP ownership, national security and private sector rights. Timely legislative intervention with India's growth in the space economy is crucial to ensure legal certainty, protecting innovation and global competitiveness.[5]

Conclusion

It is rightly quoted that, "Intellectual Property is the fuel that drives innovation & creativity... protect it fiercely." Keeping in mind these ideas of beneficial intellectual property and the need for its protection, we can conclude that, similar to any other technological innovation, Satellite Technology is a creation of the mind which deals with outer space complexities, and this complex field requires adoption of an IP strategy that provides protection appropriate to the circumstances, and helps to ensure commercial success for innovators. Out of the various available IP protection patents, Trade Secrets are most often adopted, while each of them has its own utility and benefits, the risks associated with them are also a concerning issue; dodging these risks must be of paramount importance for those looking for efficient protection. In cases of Patent, the complexities associated with Multijurisdictional application pose a grave threat to those looking for protection; on the other hand, in cases of Trade Secret, its viability is shaky due to easy breach of contracts and malpractices of a nature. Through this research, we have not only understood the aspect of IP protection for Satellite Technology but have also dealt with the National and International perspectives for the same. We can easily identify that Indian and International opinion on the protection of Technological innovation is more or less based on the sole idea of protection, which has a commercial utility and which might provide for the advancement of mankind. In

5 Patrick-André Salin, Satellite communication regulation in the early 21st century, p.16.

conclusion, it is essential for every innovator to be cautious, vigilant and surround oneself with a team that is efficient in legally protecting oneself and the innovation in all its forms.

Part IV

Trademarks, Geographical Indications, and New Frontiers of IP

Chapter 12

Trademark Protection Beyond Earth: Legal Framework and Emerging Challenges in Outer Space

-Neha Singh and Shivang Tripathi

Introduction

With the advent of the 21st century, there has been a tremendous increase in activities in space and a shift from state-led scientific exploration to a burgeoning era of commercialisation dominated by private entities.[1] Commercial entities and state space agencies are involved in various activities beyond Earth's orbit, including space tourism, resource extraction from outer space, advanced scientific research, and the establishment of orbital and potentially off-world habitats.[2] Natural to this extension into space is the increased emphasis on branding and the commercial label.

Companies such as SpaceX prominently display their branding on their rockets and spacecraft, establishing brand presence and goodwill in the nascent space market.[3] NASA, although its scientific work is in the public domain, has an international trademark portfolio as part of its effort to avoid private misperceptions of its logos, logotypes, or other personal

1 V Vasantha, "Global Opportunities and Challenges in the Space Economy", *Sri Lanka Journal of Economic Research,* vol. 12(1)(2024), pp. 81-94 at p. 82 available at: 677371347f30a.pdf accessed on 14 May, 2025.

2 *Ibid.*

3 *Ibid* at p. 84.

identity identifiers.[4] This policy is intended to prevent the unauthorised commercial use of the NASA identity in a manner that would falsely imply endorsement by the agency.[5] Private space companies, via companies like Blue Origin, have also begun engaging in proactive branding by trademarking names like "New Shepard" to their space vehicles in an attempt to develop brand recognition and distinguish between their products.[6] This shows that companies involved in space ventures want to develop and enhance their brand images, in much the same way Earth-based companies do, creating goodwill and prophesying a new world of things and services to buy.[7] Thus, it has become imperative to provide legal protection to trademarks in outer space, where the concept of territoriality and appropriation by states does not exist.

This chapter seeks to fulfil this purpose by critically examining the existing legal framework, as pertaining to the protection of trademarks, the problems raised by space commercialisation, and proposals for ensuring the world is left with a strong international system that is capable of adapting to the new realities of the nascent space age.

Understanding Trademark in Context

Intellectual property (IP) is the result of the creation of human minds[8] , and the World Intellectual Property Rights Organisation (WIPO) defines a trademark as a sign that distinguishes the products of one enterprise from

4 Jeffry L. Hinger, "Inside Track: NASA", *WTR*, 03 October, 2014 available at: https://www.worldtrademarkreview.com/article/inside-track-nasa#:~:text=Heninger%20confirms% 20that%20while%20the,less%20aggressive% 2C%E2%80%9D%20he%20explains. accessed on 14 May, 2025.

5 Jonathan Bailey, "NASA: Copyright and Trademark in Space", *Plagiarism Today*, 4 November, 2024 available at: https://www.plagiarismtoday.com/2024/11/04/nasa-copyright-and-trademark-in-space/ accessed on May 12, 2025

6 Bhavpreet Soni, "Space Law, Commercialization of Outer Space and IPR", *Soni's Vision*, 27 September, 2024, available at: https://www.sonisvision.in/blogs/space-law-commercialization-of-outer-space-and-ipr accessed on 15 May, 2025.

7 *Id.*

8 Evgenia Yvonni Tseloni, "Protection of Patent in Outer Space Could Blockchain Technology be a Sufficient Solution?", *Proceedings of the International Institute of Space Law*, vol.66(8) (2023), pp. 429-443, p. 429, 430 available at: https://orbilu.uni.lu/bitstream/10993/63793/1/Protection_of_Patents_in_Outer_Space_Could_Blockchain_Technology_Be_a_Sufficient_Solution-2.pdf accessed on 15May, 2025.

those of others.[9] A trademark provides its owner with the exclusive right to use a specific name, logo, or symbol in connection with a designated product.[10] Unlike other branches of IP law, such as copyright and patents, which aim to foster creativity and innovation, trademark law primarily seeks to encourage economic investment by protecting brand identity.[11]

In the evolving domain of space commerce, trademarks have become essential for branding ventures such as lunar bases, orbital hotels, and interplanetary enterprises. Trademarks are now commonly seen on spacecraft, payloads, and even astronaut uniforms.[12] With the rise of activities like space tourism, asteroid mining, satellite repair, and lunar exploration, the use of trademarks for marketing and commercial purposes is expected to grow substantially.[13]

However, this commercialisation also gives rise to complex legal questions. For instance, if a company's trademark is displayed on a rover operating on the Moon or on a satellite in Earth's orbit, does trademark protection apply globally or only within the jurisdiction where it was originally registered? Could a foreign competitor legally use a similar mark in outer space without infringing on intellectual property rights? The absence of clear legal frameworks and precedents leaves brand owners exposed to potential misuse, counterfeiting, and dilution, particularly in a realm where enforcement mechanisms are practically non-existent.[14]

---

9 "Trademarks", *WIPO*, available at: https://www.wipo.int/en/web/trademarks accessed on 15 May, 2025.

10 *Ibid.*

11 Ronald A. Cass and Keith N. Hylton, *Laws of Creation: Property Rights in the World of Ideas*, (Harvard University Press, Cambridge, 2013), pp. 126-127.

12 Zeldine O' Brien, "Advertising in Space: Sales at the Outer Limits", in Jai Galliott, (ed.), *Commercial Space Exploration: Ethics, Policy and Governance* (Routledge, New York, 2016), p. 91.

13 Aditya Pandey, "Beyond Earth: Unravelling the Intricacies of Intellectual Property Rights in Space Exploration", *Khurana & Khurana*, 3 Match, 2025 available at: https://www.khuranaandkhurana.com/2025/03/03/beyond-earth-unravelling-the-intricacies-of-intellectual-property-rights-in-space-exploration/#:~:text=Since%20private%20companies%20are%20beginning%20to%20market%2D,trademark%20registration%20will%20be%20even%20more%20necessary accessed on16 May, 2025.

14 Clark W. Lackert, "Trademarks in Outer Space: Supporting the Off-Eorld Economy", *WIPO Magazine*, 10 December, 2021 available at: https://www.wipo.int/web/wipo-magazine/articles/trademarks-in-outer-space-supporting-the-off-world-economy-42331#:~:text=Existing%20international%20approaches%20to%20outer,control%20of%20the%20United%20States. accessed on 16 May, 2025.

Additionally, the matter of legal jurisdiction in outer space complicates matters further. The principle of sovereignty, a foundational concept in international law, does not apply in space.[15] The Outer Space Treaty of 1967 (OST) explicitly prohibits national appropriation of outer space,[16] thereby creating a legal void concerning which national laws govern commercial activities and how disputes should be adjudicated.

The Dispute: Territorial Marks in a Non-Territorial World

The essential incompatibility of trademark territoriality with the non-territorial legal framework of outer space poses a significant problem in safeguarding trademarks in this expanding new frontier.[17] This fundamental conflict is central to the legal void on the expansion of trademark protection into space. This core clash lies at the heart of the legal vacuum surrounding trademark protection beyond Earth. Trademark law, as it has evolved, is intrinsically linked to the concept of national borders and the sovereign authority of states to grant and enforce exclusive rights within their defined territories[18], for instance, the U.S. Lanham Act and the European Union Intellectual Property Office (EUIPO) function based on the principle of territoriality and trademark projection cannot be granted beyond the state where the trademark is registered. Outer space, conversely, is expressly declared as non-appropriable for national purposes.[19] This generates a theoretical "territoriality paradox" between the two orders.[20] While trademark law relies on territorial boundaries for its application,

15 Von Der Dunk, Frans, "Sovereignty and Space: When and Where Shall the Twain Meet?", in Gerard Kreijen, and others (eds), *State, Sovereignty, and International Governance* (Oxford, 2002; online edn, Oxford Academic, 22 Mar. 2012), https://doi.org/10.1093/acprof:oso/9780199245383.003.0020, accessed on 20 May 2025.

16 Article III, Treaty on Principles Governing the Activities of States in the Exploration and Use of Outer Space, including the Moon and Other Celestial Bodies, 1967.

17 Deva Dutta, "Role of Intellectual Property Rights in Space Law", *India Legal*, 8 April, 2023 available at: https://indialegallive.com/laws-research-indepth/role-of-intellectual-property-rights-in-space-law/ accessed on 12 May, 2025

18 Chitra B T and Anshul Sajit, "Territoriality Challenges for Trademark Protection in a World Without Borders", *International Journal of Legal Studies*, vol. 1(2)(2024), pp. 18-23, p. 19 available at: https://iaeme.com/Home/issue/IJLS?Volume=1&Issue=2 accessed on 15 May, 2025.

19 Article II, Treaty on Principles Governing the Activities of States in the Exploration and Use of Outer Space, including the Moon and Other Celestial Bodies 1967.

20 Zhijie Chen, "Theoratical Territoriality Paradox for the Intellectual Property Protection in Outer Space and its Regulatory Approach for reconciliation", *Journal of East Asia and International Law*, vol. 13(1) (2020), pp. 52-74, p. 53.

space law actively prohibits the establishment of such boundaries for the purpose of national sovereignty.[21]

Despite the underlying conflict, Article VIII of the OST, when interpreted alongside Article II(1) of the Registration Convention, presents a possible means of addressing this paradox, at least in relation to space objects.[22] By granting the launching state jurisdictional control over its properly registered spacecraft, the article creates the possibility for that state's national laws, including trademark laws, to extend to activities aboard or associated with those objects.[23] This method effectively makes a registered spacecraft a "quasi-territory" of the launching state in legal terms.[24]

The application of national patent laws to spacecraft under the launching state's jurisdiction, as permitted by the above-mentioned Article, serves as a useful parallel for exploring the potential extension of trademark protection.[25] For example, the United States adopted its patent laws in outer space, enacting the U.S. Space Act 2015.[26] Section 105 of the Act applies U.S. patent law to objects launched into space.[27] This reflects the realisation that intellectual property rights have caught up with inventions made or used aboard space objects registered by states, with the launching state's jurisdiction providing a form of legal authority.[28] That ruling arguably could be extended to trademark law, where the trademark laws of the launching state might be applied to branding and commercial identification of goods and services in connection with its registered space objects.

But there are limitations to such types of solutions. This is largely aimed at what happens on space objects, on or beneath the surface of space objects, and may not extend to other commercial activities on other celestial

21 *Ibid.*

22 *Ibid.*

23 Sandeepa Bhat, "Invention in Outer Space Need for Reconstruction of the Patent Regime",) *Journal of Space Law*, Vol. 36(1) (2010), pp. 1-17, p. 12.

24 *Ibid.*

25 *Ibid.*

26 Section 105 of the U.S. Commercial Space Launch Competitiveness Act (CSLCA), 2015 (51 U.S. Code § 105)

27 *Ibid.*

28 Laurie Burlingame, Anastasia Dergacheva, *et.al.*, "Exploring the Legal Frontier of Space and Satellite Innovation", *Morgan Lewis*, 6 May, 2025 available at: https://www.morganlewis.com/pubs/2025/05/exploring-the-legal-frontier-of-space-and-satellite-innovation accessed on May 12, 2025.

bodies, or in other extra-terrestrial settings. For example, a spacecraft from country 'A' displaying a registered trademark operates near another spacecraft from country 'B' with a visually similar, unregistered mark. If confusion arises, there is no clear mechanism to resolve this conflict.

An area where territoriality is slightly relaxed is in the "well-known marks" doctrine.[29] This rule makes it possible for some marks to become so famous that they can be protected in countries where they are not effectively registered.[30] If a mark has become famous in a country, even without any (or any significant) local business presence, it might be protected against competing usage.[31] While this doctrine offers a limited form of extraterritorial reach, its applicability to trademarks used primarily or exclusively in outer space remains uncertain. For example, whether a trademark used on a lunar base would be considered "well-known" on Earth or not.

Furthermore, the enforcement of IP rights beyond airspace may clash with space law principles like open access and the principle of the common heritage of mankind.[32] The OST advocates for the exploration and use of outer space for the benefit of all countries, rather than serving the interests of a select few.[33] Granting exclusive rights through trademarks could potentially restrict access to or the use of certain terms, logos, or brand identifiers in space, potentially hindering scientific collaboration, the free flow of information, or the development of space resources for the benefit of all.[34] Hence, any trademark protection regime that might be introduced for space should be carefully balanced with the imperatives of open access and the equitable use of the space domain.

A major challenge lies in the absence of clear provisions addressing intellectual property rights, including trademarks, within the current international space treaties.[35] The OST and the other treaties regulating

29 Chitra, *note 18*, p. 22. Also see, *N.R. Dongre v. Whirlpool Corporation*, 1996 PTC (16) 583 (SC).

30 *Ibid.*

31 *Ibid.*

32 Deva, *note 17.*

33 Article I para 1 of OST.

34 Deva, *note 17.*

35 MD Jewel Ali, "From Earth to Orbit: Converging Space Law and Intellectual Property Rights to Safeguard Innovation Beyond Earth", *International Journal Of Legal Sciences and Innovation*, vol. 6(5) (2024) pp. 210-228, p. 218 available at: https://ijlsi.com/wp-content/uploads/From-Earth-to-Orbit-Converging-Space-Law-and-Intellectual-

activities beyond Earth's orbit are largely concerned with principles of peaceful utilisation, non-appropriation, state responsibility and liability.[36] The absence of specific provisions addressing how intellectual property rights acquired on Earth should be recognised and enforced in space creates a legal vacuum and considerable uncertainty for commercial actors. Absence of clear international guidance and uncertainty of the availability and enforceability of trademark rights in space may deter investment and innovation in the space industry.[37]

Issues of Enforcement and Jurisdiction for Outer Space

The absence of territorial boundaries in outer space presents a fundamental challenge to the traditional enforcement mechanisms of trademark law, which are inherently tied to national jurisdictions. Without established sovereign territories, it is unclear which legal system would have the authority to adjudicate trademark disputes arising in space. For example, if a lunar base violates a trade name, there is no established body of law to dictate whether lawsuits would be filed and tried under the laws of any of the nation-states to which the litigants might belong.

In addition, there is no central international framework dealing specifically with trademarks in outerspace.[38] No treaty in force and no international authority has been given express competence in respect of the registration and protection of trademarks related to space activities. The lack of legal support and an enforcement framework here represents an enormous challenge for trademark holders, wanting to defend their brand in space.[39]

Jurisdictional uncertainty complicates enforcement.[40] Space actors frequently include more than one country as well as the private sector, and

Property-Rights-to-Safeguard-Innovation-beyond-Earth.pdf accessed on 15 May, 2025.

36 "International Space Law Explained", *United Nations* available at: https://www.un.org/en/peace-and-security/international-space-law-explained accessed on May 15, 2025.

37 T. Leepuenghtham, *The Protection of Intellectual Property Rights in Outer Space Activities*, (Edward Elgar Publishing Limited, UK, 2017) p. 3.

38 Clark W Lackert, "IP in Outer Space: The Next Frontier", *International Trademark Association*, 8 December, 2021 available at: https://www.inta.org/perspectives/features/ip-in-outer-space-the-next-frontier/ accessed on 12 May, 2025.

39 "IP in Space", *International Trademark Association*, December 2022 available at:https://www.inta.org/wp-content/uploads/public-files/perspectives/industry-research/221207_ipinspace_report.pdf accessed on 12 May, 2025,

40 *Ibid*, p. 13.

it is not clear which national laws would apply in any particular case.[41] For example, a spacecraft launched by a particular entity in one country with one group of crew members of varying nationality to perform a business activity may infringe a trademark registered in a third country. Adjudicating these conflicts of law in the absence of a clear international accord is a complex legal problem.

Enforcement of the trademark on such a scale in the expansive and distant confines of space remains a challenge.[42] Being exemplary for trademark enforcement, monitoring for and detecting possible infringement on a moon base, on board a spaceship flying through deep space, would be a difficult and resource-consuming task.[43] There still remains the need for innovative measures and international cooperation for obtaining evidence of an infringement and legal measures taken over a potentially great distance.

Existing space law treaties typically lack compulsory dispute resolution mechanisms, with the Liability Convention being the sole instrument that outlines a procedure specifically for addressing physical damage.[44] The Optional Rules for Arbitration of Disputes Relating to Outer Space Activities have also been framed by the Permanent Court of Arbitration (PCA).[45] These mechanisms, primarily designed for other types of controversies, may be readapted or used as a model to establish the mechanisms to resolve IP matters in outer space.

Comparative Law Solutions and Proposals for Reform

Realising the necessity for legal certainty, the legal academia, international organisations, and national bodies have proposed numerous reforms to the question of trademark protection in space. One of them is to enhance

41 Dimtri Linden, "The Impact of National Space Legislation on Private Space Undertaking: Regulatory Competition vs. Harmonization", *Journal Of Science Policy & Governance*, vol. 8(1) (2016), available at: https://www.sciencepolicyjournal.org/uploads/5/4/3/4/5434385/linden_nationalspacelegislation.pdf accessed on 15 May, 2025.

42 Clark, *note* 14.

43 *Ibid.*

44 Article IV , Convention on International Liability for Damage Caused by Space Objects 1971.

45 Caroline Arbaugh, "Gravitation Towards Sensible Resolution: The PCA Optional Rules for the Arbitration of Disputes Relating to Outer Space", *Georgia Journal of International Comparative Law*, vol. 42(2013), pp. 826-850, p. 826.

the application of national legislation.[46] Some countries have already done so. For instance, as previously mentioned, the United States has enacted legislation to govern inventions created on space objects, or those in which the U.S. has involvement or risk, and over which it holds jurisdiction or control.[47] Although this affords some protection for events emerging from these countries, there is little global coordination to ensure full coverage.

The ISS Intergovernmental Agreement (IGA) provides a precedent of an international agreement that considers intellectual property in the space context, mainly patents. Article 21 of the agreement states that, regarding intellectual property rights, any action taken on or within an ISS element is deemed to have occurred solely within the territory of the nation where the element is registered.[48] This sets a precedent for assigning legal jurisdiction in space to the nation where a spacecraft is registered, a principle that could be expanded to include trademarks in future agreements.[49] However, the IGA is a private contract and does not create universally binding terms for third parties.[50]

The World Intellectual Property Organisation (WIPO) is also exploring potential resolutions, such as expanding the Madrid System for international registration of trademarks to cover a new designation for "Outer Space".[51] This approach would enable trademark owners to obtain global protection up to outer space by using one application model based on a system already in use and accepted internationally.[52] The International Trademark Association (INTA) published a comprehensive white paper suggesting ten key avenues toward developing a legal framework for IP in outer space, such as expanding the Madrid System, extending national regimes, entering into private agreements, establishing a voluntary IP repository for space, employing existing national jurisdictions, and developing a new instrument for IP in space.[53]

46 IP in Space, *note 39*, p. 19.

47 Section 105, *note 26.*

48 Leepuenghtham, *note 39*, pp. 167-168.

49 Clark, *note 38.*

50 M. Weisfeiler, "Patent Law in Space", *Boston College Intellectual Property & Technology Forum*, pp. 1-9(2019), p. 3.

51 Clark, *note 14.*

52 Clark, *note 38.*

53 IP in Space, *note 39, p.18.*

A frequent suggestion is that a new treaty should be concluded to serve as an international instrument focused on intellectual property rights generally, including trademarks, in outer space.[54] Such an agreement could provide clear rules on the acquisition, application, protection and enforcement of trademark rights in the special area of space activities.[55] It would have to deal with basic issues such as jurisdiction, law applicable and dispute resolution mechanisms.[56]

Where a full legal framework is lacking, private contractual arrangements are also under consideration as stopgap measures.[57] Part of the parties arranging for space activities could also be the inclusion of particular clauses in the contracts, clarifying issues of ownership of IP, the right to use, and the manner in which they can be enforced, also possibly providing for the selection of applicable law and the authority of a court or binding arbitration to settle disputes.[58]

A second proposal is the creation of space-specific IP registries.[59] These could be localised registries for intellectual property rights within specific space regions, such as lunar bases or orbital stations, to provide public notice of IP claims and potentially facilitate more localised enforcement mechanisms.[60]

National initiatives, such as the recent space economy reform in Italy, which introduces provisions for the authorisation and registration of space objects, also highlight a growing recognition at the national level of the need to address the legal gaps in space.[61] Although not mentioning intellectual property, this reform is the first step in setting up an overall legal system for the space industry, eventually involving IP rights.

54 Clark, *note 14.*

55 *Ibid.*

56 Clark, *note 38.*

57 IP in Space, *note*

58 Clark *note 38.*

59 IP in Space, *note 39*, pp. 20-21

60 *Ibid.*

61 Hoda Ghassabian, "Regulating Access to Outer Space-The First Italian Law on Space Economy", *Lexology*, 9 July, 2024 available at: https://www.lexology.com/library/detail.aspx?g=4223aa48-553e-4c03-b222-25c304eb59e3 accessed on 18 May, 2025.

Suggestive Framework: Towards an International Uniform Framework

There has never been a more urgent time to give effect to an effective system of trademark protection for the commercial exploitation of space operations, on an international basis. Such an approach likely needs to be multi-layered, consisting of short-term adaptations of things that are already in place, as well as adopting new longer-term solutions.

First, in order to leverage the OST provision, international endeavours should be directed towards the elucidation and the advancement of the use of the national trademark laws of the country from whose ground or with whose permission the launching or registering is carried out as regards spacecraft and their operations. International standards might be established to give uniform interpretation and effect to national laws in this novel environment, offering a more immediate, if narrow, ground for trademark protection in space.

Second, in order to expand the functional ambit of the Madrid System, there should be vigorous advocacy at the WIPO level for the incorporation of "Outer Space" as a territorial body under the Madrid Protocol. The upside would be that trademark owners could apply for international registration with worldwide effect (analogously to international trademarks), using a pre-existing and highly effective mechanism intended for the protection of trademarks worldwide. Such expansion could be discussed, and amendments to the Madrid Protocol required to cater for the same could be developed by WIPO.

Third, it is suggested that industry trade associations, law firms, and multinational bodies work together to develop standard model clauses for space contracts for aspects of trademarks, which clearly articulate who owns, uses, and what to do in the event of a dispute about a trademark. Such terms should also provide for the choice of law and jurisdiction as well as for arbitration, thus giving swift and practical answers to commercial players interested in exploiting outer space.

Fourth, efforts must be made at the United Nations to engage in discussions on and negotiation of a new international agreement, focused on intellectual property rights in space, especially trademarks. Such a treaty should seek to establish a definitive and universally accepted architecture that includes, but is not limited to, the definition of key terms, the determination of the provision of acquisition and protection of trademarks in outer space and how trademark law can be enforced.

Fifth, creation of a new international body (e.g., WIPO or the United Nations Office for Outer Space Affairs (UNOOSA)), or empowering an existing one with the responsibility of managing intellectual property rights, including trademarks, relating to outer space. Such a body might further take care of rule-making, administration of a possible international registry for space trademarks and, potentially, conflict resolution.

Sixth, when permanent human settlements or significant commercial outposts are established to colonise outer space and other astronomic bodies such as the moon or Mars, whether it is feasible to build the local IP registries with a certain jurisdiction to register the IP should be considered. Such registries could offer a more localised (perhaps more effective) vehicle for registering and enforcing trademark rights within these nascent space communities. The governance and legal underpinning of such registries would require careful attention at the international level.

Seventh, concrete mechanisms and fora for resolving IP-related disputes from the perspective of space activities are thus needed. These might include virtual courts or specialised arbitration boards with knowledge of both intellectual property and space law. Such mechanisms should be simple, user-friendly and as effective as possible for all stakeholders interested in engaging in space commerce, irrespective of nationality.

Conclusion

As commercial and government activities on and beyond the moon are projected to increase, the question of trademark in the context of space is no longer a theoretical matter. Given the restrictions of the territoriality principle over a non-sovereign territory, we need to reconsider the IPR regime in this new land. International cooperation is necessary to address the inherent difficulties and to create a transparent and comprehensible legal framework. By turning to a mix of short-term adaptations of current systems, medium-term development of new international legal instruments and institutions, and long-term planning of space-based solutions, the world can set a direction that nurtures innovation, stimulates investment and establishes a level playing field in the emerging space economy. Proactively dealing with this legal frontier is the key to realising the tremendous potential of space commercialisation in the interests of all mankind.

Chapter 13

GI Can't Fly to Space: Celestial Indications, a Proposed Framework for Origin-Based Intellectual Property in Outer Space

-Yasser Shabir Chowdhary and Abhishek Mohanpuria

Abstract

On April 12, 1961, humans first transcended into the realms of space; not long after, in 1969, our first step on the moon marked the giant leap for mankind. And from that giant leap, we are at the stage where not only the steps on the moon, but civilisation in space doesn't seem beyond imagination, but a foreseeable reality. Now, not only the Government space agencies such as NASA and ISRO, but even private ones, including SpaceX and Blue Origin, have entered the domain of space exploration. Commercialisation of the resources that the final frontier has to offer does not seem far-fetched. Our exploration so far has shown an abundance of substances and minerals found in space, such as Rare Earth Minerals and Helium-3[1], which are not abundant on Earth. In this backdrop, applying *Res communis*[2], the rule stating that space belongs to all of us, seems counter-intuitive. It is well known that the Race of commercialisation is reaching Outer Space. And, Intellectual Property Law becomes indispensable

1 A.D.S. Olson, "Lunar Helium-3: Mining Concepts, Extraction Research, and Potential ISRU Synergies," paper presented at AIAA ASCEND 2021 Conference, Las Vegas, 15–17 November 2021 (NASA Kennedy Space Center, 2021).

2 A. Fellmeth and M. Horwitz, "Res Communis (Omnium)," in *Guide to Latin in International Law* (Oxford University Press, Oxford, 2009), available at https://www.oxfordreference.com/view/10.1093/acref/9780195369380.001.0001/acref-9780195369380-e-1816 (accessed 12 August 2025).

when commercialisation comes into the picture. *Prima facie*, when we see the interplay of Space Commercialisation and IP Laws, the concept of Geographical Indication comes to the forefront, wherein certain qualities or reputation is attached to a specific Geographical Location[3]. On a deeper look, the term "Geographical[4]" is found insufficient, covering only the surface of the earth and not Space. This chapter aims to propose a new term "*Celestial Indication*" covering everything in the Observable Universe, along with a discussion of existing statutes and their applicability, while suggesting policy reforms.

Introduction

In this age of Rapid expansion of space exploration and commercialisation, new legal challenges have emerged, especially in the field of Intellectual Property Law (IP). At the dawn of this age, private entities such as SpaceX, Blue Origin, etc. have set eyes on space and extra-terrestrial bodies including the Moon, Mars, Asteroids and more for the purpose of resource extraction and even the establishment of civilisation. Geographical indication (GI), a form of IP, serves as an origin-based IP linking the reputation or the quality of a product to a geographical Location/Source[5]. In this regard, the complication arises when the international laws pertaining to outer space are factored into consideration. For instance, the 1967 outer space treaty (OST) provides that "*outer space, including the moon and the other celestial bodies, shall not be subject to national appropriation by claim of sovereignty*"[6], this clubbed with the Dilemma arising from the literal interpretation of the definition of GI renders a gap between the IP protection available on earth and IP protection which we strive to achieve for the "products" from outer space. This paper proposes a new concept, "Celestial Indication" to fill that gap. Herein, we will explore the definition of the term thus proposed, "Celestial Indication", the Rationale behind it, its contrast with the existing

---

3 World Trade Organization, *Agreement on Trade-Related Aspects of Intellectual Property Rights* (TRIPS), 15 April 1994, Marrakesh Agreement Establishing the WTO, Annex 1C, 1869 U.N.T.S. 299, art. 22.1, available at https://www.wto.org/english/docs_e/legal_e/27-trips_04_e.htm.

4 Merriam-Webster, "Geographical," *Merriam-Webster.com Dictionary*, n.d., available at https://www.merriam-webster.com/dictionary/geographic (accessed 12 August 2025).

5 World Intellectual Property Organization, "Frequently Asked Questions: Geographical Indications," WIPO, accessed 18 August 2025, available at http://www.wipo.int/en/web/geographical-indications/faq_geographicalindications.

6 Ritesh Mehra, "Intellectual Property Protection in Outer Space – An Overview," ILI Law Review, Vol. II, Winter Issue (2019), pp. 144–160 at p. 144.

terrestrial GI, Identification of potential right holders and instances of practical use cases. Thereafter, a policy framework for the inculcation of the concept into the existing legal framework is proposed.

Principles of International Space Law

Any origin-based IP scheme for space must operate within the fundamental principles of Space Law. The cornerstone is the Outer Space Treaty (1967). Article I[7] and Article II[8] provide that no nation can claim territory in space, and space activities must benefit all countries. Article IX[9] imposes duties to avoid harmful contamination and interference, and the Declaration of International Cooperation (UN Res.51/122) similarly emphasises peaceful, shared use of space for the benefit of all states[10].

The 1979 Moon Agreement[11] builds on the OST, declaring that *"the Moon and its natural resources are the common heritage of mankind"* and explicitly prohibiting any organisation or state (or private person) from claiming lunar (or celestial) land or resources as property. In effect, the Moon Treaty closes a loophole in the OST by forbidding ownership of any extraterrestrial property.

More recently, non-binding frameworks like the NASA-led *Artemis Accords* (2020 onward) have begun to address space resource activities. The Artemis Accords reaffirm the OST's principles and pledge that signatories will comply with them[12]. The Artemis Accords introduce operational rules such as *"safety zones"*, where participants will notify others and coordinate

7 Treaty on Principles Governing the Activities of States in the Exploration and Use of Outer Space, including the Moon and Other Celestial Bodies (Outer Space Treaty), 27 January 1967, 610 U.N.T.S. 205, art. I.

8 Ibid., art. II.

9 Ibid., art. IX.

10 Declaration on International Cooperation in the Exploration and Use of Outer Space for the Benefit and in the Interest of All States, Taking into Particular Account the Needs of Developing Countries, UN General Assembly Resolution 51/122, adopted 13 December 1996, UN Doc. A/RES/51/122.

11 Agreement Governing the Activities of States on the Moon and Other Celestial Bodies, adopted 5 December 1979, entered into force 11 July 1984, 1363 U.N.T.S. 3 (*Moon Agreement*). Available at: https://www.unoosa.org/oosa/en/ourwork/spacelaw/treaties/intromoon-agreement.html

12 National Aeronautics and Space Administration (NASA), *The Artemis Accords: Principles for Cooperation in the Civil Exploration and Use of the Moon, Mars, Comets, and Asteroids for Peaceful Purposes*, signed 13 October 2020, available at https://www.nasa.gov/specials/artemis-accords/ (accessed 18 August 2025).

to avoid harmful interference, while still honouring the OST's free access principle[13]. Importantly, the Accords expressly recognise private extraction rights[14] and pledge that entities will have the right to possess and utilise what they extract[15]. However, the Artemis Accords are themselves not a formal treaty and defer many details (including IP issues) to further agreements.

Intellectual Property in Outer Space

In contrast to terrestrial IP, the application of IP rights to activities beyond Earth is unsettled. On Earth, IP rights are territorial; a patent or trademark is enforceable only under the laws of the country that granted it. Space law, however, establishes that outer space is not subject to national sovereignty[16]. The Outer Space Treaty (OST) requires states to supervise the space activities of their nationals and holds them responsible for those activities, but it explicitly bars any claim of sovereignty over celestial territories[17]. This creates a tension, a fundamental precept of IP is tied to the jurisdiction of a state, yet space activities transcend those boundaries.

For patents, many countries have taken the pragmatic approach of extending their domestic IP laws to space objects that are under their jurisdiction. For instance, U.S. law[18] provides that if a U.S.-registered spacecraft makes an invention in orbit or on the Moon, it can be patented in the U.S. However, there are gaps under current U.S. law; if that same space object is registered under a foreign launch state, U.S. patent law would not apply to inventions on it[19]. Thus, the "territorial" metaphor is extended via the registration of space objects; a U.S.-registered object is treated like U.S. territory for IP law, and similarly for other states, but different national laws may yield

13 Ibid.

14 Andrew Brooks, "The Artemis Accords: The Necessary Incentive of Space Extraction Rights," *Columbia Journal of Transnational Law Bulletin Blog* (9 November 2020), available at https://www.jtl.columbia.edu/bulletin-blog/the-artemis-accords-the-necessary-incentive-of-space-extraction-rights (accessed 18 August 2025).

15 Artemis Accords, note 11.

16 Outer Space Treaty, note 7, arts. I–II.

17 Ibid, Art IV.

18 35 U.S.C. § 105, *Inventions in Outer Space*

19 Ibid.

inconsistent protections[20]. The WIPO "Inventions in Space" fact sheet notes that in the absence of explicit international rules, outer space objects are often treated as "quasi-territory" of their registration state[21]. But on issues like trademarks and GI, there is *no* clear regime.

In short, IP law for space is still in its infancy, existing IP instruments assume earthly territory, and attempts to adapt them are piecemeal. As the International Trademark Association (INTA) cautioned, "it will take time to create the appropriate legal frameworks for protection of IP off the surface of the Earth"[22].

The Problem: Applying Geographical Indication to Space

Geographical Indication

Under the IP laws, Geographical Indication (GI) holds a special place, limiting not just to the 'intellect' part of intellectual property but extending to a territorial domain. A GI is defined as "*sign used on products that have a specific geographical origin and possess qualities or a reputation that are due to that origin*"[23]*. Further, the WTO's TRIPS agreement provides "where a given quality, reputation or other characteristics of a good is essentially attributed to its geographical origin*"[24].

Inapplicability of GI to outer space

Going deeper into the above-mentioned definitions, it is seen that at the heart of these definitions and the term in itself lies the word 'geographical'.

20 Convention on Registration of Objects Launched into Outer Space (Registration Convention), adopted 12 November 1974, entered into force 15 September 1976, 1023 U.N.T.S. 15.

21 World Intellectual Property Organization, *Inventions in Space: WIPO Fact Sheet*, available at https://www.wipo.int/publications/en/details.jsp?id=4571 (accessed 18 August 2025).

22 International Trademark Association (INTA), IP in Space: White Paper (May 2023), available at https://www.inta.org/wp-content/uploads/public-files/perspectives/industry-research/221207_ipinspace_report.pdf (accessed 18 August 2025)

23 World Intellectual Property Organization, "Frequently Asked Questions: Geographical Indications," WIPO, available at http://www.wipo.int/en/web/geographical-indications/faq_geographicalindications

24 World Trade Organization, *Agreement on Trade-Related Aspects of Intellectual Property Rights* (TRIPS), 15 April 1994, Marrakesh Agreement Establishing the WTO, Annex 1C, 1869 U.N.T.S. 299, art. 22.1, available at https://www.wto.org/english/docs_e/legal_e/27-trips_04_e.htm

The word geographical is defined as "*of or relating to geography*"[25]. Further, the term geography is defined as "*a science that deals with the description, distribution, and interaction of the diverse physical, biological, and cultural features of the earth's surface*"[26]. As such, an interpretation is derived that 'geography'/ 'geographical' pertain only to the *surface of the earth.* Consequently, the conclusion is drawn that the term GI is confined only to the surface of the earth and does not extend to the domain of space. Due to this insufficiency/ gap which appears in the legal terminology, this paper aims to propose a new term along with the policy framework.

Proposal: Celestial Indication (CI)

To reconcile the need for origin-based labelling with space law principles, we propose a new IP concept: The Celestial indication (CI). A CI is proposed to be a sign or a label to be applied to a product to certify that it is derived from a specific extra-terrestrial location (for example, Moon, Asteroid, Mars, etc.), irrespective of the nature of the celestial body. It will act as a sign that the product's quality, composition or reputation stems from a particular origin from the outer space. Anything which falls beyond the jurisdiction of Geography or in simpler terms 'in Outer space', will fall under the domain of Celestial Indication.

For instance, Helium-3, a rare isotope of helium believed to be abundant on the Moon[27], is a promising fuel for nuclear fusion[28]. A "Lunar Helium-3" CI would provide a brand for this valuable resource, signalling its origin.

Definition

Drawing inspiration from Article 22 of TRIPS[29], a CI is defined as following "*Celestial Indications are indications which identify a good as originating from a celestial body, region on a celestial body or another extraterrestrial*

25 Merriam-Webster, "Geographical", *Merriam-Webster.com Dictionary* (n.d.), available at https://www.merriam-webster.com/dictionary/geographic (last visited 12 August 2025).

26 Merriam-Webster, "Geography", *Merriam-Webster.com Dictionary* (n.d.), available at https://www.merriam-webster.com/dictionary/geography (last visited 12 August 2025).

27 Aaron D. S. Olson, *Lunar Helium-3: Mining Concepts, Extraction Research, and Potential ISRU Synergies* (NASA Kennedy Space Center, FL, 32899, U.S.A.).

28 Wittenberg, L. J., Santarius, J. F., and Kulcinski, G. L. "Lunar Source of 3He For Commercial Fusion Power." Fusion Technology, Vol. 10, 1986, pp. 167–178.

29 TRIPS Agreement, Art. 22.

source, where a given quality, reputation or other characteristic of the good is essentially attributable to its extraterrestrial origin, notwithstanding whether such region falls under the claimed territory, jurisdiction or sovereignty of a Member State or otherwise."

Nature and Scope

A CI shall be defined through an International Agreement or a Treaty. Further, the enforcement will fall under the jurisdiction of an International Organisation, be it an existing one like WIPO or administered through the establishment of a pristine organisation. A comprehensive discussion on the same is pursued under *Section 5* of this Paper.

Why Do We Need 'Celestial Indication'?

In the rapid advancement of space exploration and commercialisation, the development of "celestial indication" as an important head under intellectual property is necessitated. The arguments for its establishment are not merely a legal formality but driven by economic, scientific, legal and strategic considerations.

Economic justification: Branding advantage and market development

CI offers a significant branding advantage for products derived from or manufactured in extraterrestrial environments. Just as GIs command premium prices for their authenticated origin and quality on Earth, CI will create a new luxury market for 'space-grade' or 'celestial-origin' goods, especially considering that the global space industry is projected to reach over $ 1 trillion[30].

Scientific Justification: Authenticity for Research Materials

In the scientific community, there is a heavy reliance on certification of the authenticity and precise origin of materials needed for research and experimentation. CI will provide a verifiable certification of the origin of extraterrestrial samples, ensuring the integrity of scientific research and findings. Without such a certification, the market could be flooded with unverified or fraudulent claims, which would undermine scientific progress.

30 INTA, note 21.

Legal Justification: Prevention of False Claims and Unfair Competition

There is a legal vacuum pursuant to the absence of an origin-based IP framework for space. As it stands now, there is no standard mechanism for the prevention of false claims of celestial origin goods. This creates an opportunity for consumer deception, unfair competition and loss of reputation of genuine products originating from space. CI would create a legal framework for rights holders, allowing them to challenge unauthorised use of Celestial Indications, protecting legitimate businesses and promoting fair trade practices, similar to how GIs protect against 'free-riding' on Earth[31].

Strategic Justification: Encouraging International Cooperation

CI requires international consensus to be an acceptable standard. Developing a global framework for CI will serve as a catalyst for broader discussions and collaboration on space trade rules, resource management, and dispute resolution. This will serve as ground zero to prevent future conflicts over resource claims, ensuring a stable and predictable legal environment essential for economic collaboration.

Proposed Policy Framework

Possible Claimants of a Celestial Indication

Challenges (why allocating CI rights is legally and practically hard): Any credible discussion of who may hold Celestial Indications must start by acknowledging the legal, technical and policy obstacles that differentiate space from earthbound GI regimes.

Non-sovereignty and Treaty Constraints: As established by the Outer Space Treaty (OST), the absence of territorial sovereignty means there is no analogue of a national jurisdiction that can create and police GIs in the terrestrial sense; a CI regime must therefore avoid doing indirectly what the OST forbids directly, i.e., it must not amount to claiming territory[32].

31 Evan Glatt, "Time to Stop TRIP-ing: The World Needs a New Geographical Indications Agreement", *Brooklyn Journal of International Law*, vol. 50 (2024), pp. 232-274, available at https://brooklynworks.brooklaw.edu/bjil/vol50/iss1/8 (accessed 18 August 2025).

32 Treaty on Principles Governing the Activities of States in the Exploration and Use of Outer Space, including the Moon and Other Celestial Bodies, GA Res. 2222 (XXI), adopted by the General Assembly on 19 December 1966, UN Doc. A/RES/2222(XXI).

A. **Fragmented Jurisdiction and Enforcement Gaps:** Jurisdiction over space activities is allocated by state responsibility[33] and by registration of space objects, but enforcement of label-use or false-origin claims ultimately occurs in terrestrial markets. This creates multi-jurisdictional complexity: the launching/registration state, states of sale, and states where enforcement actions are brought may all have different rules, creating uncertainty about which courts will hear CI disputes and which laws govern.

B. **Verification & Provenance Proof:** A CI must promise that a product truly came from a named celestial source. In practice, this requires reliable technical provenance (telemetry, isotope/spectral markers, custody chains). Establishing robust, internationally accepted tests for 'off-earth origin' is trivial and will be a continuous scientific and standardisation exercise.

C. **Risk of De Facto Appropriation and Equity Concerns:** If CI rights are granted exclusively to early movers (private companies or a few states), there is a real risk that brand exclusivity could become economic appropriation of a commons resource, contrary to the OST and the Moon Agreement's "province of all mankind". Any CI system therefore, needs safeguards (time limits, transparency, benefit-sharing) to mitigate perceived privatization[34].

D. **Competition & Strategic Hoarding:** The first actor to market may attempt to 'lock' desirable CI labels, creating market distortions. Without international standards and oversight, a race dynamic may produce a patchwork of unilateral claims.

Who may reasonably claim CI rights? This chapter proposes that the primary focus of the concept of Celestial Indications (CI) should rest upon the region, celestial body, or extraterrestrial source itself, rather than on the immediate conferral of proprietary rights to individual claimants, which should be secondary in nature. A framework of collaboration and collective benefit with essential safeguards is proposed over one where exclusive rights are given to a specific state or a particular entity. With this context, below are certain plausible categories of CI claimants:

33 OST, Art IV, Note 7.

34 *Agreement Governing the Activities of States on the Moon and Other Celestial Bodies* (Moon Agreement), adopted by UN General Assembly Resolution 34/68, 5 December 1979, opened for signature 18 December 1979, entered into force 11 July 1984, 1363 U.N.T.S. 3.

A. Private Extracting Companies (Operators)

These entities finance and execute extraction missions, assume commercial risk, and add value to raw resources. Granting them CI use rights is similar to awarding a trademark or certification mark to an economic entity that actually performs the production. Rights should be conditioned on demonstrable extraction, transparency obligations, and non-exclusive recognition frameworks so rights do not imply territorial exclusion[35].

B. Mission Consortiums or Joint Ventures

Many space operations are collaborative. A CI could be held by a consortium acting collectively; this mirrors terrestrial producer associations that jointly manage GIs. Joint ownership can allocate rights fairly among contributors.

C. International or Intergovernmental Bodies (Neutral Registrars)

A registry administered by UNOOSA/WIPO would lend neutrality and facilitate multilateral recognition, which is critical to preventing unilateral naming schemes.

D. Producer Associations & Collectives

If several producers extract from broadly defined zones, a collective (modelled on GI producer boards) could hold and enforce the CI, set standards, and manage compliance. This model promotes shared governance and may address equity concerns.

E. Scientific or Public-interest Holders (limited cases)

Where provenance matters primarily for research and public trust, an academic or governmental body may hold a CI-like certification to safeguard chain-of-custody and ensure data access, rather than for commercial monopoly.

F. Hybrid Models (State-authorised private holders with obligations)

States could license CIs to private firms but attach conditions: transparency, a limited exclusivity term, technology/knowledge

35 International Trademark Association (INTA), *IP in Space, Executive Summary and Recommendations* (May 2023).

sharing obligations, and contributions to society. Such hybrids reconcile private incentives and public interest.

Eligibility criteria that would make CI claims defensible

To reduce disputes and align CI with space law, registration/recognition should require a strict, demonstrable threshold:

A. **Physical extraction and primary custody:** proof that the claimant performed the extraction or was the legitimate custodian at the point of extraction (telemetry logs, chain of custody).

B. **State Authorisation:** evidence of authorisation by a launching or registration state consistent with Article VI OST.

C. **Scientific provenance markers:** isotopic signatures, spectral analysis or other forensic markers uniquely indicating extra-terrestrial origin, certified by accredited labs.

D. **Transparency and data disclosure:** a baseline requirement to publish permitted metadata (location coordinates, mission timeline) to the CI registry for audit.

E. **Non-appropriation safeguards:** clauses making clear that CI use does not confer exclusive access or territorial rights; other actors may operate and seek their own CI for the same or overlapping zones.

F. **Time-limited exclusivity with renewal conditions:** to prevent perpetual monopolies, initial exclusivity could be limited and contingent on ongoing compliance and sharing obligations.

Proposed Allocation and Governance Models

A. **First-Registration with Robust Safeguards:** The actor that first proves extraction and fulfils registry criteria obtains CI recognition for a fixed term; renewal requires continued compliance and public reporting. This model encourages early investment while preserving later competition.

B. **State-License and International Recording:** Launching states license CI use domestically and record the license in an international registry, enabling multilateral recognition and enforcement in other jurisdictions.

C. **Collective or Association Model:** Producers extracting from a defined celestial area form an association that defines standards, certifies products, and jointly manages the CI.

D. **International Certification Authority:** An international certifier accredits third-party verifiers (labs/inspections), maintains the registry, and issues CI numbers; enforcement remains in national courts under treaty obligations.

Conclusion

As humanity moves beyond Earth, intellectual property law must evolve to address new frontiers. Traditional GI regimes, which rely on national territories and centuries-old regional identities, cannot operate as is in space's extra-terrestrial commons. Celestial Indications offer a way forward, an origin-based labelling system that coexists with space law's non-appropriation principles. Under CI, products derived from the Moon, Mars, Asteroids, among other bodies, could carry legally protected names certifying their origin and distinctive qualities. This would protect honest actors and consumers, while spurring investment by granting value to place-based branding of space resources.

The idea of CI builds on established IP logic but adapts it to outer space. It recognises that, even without national borders, location matters for reputation and quality in the space economy. By carefully crafting a CI framework through international cooperation, possibly via a new treaty or agreement, states and companies can ensure that the commercialisation of space resources proceeds transparently and fairly. In doing so, they uphold the Outer Space Treaty's spirit of benefiting all humanity, while giving innovators the incentive of a protected brand identity.

Technology has raced ahead of law, but by proposing CI, we aim to catalyse a discussion on the 'when' and 'how' of space IP, not an 'if'. A robust CI regime would be a pioneering addition to space governance, helping to guide the policy and legal development needed in the coming era of interplanetary commerce.

Part V

Agriculture, Biodiversity, and Space Sustainability

Chapter 14

Space Agriculture and Plant Variety Protection in Outer Space: Reconciling Intellectual Property Rights with Space Law Principles

-Sakshi

Abstract

Outer space agriculture and IP law On Earth, plant variety protection (PVP) is governed by frameworks such as the International Union for the Protection of New Varieties of Plants (UPOV, 1961, revised 1991), the Agreement on Trade-Related Aspects of Intellectual Property Rights (TRIPS, 1994), and national laws such as India's Protection of Plant Varieties and Farmers' Rights Act (PPVFR, 2001). These laws reward breeders while safeguarding farmers' rights. However, their application to outer space remains uncertain. Meanwhile, outer space activities are regulated by treaties such as the Outer Space Treaty (1967), which states that outer space is not subject to national appropriation and must benefit all humanity. This raises a potential conflict: how can exclusive IP rights be granted in an environment that international law declares as non-appropriable?

This chapter explores the emerging intersection of intellectual property law and space law, focusing on the protection of plant varieties and agricultural innovation beyond Earth. With the rise of private space enterprises, extraterrestrial agriculture, and the use of the International Space Station (ISS) for research and breeding of novel plant varieties, existing legal frameworks face unprecedented challenges. The chapter examines how current international agreements-such as the UPOV Convention and the Outer Space Treaty- apply (or fail to apply) to plant breeders' rights (PBRs) in outer space environments. Also, this chapter explores questions like when plant breeding takes place aboard a space station or on a celestial body, which national laws govern the resulting intellectual property rights? Current research by leading space agencies, notably NASA, has demonstrated the tangible feasibility of space agriculture; for example, the Vegetable Production Unit (Veggie) and the Advanced Plant Habitat (APH) on the International Space Station (ISS) have successfully grown a variety of plant species. These experiments confirm that despite the unique challenges of microgravity, radiation, and limited resources, plants can meet their needs and they can thrive in space. The Article rigorously and comprehensively examines the challenges and opportunities in extending IP rights to "outer space plant varieties and space agricultural activities."

Introduction

Plants provide significant psychological benefits to astronauts, fostering a sense of connection to nature and improving well-being in isolated extraterrestrial environments.[1] With multiple countries and private companies now engaging in space activities, the salience of intellectual property rights in outer space will increasingly become more prominent.[2] This Article delves into the novel and critical field of intellectual property protection for novel plant varieties developed in outer space. As humans begin to imagine living and working beyond Earth — on space stations, the Moon, or even Mars — growing and developing new types of plants in these environments is becoming more likely. For the purpose of this article, the article pursues answers to the following key questions: Whether our current laws that protect new plant varieties still work in space? Moreover, if not, how should we change these laws to fit these new conditions?

Encouraging innovation in Space agriculture is essential for humans to prepare for long-term space missions—to the Moon, Mars, and beyond—there is a growing need for self-sustaining food systems. Transporting food from Earth to space is expensive, inefficient, and impractical for long-

1 Exploring plant responses to altered gravity for advancing space agriculture available at < https://www.researchgate.net/publication/391617425_Exploring_plant_responses_to_altered_gravity_for_advancing_space_agriculture> accessed on aug 1 2025

2 Available at;<https://www.wipo.int/en/web/patents/topics/outer-space> accessed on 1 aug 2025

duration missions or permanent colonies. Space agriculture helps solve this by:- Reducing dependency on Earth-based supply chains, supporting human life in space through fresh food, oxygen, and water recycling, enabling closed-loop life-support systems, encouraging scientific breakthroughs in crop resilience and genetic adaptation. However, innovation will not happen without proper incentives. That is where Plant Variety Protection (PVP) laws and breeders' rights become important: they encourage scientists and companies to invest time, resources, and expertise into developing new plant varieties suitable for outer space.

Protecting Breeders' Rights Matters because breeding a new plant variety—especially one that can survive space conditions like microgravity, radiation, or limited water—is difficult. It requires a significant R&D investment, advanced biotechnology, and experimental trials (often in high-risk environments like the ISS[3]). If the developers of these new space-adapted plant varieties are not granted exclusive rights to control and profit from their innovations, there is little commercial motivation to continue such work. Breeders' rights under frameworks like the UPOV Convention[4] allow:- Exclusive commercial use (selling seeds, licensing, etc.), legal protection from unauthorised reproduction or use of their variety, recovery of investment and profits from innovation. This is especially relevant to private space enterprises or biotech startups that want a return on their investment.

Outer Space Agriculture Missions and the Need for the Development of Agricultural Activities in Outer Space

Achievements in Outer Space Agriculture

1. **Early Experiments**: The idea of growing plants in space is not new. The Soviet Union carried out the first experiments in the 1970s aboard the Salyut space stations, where cosmonauts managed to sprout seeds and study plant development under microgravity. Later, the United States began similar studies during the Skylab missions (1973–1974)[5]. These early attempts were modest but proved that plant life could germinate and survive in orbit.

3 International Space Station

4 International Convention for the Protection of New Varieties of Plants, 1991

5 https://www.nasa.gov/skylab/#

2. **The National Aeronautics and Space Administration's (NASA) Contributions**: NASA has been at the forefront of space agriculture research. Its Veggie Plant Growth System, first activated on the International Space Station (ISS) in 2014, successfully grew red romaine lettuce.[6] In 2015, astronauts consumed the lettuce after testing for safety. Since then, crops like mustard greens, radishes, and zinnias have also been grown in orbit. These experiments show that controlled plant growth is possible even in space. "As NASA plans long-duration missions to the Moon and Mars, a key challenge is figuring out how to feed crews during their weeks, months, and even years in space. Food for crews aboard the International Space Station is primarily prepackaged, requires regular resupply deliveries aboard cargo spacecraft, and degrades in quality and nutrition. But what if astronauts could grow some of their own food in microgravity? Researchers are exploring the idea by testing various crops and equipment to figure out how to do this without a lot of extra hardware or power. To date, NASA has grown a variety of plants, including lettuces, tomatoes, and radishes – and learned a lot about how to successfully do so in the process."[7] NASA has advanced hydroponic and aeroponic systems, allowing plants to grow without soil, as carrying soil into space is impractical.

3. **Gardens in Space[8]:** As humanity prepares for longer missions beyond Earth, the ability to grow food in space is becoming increasingly essential. NASA has been actively developing innovative systems to support plant growth in microgravity environments. One such system is the **Vegetable Production System**, or *Veggie*, a compact, low-power chamber designed to grow six plants at a time. Using fabric "pillows" filled with seeds, astronauts care for these plants manually, much like tending a small garden at home. An improved version, known as **Veggie PONDS** (*Passive Orbital Nutrient Delivery System*), replaces the seed pillows with holders that contain small water reservoirs, allowing for more efficient hydration. In contrast, the **Advanced Plant Habitat** offers a fully automated environment for growing plants, requiring minimal crew involvement. Together, these systems mark significant

6 NASA, "Veggie Plant Growth System Activated on Space Station" (2014), available at: <https://www.nasa.gov >accessed 21 August 2025.

7 Station Science 101: Plant Research, available at: <https://www.nasa.gov/missions/station/ways-the-international-space-station-helps-us-study-plant-growth-in-space/ >last visited on 31 July 2025

8 Ibid, < https://www.nasa.gov/missions/station/ways-the-international-space-station-helps-us-study-plant-growth-in-space/>

progress in enabling sustainable agriculture in space, paving the way for future long-duration missions and potential space colonisation.[9]

4. **India (ISRO[10]):** CROPS stands for Compact Research Module for Orbital Plant Studies which is an unmanned experimental module designed to develop ISRO's capabilities for growing and sustaining plants in space. CROPS first mission (CROPS – 1) is designed to demonstrate germination of a seed and growth of a plant up to the two-leaf stage in space. It is an airtight container of diameter 300mm and height 450mm simulating an Earth-like environment in space, except for gravity.[11] As part of the CROPS (Compact Research Module for Orbital Plant Studies) experiment, ISRO has demonstrated the germination and growth of cowpea (also known as lobia) seeds in a microgravity environment on the PSLV-C60 mission. The experiment was conducted on the PSLV Orbital Experiment Module (POEM-4) platform. These early steps highlight India's interest in developing the capacity for future space farming, especially in the context of long-term missions. An Indian astronaut, Shubhanshu Shukla, also reportedly grew methi and moong seeds aboard the ISS as part of a study on microgravity's influence on germination and early plant development.[12]

5. **Russian and Chinese Experiments:** "The journey of space agriculture began during the early days of the space race, with initial experiments focused on understanding how plants grow in microgravity. One of the earliest milestones was the Russian mission in 1960, which successfully grew a flax plant in space. This achievement laid the groundwork for more sophisticated experiments conducted by NASA and other space agencies." [13] Russia has continued its long tradition of agricultural

9 Ibid.

10 Indian Space Research Organisation

11 CROPS: A Leap in Space Biological Experiments available at< https://www.isro.gov.in/CROPS.html >

12 Available at: < https://www.thehindu.com/sci-tech/science/shubhanshu-shukla-turns-farmer-in-space-grows-methi-moong-seeds/article69791495.ece> accessed on Aug 1, 2025

13 Space Agriculture Expanding Horizons: The Impact and Opportunities of Space Agriculture in Space Commercialisation available at<https://www.meegle.com/en_us/topics/space-commercial/space-agriculture>

studies in orbit. The LADA[14] greenhouse module aboard the ISS was developed by Russia, which was launched in 2002, and has been used continuously for growing plants in the Russian segment. LADA has supported a series of experiments on fundamental plant biology and space farming, growing multiple generations of sweet peas, wheat, tomatoes, and lettuce.

China conducted its first space breeding experiment in 1987, launching packets of seeds on a satellite and returning them to Earth after exposure to cosmic radiation. Since then, hundreds of plant species seeds have travelled with dozens of the country's retrievable satellites and Shenzhou spaceships. At a crop breeding centre in Shanghai, rice ears have turned yellow and fully matured after over 100 days of growth. These rice seeds were part of a 6-month-long breeding experiment conducted aboard China's space station Tiangong (Heavenly Palace) in 2022. They were planted upon return to Earth and have yielded plentiful harvests. The 120-day rice experiment on the Tiangong space station in 2022 represented an achievement as it is the first time ever that rice has been cultivated from germination to reproduction in orbit, showcasing the complete life cycle of this crop. Previously, such seed-to-seed cultivation had only been achieved with Arabidopsis, canola, peas and wheat on the International Space Station. The space-bred rice tastes sweeter and has more energy due to higher content of glucose and fructose, and the density of rice leaves also differs.[15] China has already commercialised certain varieties of rice that originated from space mutation breeding.

Example of space agriculture patent: Passive Nutrient Delivery System (PONDS) (U.S. 10,945,389): This technology employs a wicking material to passively link a water/nutrient reservoir to a growth cylinder where seeds are germinated and plants are produced. According to the '389 patent, PONDS addresses limitations with existing International Space Station plant-production technology by providing consistent delivery of water/nutrients, improving oxygen transfer to plants, and allowing users to determine how much water is being applied.[16] PONDS was developed to

14 Reference guide too ISS, P 29 Available at < https://www.nasa.gov/wp-content/uploads/2022/06/508318main_iss_ref_guide_nov2010.pdf>

15 Scientists Harvest Sweet Space-grown Rice, available at < https://english.cas.cn/newsroom/cas_media/202411/t20241107_693870.shtml> accessed on 21 July 2025

16 Reaching for the stars: biotechnological patents, challenges, and opportunities in outer space By Bree Vculek and David H. Holman available at < https://www.reuters.com/

improve water and nutrient delivery for plants grown on the International Space Station (ISS). [17]

Significance of These Achievements: These achievements show that plants can be grown in microgravity, although their development differs from Earth conditions. Seeds exposed to space often develop new traits, some of which may be commercially useful. Space agriculture is no longer an experimental science but a strategic necessity for future missions to the Moon and Mars. At the same time, these developments bring up the legal question of ownership. If a new variety of rice is created because it was exposed to cosmic radiation in orbit, who owns the rights? The astronaut who carried it? The state that funded the mission? Or the private company that later develops it?

Outer Space Law Treaties and Agreements

The Committee on the Peaceful Uses of Outer Space is the forum for the development of international space law. International space activities are mainly regulated by a set of treaties developed under the United Nations Committee on the Peaceful Uses of Outer Space (UNCOPUOS).[18]

The Committee has concluded five international treaties and five sets of principles on space-related activities. The five core treaties are often called the "UN Space Treaties". These five treaties deal with issues such as the non-appropriation of outer space by any one country, arms control, the freedom of exploration, liability for damage caused by space objects, the safety and rescue of spacecraft and astronauts, the prevention of harmful interference with space activities and the environment, the notification and registration of space activities, scientific investigation and the exploitation of natural resources in outer space and the settlement of disputes. Each of the treaties stresses the notion that outer space, the activities carried out in outer space and whatever benefits might be accrued from outer space should be

---

legal/litigation/reaching-stars-biotechnological-patents-challenges-opportunities-outer-space-2024-08-28/> accessed on Aug 1, 2025

17 Available at< https://technology.nasa.gov/patent/KSC-TOPS-81> accessed on Aug 1 , 2025

18 United Nations Office for Outer Space Affairs (UNOOSA), "UN Treaties and Principles on Outer Space" (2020), available at: <https://www.unoosa.org >accessed 21 August 2025.

devoted to enhancing the well-being of all countries and humankind, with an emphasis on promoting international cooperation.[19]

A The Outer Space Treaty 1967 (OST)[20]: The OST is the most important legal framework for outer space. It sets out key principles:

Benefit of all humankind (Art. I): OST states that exploration must be carried out for the benefit of all."The exploration and use of outer space, including the moon and other celestial bodies, shall be carried out for the benefit and in the interests of all countries, irrespective of their degree of economic or scientific development, and shall be the province of all mankind. Outer space, including the moon and other celestial bodies, shall be free for exploration and use by all States without discrimination of any kind, on a basis of equality and in accordance with international law, and there shall be free access to all areas of celestial bodies. There shall be freedom of scientific investigation in outer space, including the moon and other celestial bodies, and States shall facilitate and encourage international co-operation in such investigation."[21]

Non-appropriation principle (Art. II): Article II of the OST states that -Outer space, including the moon and other celestial bodies, is not subject to national appropriation by claim of sovereignty, by means of use or occupation, or by any other means.[22]which implies that- no nation can claim sovereignty over outer space or celestial bodies.[23]

Peaceful purposes (Art. IV): Space must only be used for peaceful activities."States Parties to the Treaty undertake not to place in orbit around the earth any objects carrying nuclear weapons or any other kinds of weapons of mass destruction, install such weapons on celestial bodies, or station such weapons in outer space in any other manner. The moon and other celestial bodies shall be used by all States Parties

19 Space law Treaties and Principles available at https://www.unoosa.org/oosa/en/ourwork/spacelaw/treaties.html acess on 32 july 2025

20 GA Resolution 2222 (XXI). Treaty on Principles Governing the Activities of States in the Exploration and Use of Outer Space, including the Moon and Other Celestial Bodies available at < https://www.unoosa.org/oosa/en/ourwork/spacelaw/treaties/outerspacetreaty.html> accessed on 22 July 2025

21 Ibid.,Art. I

22 Ibid, Art. II

23 Outer Space Treaty, 27 January 1967, 610 UNTS 205, Art. II.

to the Treaty exclusively for peaceful purposes. The establishment of military bases, installations and fortifications, the testing of any type of weapons and the conduct of military manoeuvres on celestial bodies shall be forbidden. The use of military personnel for scientific research or for any other peaceful purposes shall not be prohibited. The use of any equipment or facility necessary for peaceful exploration of the moon and other celestial bodies shall also not be prohibited."[24]

Jurisdiction (Art. VIII): A state has jurisdiction over its objects and personnel in space."A State Party to the Treaty on whose registry an object launched into outer space is carried shall retain jurisdiction and control over such object, and over any personnel thereof, while in outer space or on a celestial body. Ownership of objects launched into outer space, including objects landed or constructed on a celestial body, and of their component parts, is not affected by their presence in outer space or on a celestial body or by their return to the Earth. Such objects or component parts found beyond the limits of the State Party to the Treaty on whose registry they are carried shall be returned to that State Party, which shall, upon request, furnish identifying data prior to their return."[25]

For plant variety protection, the OST creates uncertainty. While it bans ownership of outer space itself, it does not explicitly mention intellectual property rights in inventions or plant varieties developed in space. This leaves open whether private rights can exist without violating the "benefit of all mankind" clause. The exploration and use of outer space, including the Moon and other celestial bodies, shall be carried out for the benefit and in the interests of all countries, irrespective of their degree of economic or scientific development, and shall be the province of all mankind.

Outer space, including the Moon and other celestial bodies, shall be free for exploration and use by all States without discrimination of any kind, on a basis of equality and in accordance with international law, and there shall be free access to all areas of celestial bodies. There shall be freedom of scientific investigation in outer space, including the Moon and other celestial bodies, and States shall facilitate and encourage international co-operation in such investigation.[26] Outer space, including the Moon and

24 Ibid.,Art IV

25 Ibid., Art. VIII

26 Treaty on Principles Governing the Activities of States in the Exploration and Use of Outer Space, including the Moon and Other Celestial Bodies available at: < https://

other celestial bodies, is not subject to national appropriation by claim of sovereignty, by means of use or occupation, or by any other means.[27]

While recognising the importance of intellectual property for the exploration of outer space and the further development of science and technology, questions have been raised as to whether the protection and enforcement of intellectual property rights may conflict with the said fundamental principles in terms of access to knowledge and information derived from space activities and in terms of the freedom of exploration and use of outer space.[28]

B. The Rescue Agreement 1968[29]: "The Agreement, elaborating on elements of V and VIII of the Outer Space Treaty, provides that States shall take all possible steps to rescue and assist astronauts in distress and promptly return them to the launching State, and that States shall, upon request, provide assistance to launching States in recovering space objects that return to Earth outside the territory of the Launching State. "[30]The Agreement on the Rescue of Astronauts obliges states to help astronauts in distress. While not directly linked to agriculture or plant varieties, it reinforces the principle of cooperation and humanitarian obligations in space.

C. The Liability Convention 1972[31]: The Convention on International Liability for Damage Caused by Space Objects makes states responsible for damage caused by their space objects.[32] While mainly about physical damage, it could indirectly apply if, for example, a plant variety experiment leaked harmful biological material. However, it does not cover ownership or intellectual property rights.

---

www.unoosa.org/pdf/gares/ARES_21_2222E.pdf> accessed on 1 aug 2025

27 Ibid., Art II.

28 Available at: <https://www.wipo.int/en/web/patents/topics/outer-space> accessed on 1 aug 2025

29 Resolution 2345 (XXII)), Agreement on the Rescue of Astronauts, the Return of Astronauts and the Return of Objects Launched into Outer Space 1968

30 UNOOSA, available at<https://www.unoosa.org/oosa/en/ourwork/spacelaw/treaties/introrescueagreement.html> accessed on 24July 2025

31 Convention on International Liability for Damage Caused by Space Objects, 29 March 1972 available at < https://www.unoosa.org/oosa/en/ourwork/spacelaw/treaties/introliability-convention.html> accessed on 24 July 2025

32 Ibid.

D. **The Registration Convention 1976[33]:** The Convention on Registration of Objects Launched into Outer Space requires states to register their space objects with the UN.[34] Jurisdiction flows from registration. This matters for IP because it means that inventions or plant varieties created aboard a registered object (e.g., a US module on the ISS) could fall under the jurisdiction of that state.

E. **The Moon Agreement 1979[35]:** The Agreement Governing the Activities of States on the Moon and Other Celestial Bodies declares the Moon's resources as the "common heritage of mankind."[36] However, very few states have ratified it (not India, the US, Russia, or China). The agreement also talks about developing a regime to govern exploitation of lunar resources, but this regime was never established. Its language is closer to the UNCLOS deep seabed regime, but since major space powers have not ratified it, its effect is limited.

F. **The Artemis Accords 2020[37]:** The Artemis Accords, led by the United States and signed by several countries (including India), are not treaties but political commitments. They promote transparency, interoperability, and peaceful exploration.[38]They also support the idea of resource utilisation by private actors, provided it complies with OST principles. The Accords do not directly mention intellectual property or plant varieties, but they represent a shift towards recognising private commercial interests in outer space.

International IP Laws on Plant Variety and Agriculture

Plant Variety Protection refers to the grant of exclusive rights to breeders over new plant varieties that are distinct, uniform and stable, enabling them to commercialise seeds and plants propagating materials with an objective to encourage agricultural innovation.

33 3235 (XXIX). Convention on Registration of Objects Launched into Outer Space 1976 available at< https://www.unoosa.org/oosa/en/ourwork/spacelaw/treaties/registration-convention.html> accessed on 24 July 2025

34 Ibid.,

35 34/68. Agreement Governing the Activities of States on the Moon and Other Celestial Bodies The General Assembly,< https://www.unoosa.org/oosa/en/ourwork/spacelaw/treaties/moon-agreement.html> accessed on 24 July 2025

36 Ibid.

37 Available at <https://www.nasa.gov/artemis-accords/>

38 Artemis Accords, 13 October 2020, available at: https://www.nasa.gov accessed 21 August 2025.

According to the International Convention for the Protection of New Varieties of Plants, 1991 (UPOV, 91), **"breeder"**[39] means - the person who bred, or discovered and developed, a variety, - the person who is the employer of the aforementioned person or who has commissioned the latter's work, where the laws of the relevant Contracting Party so provide, or - the successor in title of the first or second aforementioned person, as the case may be;

- **"breeder's right"**[40] means the right of the breeder provided for in this Convention;
- **"variety"**[41] means a plant grouping within a single botanical taxon of the lowest known rank, which grouping, irrespective of whether the conditions for the grant of a breeder's right are fully met, can be

  -defined by the expression of the characteristics resulting from a given genotype or combination of genotypes,

  -distinguished from any other plant grouping by the expression of at least one of the said characteristics and

  -considered as a unit with regard to its suitability for being propagated unchanged;

Condition for grant of breeder's rights: The breeder's right shall be granted where the variety is (i) new, (ii) distinct, (iii) uniform and (iv) stable. [42]

A notable feature of PVPCs is the inclusion of exemptions[43] that permit other breeders to use the protected varieties as parent material for developing new varieties, and allow farmers to save seeds from their harvest for subsequent plantings on their own land. Separately, plant patents, issued by the Patent and Trademark Office (PTO), cover asexually reproduced plants, with the exception of tuber-propagated plants like potatoes. These patents grant the owner the right to exclude others from asexually reproducing, using, selling, or importing the patented plant or its parts for 20 years from the

39 UPOV,1991 Art. 1(iv)

40 Ibid.,Art. 1(v)

41 Ibid.,Art. 1(vi)

42 Ibid., Art. 5

43 Ibid., Art. 15

application filing date. The 1991 Act expands rights and restricts farmers' exemptions.

However, the UPOV Conventions do not currently address the unique challenges posed by space-grown mutations or varieties developed through cosmic radiation or altered gravity, highlighting the urgent need for further regulation in this area. But the problem is UPOV is designed for crops grown on Earth. If a plant develops new traits in orbit, can it qualify as "new" under UPOV rules? And which country has jurisdiction to grant protection? If the seeds were carried on a multinational mission, disputes may arise over who the breeder really is.

The TRIPS Agreement (1994)[44]

The WTO Agreement on Trade-Related Aspects of Intellectual Property Rights (TRIPS) sets minimum standards for IP protection. Article 27.3(b) requires members to provide some form of protection for plant varieties—either by patents, a *sui generis* system, or a combination.[45] TRIPS gives flexibility to states, but it also strengthens the private rights of breeders. If a space-bred variety is brought to Earth, private corporations could claim exclusive rights, limiting access. This may clash with space law, where Article I of the OST states that exploration "shall be carried out for the benefit and in the interests of all countries."

The Convention on Biological Diversity (CBD 1992)[46]

The CBD focuses on sovereignty over genetic resources. Article 15 says that states have the right to regulate access to their genetic resources and should share benefits fairly.[47] If applied to outer space, the CBD raises difficult questions. Outer space has no sovereign state. So, who owns seeds developed in orbit? Can one state or company monopolise them, or should the benefits be shared with all humanity? The Nagoya Protocol (2010),

44 Trade-Related Aspects of Intellectual Property Rights (TRIPS) available at < https://www.wto.org/english/tratop_e/trips_e/trips_e.htm> accessed on 24 July 2025

45 Agreement on Trade-Related Aspects of Intellectual Property Rights (TRIPS), 15 April 1994, Art. 27.3(b).

46 Available at <https://www.un.org/ldcportal/content/convention-biological-diversity-and-its-protocols. Accessed on 24 July 2025

47 Convention on Biological Diversity, 5 June 1992, Art. 15.<https://www.cbd.int/doc/legal/cbd-en.pdf>

which builds on the CBD, stresses fair and equitable benefit-sharing.[48] This principle could guide how space-bred plant varieties are treated.

FAO International Treaty on Plant Genetic Resources (2001)[49]

The FAO Treaty promotes the conservation and sustainable use of plant genetic resources. It also sets up a multilateral system where states share plant genetic materials for food security.[50] If applied to space, the FAO model could mean that plant varieties developed in orbit should be treated as part of a shared pool of resources available to all, rather than privately owned. This would align with the OST's principle of common benefit.

World Intellectual Property Organisation (WIPO)[51]

WIPO does not have a specific treaty for plant varieties in space, but it plays a role in patents and international registrations. In recent years, WIPO has also discussed the impact of space activities on IP, especially in its Standing Committee on the Law of Patents.[52] It could become a platform to develop new rules for space agriculture.

Applying PVP to Space Agriculture: whether the existing legal framework can be interpreted in a way that it can be applied concerning outer space agriculture activities and plant variety protection in outer space like Defining variety, breeders rights, farmers rights etc. concerning outer space.

Definition of Variety: UPOV 91 can be applied as prescribed conditions which are new, distinct, uniform and stable[53]. Even if a plant mutates due to space radiation, if it shows unique and stable traits, it could still qualify as a "variety" under UPOV. Breeder's Rights: Scientists or private companies that grow and develop these new space plants could be recognised as "breeders"

48 Nagoya Protocol on Access to Genetic Resources and the Fair and Equitable Sharing of Benefits, 29 October 2010,

49 FAO International Treaty on Plant Genetic Resources for Food and Agriculture, 3 November 2001, https://faolex.fao.org/treaty/docs/tre000005E.pdf

50 Ibid available at https://faolex.fao.org/treaty/docs/tre000005E.pdf

51 World Intellectual Property Organization (WIPO), "Report of the Standing Committee on the Law of Patents" (2020), available at: https://www.wipo.int accessed 22 August 2025.

52 World Intellectual Property Organization (WIPO), "Report of the Standing Committee on the Law of Patents" (2020), available at: https://www.wipo.int

53 Ibid., Art 5

and can be allowed to claim legal rights over them. DUS Criteria in Space: The conditions for distinctness, uniformity, and stability might need new testing standards, because plants behave differently in zero gravity.

Jurisdictional Ambiguities and Enforcement in the Final Frontier:The territorial nature of intellectual property rights, coupled with the non-territorial domain of outer space, creates significant jurisdictional ambiguities and formidable challenges for the enforcement of plant variety rights. National laws are inherently territorial, designed to apply primarily within a country's borders.[54] This fundamental characteristic poses a direct challenge to their application in outer space, which is not subject to any single national sovereignty.

Farmers' Rights in Space: Just like on Earth, astronauts or future space colonists might want to save and reuse seeds. Laws may need to clarify who counts as a "farmer" in space and whether they have similar rights.

International Legal Gap: Right now, no law clearly covers space-grown plants. UPOV and other treaties don't say what happens when a plant is bred in orbit or on Mars. We need new legal rules or extensions of current laws to deal with these issues. Given the limitations of merely adapting existing terrestrial frameworks, developing a new sui generis (unique) intellectual property regime specifically for space biotechnology, including plant varieties, merits serious consideration. The Agreement on Trade-Related Aspects of Intellectual Property Rights (TRIPS) already permits member states to adopt sui generis legal regimes for plant varieties, providing flexibility to tailor protection to specific contexts.[55]

Conflict Between IP Laws and Space Law: On Earth, UPOV, TRIPS, and CBD balance breeder's rights and public interest (though not perfectly). But in space: UPOV's DUS criteria may be difficult to apply when plants mutate unpredictably. TRIPS promotes private monopolies, while OST calls for benefit to all. CBD assumes national sovereignty, which does not exist in space. This shows the urgent need to adapt existing IP laws for outer space, or create a new treaty that combines both space law and IP law.

Principles of Space Law and Their Impact on IPR: Lets examine how core principles of space law affect intellectual property rights in outer space.

54 Intellectual Property and space activities available at <https://www.wipo.int/documents/d/patents/docs-en-topics-outer-space-ip_space_wipo-contribution_oecd_2004.pdf> access on Aug 1, 2025

55 Available at < https://www.undp.org/sites/g/files/zskgke326/files/publications/TowardaBalancedSuiGenerisPlantVarietyRegime.pdf> accessed on 1 Aug 2025

1. Principle of Non-Appropriation: Article II of the OST says: "Outer space, including the Moon and other celestial bodies, is not subject to national appropriation by claim of sovereignty, by means of use or occupation, or by any other means."[56] This means no country can own a part of space. But what about intellectual creations? If a company breeds a new wheat variety in orbit, is that "appropriating" outer space, or is it just using resources legally? The lack of clarity creates legal uncertainty.

2. Principle of Freedom of Exploration: Article I of the OST says: "Outer space shall be free for exploration and use by all States without discrimination."[57] If plant varieties developed in orbit are patented and restricted, this could limit other states' freedom to use space resources. Private monopolies may therefore conflict with the principle of free exploration.

3. Jurisdiction and Control: Article VIII of the OST says that states keep jurisdiction over their objects in space.[58] For example, if a plant experiment is done in the US module of the ISS, US law applies. But what if seeds move between modules? Or if astronauts from different countries jointly work on them? Jurisdiction then becomes messy. This shows why multilateral agreements (like the ISS Intergovernmental Agreement) are needed to decide IP rights.

4. Principle of Benefit to All Humankind: Article I of the OST also says: "The exploration and use of outer space shall be carried out for the benefit and in the interests of all countries, irrespective of their degree of economic or scientific development."[59] This clash directly with private monopolization. If one company owns a space-bred variety, does that violate the duty to share benefits with all? Some argue that like the seabed under UNCLOS, outer space should follow a common heritage approach, with benefits shared globally.

5. The "Common Heritage of Mankind" Concept: The Moon Agreement goes further, declaring the Moon's resources the "common heritage of

56 OST,Art.II

57 Ibid., Art.I

58 Ibid., Art VIII

59 Ibid., Art. I

mankind."[60] This idea is similar to how the deep seabed is regulated under UNCLOS. It means resources should not be owned privately but used for the benefit of all. Although the Moon Agreement has few ratifications, the concept of common heritage could be applied to plant varieties developed in space. This would suggest that they should be put in a global pool, accessible to all nations.

6. Tension Between Innovation and Public Good: On one side, private breeders and corporations argue that strong IP rights are needed to encourage investment. Without patents or PVP, no one will fund costly experiments. On the other side, space law emphasises that space activities must benefit all.

The solution may lie in a middle path: granting limited IP rights but requiring benefit-sharing, like the CBD and FAO Treaty do on Earth. This way, innovation is rewarded, but no one is completely excluded.

Intellectual Property Rights on the International Space Station (ISS): The International Space Station (ISS) is one of the best examples of how multiple states cooperate in outer space. It is governed by the Intergovernmental Agreement (IGA) of 1998, signed by the United States, Russia, Canada, Japan, and European partners.[61] The IGA provides that each state retains jurisdiction and control over its own modules. This means that if an invention is made inside the US module, US law applies. Article 21 of the IGA deals with intellectual property and says that "for the purposes of intellectual property, activities occurring in or on a flight element shall be deemed to have occurred only in the territory of the Partner State of that element."[62] This rule is important for plant variety protection. If a new variety is developed in the US module, US patent or plant variety law would govern. But if the seeds are moved into the Japanese module, Japanese law applies. Such rules help avoid disputes, but they are not always clear when astronauts from different states jointly participate in experiments.[63] The ISS therefore shows both the possibility of legal clarity

60 34/68. Agreement Governing the Activities of States on the Moon and Other Celestial Bodies The General Assembly,< https://www.unoosa.org/oosa/en/ourwork/spacelaw/treaties/moon-agreement.html> accessed on 24 July 2025

61 Intergovernmental Agreement on Space Station Cooperation (IGA), 29 January 1998, TIAS 12927.

62 Ibid, Art. 21.

63 https://ppp.worldbank.org/library/outer-space-treaty

(through agreements) and the limits of national law when dealing with international projects.

The Role of Private Companies: Space exploration is no longer limited to states. Private companies like SpaceX, Blue Origin, and Axiom Space are planning commercial space stations. Corporations are also investing in space agriculture projects, since long-term missions will require food sustainability. The issue is that private companies depend on strong intellectual property protection to justify their investments. They may push for patents and plant breeders' rights over space-grown crops. However, this could clash with the OST, which says that "the exploration and use of outer space shall be carried out for the benefit and in the interests of all countries."[64] A balance may be needed that allows private rights to encourage innovation, but ensures benefit-sharing mechanisms so that no single company controls essential food sources in space. This is similar to the way the FAO Treaty promotes the sharing of genetic resources on Earth. Applying that model to space could ensure fairness while respecting commercial interests.

Case Law and Precedents: There are no direct cases yet on plant variety protection in outer space. But some terrestrial and space-related cases provide guidance. Diamond v. Chakrabarty (US Supreme Court, 1980)[65]: The Court held that "a live, human-made microorganism is patentable subject matter under 35 U.S.C. §101."[66] This case shows that even living organisms created through human effort can be protected by IP law. By analogy, a space-bred plant variety could also qualify. Monsanto Technology LLC v. E.I. DuPont (2013): This case confirmed that strong IP rights exist for genetically modified plants.[67] It highlights how private corporations defend breeder's rights vigorously, which may also happen with space-bred crops. Bogota Declaration (1976): Though not a case, this declaration argued that geostationary orbit should be under the sovereignty of equatorial states.[68]While rejected internationally, it shows how states may attempt to claim special rights over space resources. Together, these

64 Outer Space Treaty, 1967, Art. I.

65 Diamond v Chakrabarty, 447 US 303 (1980).

66 https://supreme.justia.com/cases/federal/us/447/303/

67 Monsanto Technology LLC v E.I. DuPont de Nemours and Co., 878 F. Supp. 2d 599 (ED Mo 2012). https://www.cafc.uscourts.gov/1-05-2018-17-1032-monsanto-technology-llc-v-ei-dupont-de-nemours-opinion-17-1032-opinion-1-4-2018-1/

68 Bogota Declaration, 3 December 1976,

precedents suggest that space-bred plants could become a highly contested area, where both private rights and public interest are tested.

The Way Forward: Given the gaps between terrestrial IP law and space law, a new legal framework is needed. Possible approaches include: **Developing a Sui Generis Space Plant Treaty**: A new treaty, like the UPOV Convention but adapted to space, could define how plant varieties developed in orbit are protected. It could require proof of novelty, distinctness, uniformity, and stability, but in a way that recognises unique space conditions. **Using the ISS IGA as a Model:** Future space stations could adopt agreements similar to the IGA, with clear rules on which state's IP laws apply in each module. This would reduce jurisdictional conflicts. **Public-Private Partnerships:** States, international organisations, and private companies could jointly manage space agriculture, with agreements ensuring that both innovation and access are protected. **WIPO and UNCOPUOS Involvement:** The World Intellectual Property Organisation (WIPO) and the UN Committee on the Peaceful Uses of Outer Space (UNCOPUOS) could work together to create guidelines. This would merge IP expertise with space law principles.

Conclusion

Space agriculture is no longer science fiction. As humans prepare for long-duration missions to the Moon and Mars, the development of new plant varieties in orbit is becoming a reality. These plants may differ genetically from their Earth-based relatives due to radiation, microgravity, and other factors. Existing IP laws like UPOV, TRIPS, and CBD provide useful lessons but were created for Earth. Meanwhile, space law through the Outer Space Treaty emphasises that activities should be "for the benefit and in the interests of all countries."[69] The two systems clash when private monopolies over space-bred crops are considered. The way forward must be a balanced framework—rewarding innovation but ensuring fair access. A sui generis space law system, guided by principles of benefit-sharing and cooperation, seems necessary. Only then can plant variety protection in space support both human exploration and global food security. Innovation in space agriculture is essential for sustaining human life beyond Earth. Protecting the rights of plant breeders fuels this innovation, but it must not come at the cost of global access and equity. Outer space must remain a shared domain, and the legal system must evolve to reward innovation without enabling appropriation. To reconcile breeders' rights with space law principles, a future legal framework should recognise breeders' rights for space-

69 Outer Space Treaty, 1967, Art. I.

developed plant varieties, ensuring fair reward and commercial incentive. Establish multilateral treaties or protocols under bodies like UNCOPUOS or UPOV, clarifying how PVP laws should apply in outer space. Promote shared access to plant varieties critical to survival through international seed banks, possibly governed by neutral bodies like the UN. By leveraging their respective expertise in intellectual property, space law, and plant variety protection, these bodies can facilitate the necessary international consensus and legal development. By aligning PVP frameworks with the principles of access to all and non-appropriation, we can build a future where space farming serves both scientific advancement and the common good of all humankind.

Part VI

Jurisdictional and Regulatory Challenges

Chapter 15

Beyond Earth: Jurisdictional Challenges in Intellectual Property Protection for Outer Space Innovations

-Modi Umangkumar Champaklal

Abstract

The rapid commercialisation of outer space, driven by private space enterprises, satellite technologies, and extraterrestrial research, has intensified debates over the applicability and enforcement of intellectual property (IP) rights beyond Earth's territorial boundaries. Traditional IP frameworks, largely built around sovereign jurisdictions, encounter profound legal ambiguities when applied to outer space activities governed by international treaties such as the Outer Space Treaty (1967) and the Moon Agreement (1979).[1] This paper critically examines the jurisdictional challenges arising in protecting patents, copyrights, and trademarks for inventions and creations made, used, or commercialised in outer space environments, such as space stations, lunar bases, and orbital manufacturing facilities.

Particular focus is given to the principles of non-appropriation and the prohibition on the exercise of national sovereignty in outer space, which complicate the extension of domestic IP laws to assets located in or

1 "Protecting Intellectual Property Rights in Outer Space", *CII Blog*, 18 September 2023, available at: https://ciiblog.in/protecting-intellectual-property-rights-in-outer-space/ (last visited May 15, 2025).

originating from outer space.[2] The paper analyses evolving state practices, such as the United States' approach under the Commercial Space Launch Competitiveness Act (2015), and explores multilateral efforts to harmonise IP protections, including WIPO's discussions on space-related IP issues. Emerging questions regarding the situs of invention, applicable law in the multinational space station context, and conflict-of-laws scenarios are also addressed.[3] Ultimately, the paper argues for the development of a new international legal framework or soft-law mechanisms to balance innovation incentives with the fundamental principles of outer space law. Without adaptive legal innovation, uncertainty will stifle commercial space activities and scientific collaborations, hindering the growth of a truly sustainable space economy.

Keywords: Intellectual Property Rights, Outer Space Treaty, Jurisdictional Challenges, Space Law, Innovation Regulation

Introduction

The increasing involvement of private entities and the rise of international partnerships in outer space activities have significantly altered the character of space from a domain traditionally reserved for scientific research and governmental exploration to one increasingly driven by commercial imperatives. The development of sophisticated satellite systems, the burgeoning space tourism sector, and the prospective extraction of extraterrestrial natural resources—such as lunar minerals and asteroids—underscore the urgent need for a comprehensive reassessment of the international legal architecture governing intellectual property rights (IPRs) in outer space. These developments, while opening new frontiers for technological advancement and economic gain, have also revealed a host of jurisdictional uncertainties that threaten the enforceability and protection of IPRs in the space domain.[4]

2 Chabert, Valentina. "The Exploitation of Mineral Resources of the Moon and Celestial Bodies in International Law and Practice." *The Irish Yearbook of International Law*, vol. 16, 2021–2022, pp. 36–58. Available at: https://iris.uniroma1.it/retrieve/5c58dee9-a57c-470b-8b1b-991bc9d09f18/Chabert_Exploitation_2025.pdf (last visited May 15, 2025).

3 Azevedo, João Pedro Marques de. "The Principle of Common Heritage of Humankind in the Law of Outer Space." Ph.D. dissertation, Universidade NOVA de Lisboa, 2021. Available at: https://www.proquest.com/docview/3059430315 (last visited May 15, 2025).

4 Rajat Chawda, "Need for Intellectual Property Rights in Outer Space", *iPleaders Blog*, May 6, 2020, available at: https://blog.ipleaders.in/need-intellectual-property-rights-

The fundamental problem arises from the mismatch between the territorial nature of intellectual property regimes and the inherently non-sovereign status of outer space under international law.[5] Intellectual property rights such as patents, trademarks, copyrights, and industrial designs are traditionally granted by, and enforceable within, the jurisdiction of sovereign states.[6] However, Article II of the *Treaty on Principles Governing the Activities of States in the Exploration and Use of Outer Space, including the Moon and Other Celestial Bodies*, 1967 (commonly referred to as the Outer Space Treaty or OST), explicitly prohibits any claim of national sovereignty over celestial bodies. This non-appropriation principle has profound implications for the applicability and enforceability of domestic IP law beyond Earth's confines.[7]

Moreover, while Article VIII of the OST allows a State to retain jurisdiction and control over objects launched into outer space and personnel aboard such objects, the increasing complexity of space missions, often involving multinational partnerships and private-sector contractors, complicates the determination of which national jurisdiction is competent to adjudicate IP-related disputes.[8] For instance, a patented technology developed jointly aboard the International Space Station (ISS) may involve intellectual contributions from entities subject to different legal systems, each asserting its own claims and standards regarding inventorship, ownership, and licensing.[9]

---

outer-space/ (last visited May 14, 2025).

5 Chen, Zhijie. "The Unity of Non-Territoriality in Outer Space versus the Diversity of Territoriality in Intellectual Property: A Reconciliation Regime for Sustainable Space Commercialisation." *Hong Kong Law Journal*, vol. 52, no. 1, 2022, pp. 1–30. Available at: https://www.researchgate.net/publication/362945367 (last visited May 15, 2025).

6 Voronoi, "Total US Services Exports in 2023: $1.015 Billion", *Voronoi*, 14 May 2025, available at: https://www.voronoiapp.com/economy/Total-US-Services-Exports-in-2023-1015-Billion-1555 (last visited May 15, 2025).

7 West, Jessica, ed. *Space Security Index 2018*. Waterloo: Project Ploughshares, 2018. Available at: https://www.thesimonsfoundation.ca/sites/default/files/Space%20Security%20Index%202018.pdf (last visited May 15, 2025).

8 Treaty on Principles Governing the Activities of States in the Exploration and Use of Outer Space, including the Moon and Other Celestial Bodies, opened for signature on 27 January 1967, 610 U.N.T.S. 205, Article VIII.

9 Intergovernmental Agreement on Space Station Cooperation, signed 29 January 1998, entered into force 27 March 2001, available at: https://www.nasa.gov/specials/ippolicy/IGA.html (last visited May 15, 2025).

The ambiguity surrounding jurisdiction in outer space, therefore, creates a legal vacuum that could deter innovation and undermine investor confidence. The absence of a harmonised legal mechanism for registering and enforcing IPRs in space leads to potential risks of duplication, infringement, and misappropriation, particularly in high-stakes sectors such as proprietary propulsion systems, navigation software, and extraterrestrial mining technologies. Furthermore, the lack of clarity may disincentivise private actors from engaging in research and development activities in space, thereby stalling technological progress.[10]

To ensure a conducive environment for sustained innovation in outer space, it is imperative to develop legal frameworks that transcend the traditional territorial constraints of IP protection. One approach may involve international agreement on extending the territorial reach of national IP laws to space objects registered under the United Nations' Registration Convention, thereby attributing legal jurisdiction based on registration and ownership of space assets. Alternatively, establishing an international space-specific IP registry under the auspices of the World Intellectual Property Organisation (WIPO) could provide a uniform, transparent mechanism for recording and recognising intellectual property claims related to space innovations.[11]

In conclusion, the transition of outer space from a purely scientific frontier to a commercial arena requires urgent legal reforms in intellectual property law. The existing regime, shaped by terrestrial assumptions of jurisdiction and sovereignty, is ill-equipped to meet the challenges posed by space-based innovation. A concerted effort by the international community—combining treaty-making, institutional innovation, and harmonisation of domestic IP laws—is essential to secure intellectual property protection in a manner that fosters innovation, protects investments, and ensures equitable access to the benefits of space technology.

The Legal Landscape of Outer Space

A. The Outer Space Treaty (OST) and Its Implications

The *Treaty on Principles Governing the Activities of States in the Exploration and Use of Outer Space, including the Moon and Other Celestial Bodies,*

10 Mehra, Ritesh, "Intellectual Property Protection in Outer Space - An Overview", *ILI Law Review*, vol. 2, Winter 2019, pp. 144–159.

11 Convention on Registration of Objects Launched into Outer Space, adopted on 12 November 1974, entered into force 15 September 1976, 1023 U.N.T.S. 15.

1967—commonly referred to as the Outer Space Treaty (OST)—remains the cornerstone of the international legal regime governing activities beyond Earth's atmosphere. Adopted under the auspices of the United Nations and opened for signature in January 1967, the OST entered into force in October of the same year and now enjoys near-universal acceptance. As of 2025, it has been ratified by 113 States, with several more signatories.[12]

The OST articulates several foundational principles governing the conduct of States and other actors in outer space. Most notably, Article I declares that outer space shall be the "province of all mankind," affirming the principle of non-exclusion and mandating that the exploration and use of outer space be carried out for the benefit and in the interests of all countries. Article II enshrines the principle of non-appropriation, prohibiting States from claiming sovereignty over celestial bodies or outer space territory. Further, Article IV restricts the use of outer space to peaceful purposes, prohibiting the placement of nuclear weapons or other weapons of mass destruction in orbit or on celestial bodies.

Despite its progressive and pioneering spirit, the OST is conspicuously silent on matters related to intellectual property rights (IPRs). As space exploration has evolved from state-centric scientific endeavours into a realm of private innovation and commercial exploitation, the absence of specific provisions governing the protection of patents, trade secrets, and copyrights has created a significant legal vacuum. The OST does not define the legal status of inventions made or used in space, nor does it provide guidance on adjudicating conflicting claims to intellectual property developed in extraterrestrial environments. As a result, the application of terrestrial IP laws to space activities remains largely inferential and jurisdiction-dependent, giving rise to legal uncertainty that may disincentivise investment in space innovation.

This gap becomes particularly acute when considering that IP protection is inherently territorial, it relies on national legal systems for grant, registration, and enforcement. In outer space, where no State may exercise sovereignty, the classical territorial basis of intellectual property law becomes difficult to operationalise. Thus, while the OST provides a framework for peaceful cooperation and non-appropriation, it leaves unresolved critical regulatory questions regarding intellectual property.

12 Treaty on Principles Governing the Activities of States in the Exploration and Use of Outer Space, including the Moon and Other Celestial Bodies, opened for signature on 27 January 1967, 610 U.N.T.S. 205.

B. The Role of National Jurisdictions

While the OST avoids providing a direct mechanism for IP protection, it does offer a partial jurisdictional anchor through Article VIII, which provides that a State Party to the Treaty on whose registry a space object is launched shall retain jurisdiction and control over that object and any personnel thereon while in outer space or on a celestial body.[13] This provision enables States to extend their domestic laws, including intellectual property legislation, to spacecraft, space stations, and other registered assets in outer space. Accordingly, if a patented invention is utilised aboard a spacecraft registered with a specific State, that State's patent laws may govern the legal status of that invention.

This jurisdictional principle underpins the current regulatory model used, for example, on the International Space Station (ISS), where a multilateral agreement allows each partner nation to apply its own criminal, civil, and administrative laws—including intellectual property laws—to its respective modules. While functional for the ISS, such a solution depends on pre-existing bilateral or multilateral agreements and cannot be seamlessly extrapolated to commercial missions involving non-State actors or to new cooperative frameworks that may emerge in deep space exploration or on lunar bases.[14]

Moreover, the increasing multinational composition of space missions—where spacecraft components may be manufactured in one State, assembled in another, launched by a third, and operated jointly in space—complicates clear jurisdictional attribution. When a dispute arises concerning the infringement of a patent developed jointly on an orbital platform or during a lunar expedition, it is not always evident which State's laws would apply, nor which forum would have competence to adjudicate such matters. This lack of clarity leads to forum shopping, inconsistent enforcement, and a general erosion of predictability—an essential element in commercial innovation and licensing strategies.[15]

13 International Space University. *Guidebook on Small Satellite Programs*. SSP 2011 Final Report, Graz, Austria, 2011. Available at: https://isulibrary.isunet.edu/doc_num.php?explnum_id=279 (last visited May 15, 2025).

14 Intergovernmental Agreement on Space Station Cooperation, signed 29 January 1998, entered into force 27 March 2001, available at: https://www.nasa.gov/specials/ippolicy/IGA.html (last visited May 15, 2025).

15 Regulatory Horizons Council, *The Future Regulation of Space Technologies: Plugging the Gaps in Space*, April 2024, available at: https://assets.publishing.service.gov.uk/

As a result, the OST's jurisdictional formula, while useful in attributing responsibility for liability and control over space objects, falls short of addressing the full complexity of intellectual property protection in an increasingly privatised and diversified space economy. In the absence of a harmonised or universal regime for the registration and enforcement of space-based intellectual property rights, reliance on Article VIII alone may prove inadequate in ensuring equitable access and legal certainty for innovators operating beyond Earth.[16]

Intellectual Property Challenges in Space

A. Territoriality of Intellectual Property Rights

The most fundamental challenge to the application of intellectual property rights (IPRs) in outer space arises from their territorial nature. Traditional IP regimes are grounded in the sovereignty of States and are enforced within the bounds of national jurisdictions. Patents, copyrights, trademarks, and other forms of intellectual property are granted by national authorities and remain enforceable only within the territory of the granting State.[17] This creates a structural contradiction when applied to the domain of outer space, which is explicitly declared as non-sovereign by international legal instruments such as the *Outer Space Treaty, 1967.*

Article II of the *Outer Space Treaty* stipulates that "outer space, including the Moon and other celestial bodies, is not subject to national appropriation by claim of sovereignty, by means of use or occupation, or by any other means". Consequently, no State may assert exclusive jurisdiction over a region of outer space in the way that it does over its terrestrial territory. This absence of sovereign jurisdiction raises serious concerns about how and where IP rights can be enforced when an invention is conceived, developed, or used in space.[18]

---

media/ 6620cf9a77a30aa0c4757d35/rhc_report_on_the_future_regulation_ of_ space_technologies.pdf (last visited May 15, 2025)

16 Treaty on Principles Governing the Activities of States in the Exploration and Use of Outer Space, including the Moon and Other Celestial Bodies, opened for signature on 27 January 1967, 610 U.N.T.S. 205, Article VIII.

17 "Intellectual Property in Space: Rights in Outer Space", *IIPRD Blog*, 18 September 2024, available at: https://www.iiprd.com/intellectual-property-in-space-rights-in-outer-space/ (last visited May 15, 2025).

18 Ali, Md Jewel. "From Earth to Orbit: Converging Space Law and Intellectual Property Rights to Safeguard Innovation Beyond Earth." *International Journal of Legal Science and Innovation*, vol. 6, no. 5, 2024, pp. 210–228. Available at: https://ijlsi.com/paper/

For instance, consider a situation where a scientific breakthrough is achieved aboard a multinational orbital space station or during a lunar mission jointly undertaken by several States and private actors. Which national patent office would have the competence to register the invention? Which courts would have jurisdiction to resolve disputes over authorship or licensing? And most importantly, under what law would such questions be adjudicated? These uncertainties reflect the inadequacy of traditional territorial IP doctrines in dealing with the extraterrestrial environment, where legal authority is neither clearly demarcated nor universally accepted.[19]

The problem is further compounded by the increasing role of private space actors, who may not be directly affiliated with a national space programme and often operate through transnational partnerships. Without a coordinated international regime or at least mutual recognition mechanisms, such actors risk operating in a legal grey area. The possibility of infringement without legal recourse may discourage investment in space-based research and development, which inherently involves high financial and technological risk.[20]

Several commentators have suggested that, for the interim, intellectual property rights in space should follow the registration-based jurisdictional principle codified in Article VIII of the *Outer Space Treaty*, whereby States retain jurisdiction over their registered space objects. While this offers a partial solution, it remains limited to circumstances where the object or invention is clearly tied to a specific national registry. It does not address the increasing complexity of multinational spacecraft and collaborative innovations where ownership and inventorship span multiple jurisdictions.[21]

from-earth-to-orbit-converging-space-law-and-intellectual-property-rights-to-safeguard-innovation-beyond-earth/ (last visited May 15, 2025).

19 Aditya Pandey, "Beyond Earth: Unravelling the Intricacies of Intellectual Property Rights in Space Exploration", *Mondaq*, 7 March 2025, available at: https://www.mondaq.com/india/trademark/1594424/beyond-earth-unravelling-the-intricacies-of-intellectual-property-rights-in-space-exploration (last visited May 15, 2025).

20 European Space Policy Institute, *The Rise of Private Actors in the Space Sector: Executive Summary*, July 2017, available at: https://www.espi.or.at/wp-content/uploads/2022/06/ESPI-report-The-rise-of-private-actors-Executive-Summary-1.pdf (last visited May 15, 2025)

21 Joel A. Dennerley, "State Liability for Space Object Collisions: The Proper Interpretation of 'Fault' for the Purposes of International Space Law", *European Journal*

B. Enforcement Mechanisms

Even if questions of jurisdiction and registration are resolved, the enforcement of intellectual property rights in outer space remains a formidable challenge. Unlike Earth, where national legal systems provide established enforcement mechanisms—ranging from civil litigation to administrative action and criminal prosecution outer space lacks a centralised enforcement authority capable of investigating and adjudicating IPR infringements.

This lacuna stems from the absence of an international legal institution mandated with overseeing IP enforcement in space. While the World Intellectual Property Organisation (WIPO) provides global frameworks for IP cooperation, it has no adjudicatory or enforcement powers, particularly for activities conducted outside State jurisdictions. Moreover, the international dispute resolution mechanisms available under existing treaties, such as the arbitration provision under Article IX of the *Outer Space Treaty* or the *Permanent Court of Arbitration Optional Rules for Space Law Disputes*, are voluntary and not widely utilised in practice.[22]

Another significant barrier to enforcement arises from the collaborative and multi-jurisdictional nature of modern space missions. Space exploration and commercial activities often involve partnerships between space agencies, private corporations, and research institutions from different States. As such, even when an infringement is identified, determining the applicable law, the competent forum, and the responsible party can be an extremely complicated endeavour. For example, if a patented technology licensed in one jurisdiction is unlawfully replicated in another jurisdiction's space module or during joint operations in orbit, there may be no clear legal pathway for the rights holder to obtain redress.[23]

Furthermore, the lack of enforcement mechanisms creates perverse incentives for bad-faith actors. Without fear of liability or regulatory

---

of International Law, Vol. 29, No. 1, 2018, pp. 281–301, available at: https://academic.oup.com/ejil/article/29/1/281/4993226 (last visited May 15, 2025).

22 Lee, Ricky J. *Law and Regulation of Commercial Mining of Minerals in Outer Space*. Dordrecht: Springer, 2012. Available at: https://link.springer.com/content/pdf/10.1007/978-94-007-2039-8.pdf (last visited May 15, 2025).

23 LexOrbis, "Patents Beyond Land: Applicability and Infringement of Inventions in Outer Space", *Mondaq*, 5 September 2019, available at: https://www.mondaq.com/india/patent/842270/patents-beyond-land-applicability-and-infringement-of-inventions-in-outer-space (last visited May 15, 2025).

oversight, entities may exploit the legal vacuum to appropriate technologies developed by others, undermining innovation, research integrity, and fair competition. This situation is antithetical to the objectives of intellectual property protection, which is designed to reward innovation by granting exclusive rights to inventors for a limited duration in exchange for public disclosure.

To address these challenges, scholars and policymakers have proposed the development of an international space IP registry administered through a dedicated multilateral framework, possibly under the joint aegis of WIPO and the United Nations Committee on the Peaceful Uses of Outer Space (UNCOPUOS).[24] Such a mechanism could record inventions developed in outer space, standardise procedures for attribution and licensing, and facilitate dispute resolution through pre-agreed protocols. Another complementary approach would be the negotiation of bilateral and multilateral agreements incorporating model IP clauses applicable to cooperative space ventures.[25]

In sum, the challenges of IP enforcement in space highlight the inadequacy of existing frameworks when applied to the frontier of human innovation. A proactive legal response anchored in international cooperation and supported by technological transparency is imperative to create a robust, fair, and innovation-friendly environment beyond Earth.

Towards a Comprehensive Legal Framework

A. International Cooperation and Treaties

The protection and enforcement of intellectual property rights (IPRs) in outer space cannot be effectively realised through unilateral or fragmented national initiatives alone.[26] Given the inherently transnational and non-sovereign character of space, international cooperation is not merely desirable but essential. The development of a multilateral treaty

24 United Nations Office for Outer Space Affairs (UNOOSA), "Committee on the Peaceful Uses of Outer Space (COPUOS)", available at: https://www.unoosa.org/oosa/en/ourwork/copuos/index.html (last visited May 15, 2025).

25 Gérardine Meishan Goh, Dispute Settlement in International Space Law: A Multi-Door Courthouse for Outer Space, Martinus Nijhoff Publishers, Leiden, 2007. European Space Agency

26 "Space Law and the Geostationary Orbit: Legal Challenges and Policy Implications", *The International Journal of Emerging Research (TIJER)*, Vol. 23, No. 6, 2023, pp. 310–325, available at: https://tijer.org/tijer/papers/TIJER2306310.pdf (last visited May 15, 2025).

framework, either as a new convention or as a protocol to existing space law instruments, is critical for addressing the specific challenges posed by intellectual property in extraterrestrial contexts.[27]

Existing space treaties, such as the *Outer Space Treaty* (1967), the *Registration Convention* (1976), and the *Liability Convention* (1972), were designed at a time when space activities were largely state-driven and scientific. These instruments lack any express reference to intellectual property. In contrast, the modern era of space exploration is marked by the increasing participation of private actors, commercialisation, and the rise of space-based technological innovation, making the silence of these treaties on IP matters a significant lacuna in international space law.[28]

A new treaty or protocol should aim to:

- Codify the jurisdictional basis for IP protection in space;
- Define the applicable law in case of multinational inventions or use;
- Create a uniform mechanism for the registration and disclosure of space-based IP;
- Establish dispute resolution procedures, either through a standing tribunal or ad hoc arbitration panels.

Such a treaty could be developed under the auspices of the United Nations Committee on the Peaceful Uses of Outer Space (UNCOPUOS) in collaboration with the World Intellectual Property Organization (WIPO).[29] The integration of WIPO's expertise in IP law with UNCOPUOS's mandate on space governance would ensure that legal standards are both technically sound and internationally representative.

27 R. Saha, "Protecting Intellectual Property Rights in Outer Space", *CII Blog*, 18 September 2023, available at: https://ciiblog.in/protecting-intellectual-property-rights-in-outer-space/ (last visited May 15, 2025).

28 Convention on International Liability for Damage Caused by Space Objects, adopted by the United Nations General Assembly in resolution 2777 (XXVI) on 29 November 1971, opened for signature on 29 March 1972, entered into force on 1 September 1972, available at: https://www.unoosa.org/oosa/en/ourwork/spacelaw/treaties/introliability-convention.html (last visited May 15, 2025).

29 See, United Nations Committee on the Peaceful Uses of Outer Space (UNCOPUOS), "Legal Subcommittee Reports," available at: https://www.unoosa.org/oosa/en/ourwork/copuos/legal/index.html (last visited 12 May 2025).

Furthermore, the treaty should recognise the unique characteristics of outer space as a non-appropriable, collaborative domain. It must strike a balance between the proprietary interests of inventors and the collective interest of humanity in equitable access to space-derived technologies—a principle embedded in Article I of the *Outer Space Treaty*.[30]

B. Establishment of an International Space IP Registry

In tandem with international treaty-making, the establishment of a dedicated International Space Intellectual Property Registry is vital to provide a centralised, transparent, and reliable platform for the registration, recognition, and protection of IPRs originating in or utilised in outer space. This registry could be developed as a specialised organ under WIPO or as a joint initiative with the International Telecommunication Union (ITU) and UNCOPUOS.

The registry would serve multiple purposes:

- Offer a record-keeping mechanism for patents, copyrights, and trademarks associated with space technology and activities;
- Facilitate ownership attribution in cases of joint inventions developed by multinational space platforms;
- Act as a public notification system to prevent duplication and infringement;
- Serve as a jurisdictional anchor for determining applicable law in disputes.

Such a registry would be especially useful in addressing complex scenarios such as:

- Co-invention by scientists from different jurisdictions aboard a spacecraft;
- Use of patented technologies across national modules of space stations;
- Licensing disputes involving space-based software or satellite networks.

By making registration a precondition for enforceability, the registry would enhance legal certainty, reduce transaction costs, and build investor

30 Ibid., art. I.

confidence in the space sector.[31] Moreover, public access to the registry's database could promote technological diffusion and transparency without compromising proprietary interests.[32]

Although WIPO currently maintains the Patent Cooperation Treaty (PCT) system, which offers a unified procedure for filing patent applications across multiple countries, its terrestrial orientation limits its utility in outer space contexts. A space-specific registry, operating under sui generis rules, would fill this gap while complementing the existing global IP infrastructure.

C. Harmonisation of National Laws

Another essential component of a comprehensive legal framework is the harmonisation of national IP laws as they relate to space activities. At present, States vary widely in their approach to IP protection in space, with some extending domestic patent laws extraterritorially (e.g., the United States), while others rely solely on international frameworks or remain silent altogether. This divergence leads to jurisdictional fragmentation, legal uncertainty, and a lack of consistency in rights enforcement.

Encouraging harmonisation through model laws, regional agreements, and bilateral treaties can help reduce conflicts of law and promote legal interoperability. For instance, national space legislations could be amended to:

- Incorporate express provisions on the application of IP laws to registered space objects;[33]
- Define the legal status of inventions developed in space;
- Clarify rules on joint inventorship and licensing in multinational missions.

31 The New Focus of IPR", *Khurana & Khurana*, 19 November 2021, available at: https://www.khuranaandkhurana. com/2021/11/19/space-law-protection-the-new-focus-of-ipr/ (last visited May 15, 2025).

32 Ibid.

33 NALSAR University of Law, "Space Technology, Telecommunications and IPRs Issues", Directorate of Distance Education, available at: https://nalsarpro.org/Portals/23/Paper-II-1_2_6_Space%20Technology%2C%20Telecommunications %20and%20 IPRs%20Issues%20%281%29_1.pdf (last visited May 15, 2025).

Harmonisation efforts could draw upon successful precedents such as the Uniform Domain-Name Dispute-Resolution Policy (UDRP)[34] or the Madrid Protocol on international trademark registration, which have streamlined legal processes across jurisdictions while preserving domestic legal autonomy.[35]

Additionally, States could adopt reciprocal recognition agreements for space-related IP, akin to bilateral tax or extradition treaties, allowing rights granted in one jurisdiction to be enforceable in another in specific circumstances. Over time, such bilateral and regional efforts may coalesce into customary norms or pave the way for binding multilateral conventions.

In conclusion, achieving legal coherence in the protection of intellectual property in outer space requires a multi-tiered strategy of international rule-making, institutional innovation, and national legal reform. Together, these elements can create a forward-looking, legally certain, and innovation-friendly regime that encourages scientific advancement while ensuring equitable access and compliance with international law.

Conclusion

The rapid evolution of outer space from a domain of scientific inquiry to a commercial frontier has raised fundamental questions about the applicability, adequacy, and adaptability of existing intellectual property (IP) regimes. The territorial foundation of IP law, deeply rooted in notions of national sovereignty, finds itself ill-suited for the non-sovereign, cooperative, and increasingly privatised nature of outer space activities. As demonstrated through this study, the legal vacuum surrounding IP rights in space—particularly regarding registration, enforcement, and jurisdiction—presents significant risks to innovation, investment, and equitable access to space technologies.

While the *Outer Space Treaty* and related instruments provide a structural foundation for space law, they are silent on matters of intellectual property. The extension of national laws, as observed through the International

34 Uniform Domain-Name Dispute-Resolution Policy (UDRP): Internet Corporation for Assigned Names and Numbers (ICANN), "Uniform Domain-Name Dispute-Resolution Policy", 24 October 1999, available at: https://www.icann.org/resources/pages/policy-2024-02-21-en (last visited May 15, 2025).

35 Madrid Protocol on International Trademark Registration: World Intellectual Property Organization (WIPO), "Madrid Protocol for the International Registration of Marks", available at: https://www.wipo.int/treaties/en/registration/madrid/ (last visited May 15, 2025).

Space Station model and statutes like the United States' *Commercial Space Launch Competitiveness Act*, offer partial remedies but raise concerns about legal fragmentation and inconsistency with the non-appropriation principle. These developments underscore the urgency of developing an international legal framework that balances proprietary interests with the collective interest in space as the "province of all mankind".

The future of IP protection in outer space demands a three-pronged strategy. First, there is a pressing need for multilateral treaty-making under the joint guidance of WIPO and UNCOPUOS to codify principles specific to space-based innovations. Second, the creation of an international space IP registry would provide a transparent, accessible platform for documenting and enforcing space-related IP rights, thereby promoting legal certainty across jurisdictions. Third, the harmonisation of national space laws through model legislation and mutual recognition agreements would reduce jurisdictional conflicts and promote predictability.

Furthermore, space-related IP protection must be embedded within a human rights and development-oriented framework, ensuring that technological advancements do not disproportionately benefit spacefaring nations or commercial conglomerates at the expense of equitable access for developing countries. In this regard, the principle of the common heritage of humankind should inform the future design of legal and institutional frameworks.

In conclusion, the governance of intellectual property in outer space stands at a critical crossroads. Without proactive, inclusive, and legally robust mechanisms, the promise of space-based innovation may be undermined by uncertainty and conflict. Conversely, a comprehensive and cooperative legal architecture can serve as a catalyst for technological advancement, commercial opportunity, and international solidarity in this final frontier.

Chapter 16

Intellectual Property Protection in Outer Space: Conflicts and Practical Challenges

-Saneh Kumari & Hritwik Ravi

Abstract

The rapid expansion of commercial space activities has created a fundamental legal conflict between intellectual property rights and international space law, presenting unprecedented challenges for innovation and national security in the extraterrestrial domain. Traditional IP frameworks grant inventors exclusive control over their creations to incentivise innovation, while international space treaties, particularly the Outer Space Treaty of 1967, declare that outer space belongs to all humanity under the "*Res Communis*" principle and should benefit everyone equally, creating a core tension between exclusivity and collective access that threatens both commercial space development and defence capabilities.

This chapter addresses the critical question of how to protect intellectual property rights that drive space innovation while respecting the foundational principle that space is a shared global resource, a challenge amplified by dual-use technologies. It identifies specific challenges, firstly, major jurisdictional ambiguities exist because IP rights are territorial while outer space has no national boundaries, making it unclear which country's laws apply to space-based inventions and how to enforce patent protections beyond Earth; secondly, existing international space treaties contain no specific provisions for intellectual property rights, leaving a critical legal vacuum as private companies now drive most space innovation without clear IP protection frameworks. The chapter concludes that while a comprehensive global IP regime for space remains aspirational, immediate solutions must focus on harmonised legal frameworks, international cooperation, and adapted national regulations to protect commercial space development in an increasingly competitive space environment.

Keywords: Space Law, Intellectual Property Rights, Outer Space Treaty, Space Exploration, International IP framework.

Introduction

In the information-driven society, it is widely acknowledged that an appropriate legal regime for intellectual property protection is indispensable for the healthy development of society and technology.[1] Various states have invested substantial effort in creating national legal regimes to protect intellectual property. At the same time, we have witnessed the formation of international treaties at the international level, unifying the rules for the protection of various forms of intellectual property rights.[2] Given that space exploration and development are inherently dependent on cutting-edge technologies that require robust intellectual property rights (IPRs) protection to incentivise innovation and secure competitive advantage, the rapid expansion of space commercialisation has created unprecedented demand for clear and enforceable IP frameworks in the extraterrestrial domain. Space activities and space research are receiving more and more attention for intellectual property protection. Outer space is the area that exists beyond Earth. Space technology is the systematic application of engineering and scientific disciplines to the exploration and utilisation of outer space. The technology that is related to entering and retrieving objects or life forms from space is space technology.[3]

In the beginning, there has been little or no dispute over the fact that space is part of a larger and more cohesive system of international law.[4] The dawn of the 21st century has marked a revolutionary period in space exploration, as technological advancement and research in this area are no longer limited to the state domain; space has become a fertile ground for innovation driven by private corporations such as SpaceX, Blue Origin, and Virgin Galactic. This privatisation has opened new frontiers not only in

1 Ritesh Mehra, "Intellectual Property Protection in Outer Space – An Overview" 2 *ILI Law Review* (2019).

2 Zhijie Chen and Yun Zhao, "Intellectual Property Protection in Outer Space: Conflict in Theory and Application in Practice" 61 *Space Policy* (2022).

3 KP Abitha, "Intellectual property and outer space: The need of international harmonized legal framework" 6 *International Journal of Law* 3 (2020).

4 *Ibid.*

exploration but also in the commercialisation of space-based technologies. The participation of private entities adds to the regulatory regimes in such activities. With these developments comes the pressing need to address the legal challenges surrounding the ownership and protection of intellectual property in space.

Hence, legal clarification regarding IP protection in outer space remains in demand. In fact, discussions on the application of IP rules to space activities have lasted for several decades, but the results from these analyses have not been satisfying. Legal uncertainties concerning whether the outer space treaties will admit IP in outer space remain till now. Those principal rationales that have contributed to such legal uncertainty are related to the public-private conflict and territoriality conflict between the legal regimes of outer space and IP. The absence of explicit legal foundations for IP protection in space law creates significant barriers that may discourage private sector investment and limit active participation in commercial space activities, as companies require legal certainty to justify substantial research and development expenditures in space technologies. Consequently, there remains an urgent need for comprehensive legal clarification of IP protection mechanisms in outer space. Despite decades of scholarly discussion and analysis examining the application of IP rules to space activities, the results have been largely unsatisfactory in resolving fundamental legal uncertainties.

Intellectual Property and International Principles of Space Law

The dawn of legislation on space matters bears the mark of the United Nations. In 1957, the Soviet Union launched Sputnik, the first man-made object orbiting the Earth, thereby inaugurating the space race. The first full-fledged international treaty on space is the 1967 Outer Space Treaty,[5] followed by the 1968 Rescue Agreement,[6] the 1972 Liability Convention,[7] the 1975 Registration Convention,[8] and finally the 1979 Moon Treaty.[9] To understand the reason behind the conflict between IPR laws and the international principles governing outer space activities, one first needs a clear insight into the international laws regarding space exploration.

5 *Supra* note 2.

6 *Ibid.*

7 *Ibid.*

8 *Ibid.*

9 *Ibid.*

The 1967 Outer Space Treaty is the cornerstone of international space law. It explicitly prohibits the national appropriation of celestial bodies[10] and makes the outer space free for use and exploration by all states[11], i.e., the outer space cannot be claimed by any single state. It is regarded as "*Res Communis*" which means in the public domain or public property. The Outer Space Treaty also mandates that activities in outer space should be carried out for the benefit of all countries, irrespective of their level of economic or scientific development.[12] The treaty on a primary basis focuses on the governmental activities happening in space only. The Moon agreement, intended as a supplement to the OST, declares the moon and other celestial bodies to be the "common heritage of mankind" and prohibits ownership of any part of a celestial body by any state, organisation, or individual.[13]

Other international agreements regarding the exploration and use of outer space include the Convention on Registration of Objects Launched into Outer Space (1975), which is an expansion upon art. VIII of the Outer Space Treaty, the Agreement on the Rescue of Astronauts, the Return of Astronauts and the Return of Objects Launched into Outer Space (1968), which augments art. V and VIII of the Outer Space Treaty, and the Convention on International Liability for Damage Caused by Space Objects (1972), which adds to art. VII of the OST. However, none contains any provisions directly applicable to the question of intangible intellectual property rights.

The historical context surrounding the development of these foundational treaties reveals a deliberate emphasis on preventing the militarisation and nationalisation of space during the height of the Cold War tensions. The drafters of the Outer Space Treaty, working within the United Nations Committee on the Peaceful Uses of Outer Space (COPUOS), were primarily concerned with preventing space from becoming another theatre of superpower competition and ensuring that the benefits of space exploration would be shared equitably among all nations. This noble aspiration, however, was formulated during an era when space activities were exclusively conducted by government agencies with public funding, and the concept of private commercial space ventures was largely confined to science fiction. The treaty's language reflects this historical context,

10 Article II of the OST specifically states that "outer space, including the Moon and other celestial bodies, is not subject to national appropriation by any means.

11 Article 1.

12 Outer Space Treaty, art. I, Jan. 27, 1967, 610 U.N.T.S. 205.

13 Moon Agreement, art. 11, Dec. 5, 1979, 1363 U.N.T.S. 3.

with its emphasis on state responsibility and the absence of provisions addressing private property rights or commercial exploitation of space resources, creating a fundamental mismatch with contemporary realities where private entities drive much of space innovation and investment.[14]

While these principles foster global cooperation, they create ambiguity for private entities and IPR, as treaties do not clarify whether inventions or discoveries made in space can be patented under terrestrial laws. This legal contradiction creates a problematic environment where intellectual property rights, which depend on sovereign authority for protection and enforcement, cannot be readily applied in a domain explicitly declared beyond national appropriation. The common heritage principle of the Moon Agreement directly challenges the concept of private ownership, which is the cornerstone of IPR protection. The limited ratification of the Moon agreement further complicates its impact on IPR. Major spacefaring nations such as the United States, Russia, and China are notably absent from the list of signatories. Hence, nations that host the most private space companies are not bound by their provisions, leading to a fragmented legal landscape. This creates a practical challenge: while the OST's principles are universally accepted, the Moon Agreement's more stringent rules apply only to a small subset of states, leaving private entities in a legal gray zone.

Professor Cromer proposes a conflict between any assertion of exclusive intellectual property rights in outer space-derived geospatial data and the overarching international legal principle applied to outer space, namely, *res communis*, which designates outer space as a global common.[15] This conflict raises significant legal and ethical questions about ownership, control, and equitable sharing of space-derived data in the context of the rapidly growing commercial space industry. Hence, creating two international divergences, first, exclusivity of IP Rights versus equitable access, where IP laws grant creators exclusive control, potentially restricting access to data critical for global challenges such as climate monitoring or disaster response. Second, IP rights provide De Facto appropriation over it, undermining the non-appropriation principle of space law.

Further, present international treaties are designed state-centric, not anticipating the rise of commercialisation and privatisation of outer space, creating a gap area relating to private entities' liability. The present treaties

14 *Supra* note 1.

15 Lee Ann W. Lockridge, "Intellectual Property in Outer Space: International Law, National Jurisdiction, and Exclusive Rights in Geospatial Data" 32 *Journal of Space Law* 319 (2009).

are based on the premise of exploration and peaceful use of outer space by the state, only looking at state liability. According to the Registration Convention 1975[16], registration is compulsory for any spacecraft[17] before launching into outer space, this is to ensure that if any accident occurs, liability can be attributed to the launching state. This raises a concern that, until and unless international law exists, supplemented by national law, it is almost impossible to determine the liability of private parties. Hence, the absence of a clear provision within international law will discourage the state from employing private bodies to enter into space commercialisation.[18] On the other hand, if the state frames law in such a manner that shifts complete liability to a private body, that will also discourage private bodies from entering into space commercial transactions. Hence, aspects of space commercialisation from the manufacturer's point of view, who supply different equipment or parts to space agencies for building spacecraft, are very essential.[19]

Determination of product liability and how it will be shared by the manufacturer and the registered country in the absence of any guiding principles is a matter of concern. For fixing liability under international space law, absolute liability is the only option, that is, fixing the liability even when there is no fault. If damage has been done, the liability will be fixed automatically, irrespective of due care and caution undertaken. However, on the other hand, national space law imposes fault liability. Therefore, there is a vast difference in the determination of liability for any damage in the international and national regimes.[20]

IP Protection and the Territoriality of IPR in Space Activities

Theoretically, the essentially public nature of outer space law appears to clash with the private nature of IP law. For instance, the OST explicitly provides that States and intergovernmental organisations are two legal beneficiaries of outer space law. One can say that four fundamental forces shape the universe. The existence of everything in the universe and the explanation

16 *Ibid.*

17 *Ibid.*

18 Biswanath Gupta and Dr. Raju KD, "Commercialisation of Outer Space: Need for a Legal Regime in India" *RMLNU Law review Blog, available at:* https://rmlnlulawreview.com/wp-content/uploads/2021/04/ee79e-commercialisation-of-outer-space-activities.pdf (last visited on May 01, 2025).

19 *Ibid.*

20 *Ibid.*

of every phenomenon are attributable to the effects of at least one of these forces: gravity, electromagnetic force, weak force, and strong force. These forces are also referred to as interactions. They are fundamental because a reduction to simpler interactions is not possible. Figuratively, space law was born and is evolving as the point of convergence of a different set of four essential advancements and intellectual property. These categorical directives have informed the human approach to space and will do so in the future.[21]

Sovereignty is the most fundamental relation between states, rooted in territory, population, authority, and recognition. A state's sovereign jurisdiction is central to securing and enforcing IP rights. The sovereignty challenges appear when the IP rights are contemplated in outer space, where the claim of sovereignty cannot be made. On earth, a state's sovereign jurisdiction is central to securing and enforcing IP rights, which are inherently territorial and limited to the geographical area where they are registered for a specific duration. Although in the present advanced multilateral treaty framework, such as the Agreement on Trade-Related Aspects of Intellectual Property Rights (TRIPS)[22], is facilitating the securing and enforcement of such IP rights is virtually global, since a member state to a treaty may provide national treatment to a foreign IP right and secure or enforce such foreign IP rights under its jurisdiction through its domestic law. This framework has significantly expanded the scope of IP protection on Earth. However, the territoriality creates complex problems when innovation occurs in outer space, as space is not subject to national sovereignty or territorial claims.

The fundamental challenge of applying territorial IP law to the non-territorial domain of outer space becomes even more pronounced when considering the dynamic nature of space-based operations. Unlike terrestrial intellectual property disputes, which can be resolved within established jurisdictional frameworks, space-based innovations often involve multiple moving platforms, international collaborations, and constantly changing spatial relationships that defy traditional territorial concepts. For instance, a satellite manufactured in one country, launched from another, operated by a multinational consortium, and providing services to global customers creates a complex web of potential jurisdictional claims that existing IP law is ill-equipped to handle. The situation becomes even more complicated when considering innovations that occur during space missions, where

21 *Supra* note 1.

22 *Ibid.*

the location of the invention may be constantly changing as spacecraft move through different orbital regimes or travel between celestial bodies, making it virtually impossible to determine which terrestrial jurisdiction should apply.

The emergence of commercial space stations, lunar bases, and other permanent or semi-permanent space installations further complicates the territorial application of IP law. While the International Space Station operates under a specific intergovernmental agreement that assigns jurisdictional authority based on the national origin of different modules, this model may not be practical or desirable for purely commercial space installations. Private space stations operated by companies like Axiom Space or planned lunar facilities for resource extraction raise questions about whether IP rights should be determined by the nationality of the operating company, the launch state, the state of registration, or some other criteria. The absence of clear legal precedents for these scenarios creates uncertainty that could discourage investment in space-based research and development, as companies cannot be certain that their innovations will be adequately protected or that they will be able to enforce their rights against potential infringers.

Space presents a unique challenge, as also seen above, that it is governed by international treaties such as the Outer Space Treaty, a cornerstone of international space law, which declares outer space, including the Moon and other celestial bodies, as the "province of all mankind" and also prohibits any national appropriation of space.[23] It ensures that no country has sovereignty over parts of space. This gives rise to questions about how territorial IP laws can be applied to space activities and innovations that occur in a domain beyond territorial boundaries. Neither national laws nor international conventions deal with infringement of the intellectual property used or made in outer space.

For instance, patents are a most crucial form of intellectual property for space-based innovations. With the new technology, such as satellite communications, space mining technologies, etc, patents will be a major aspect of a space tech start-up's IP strategy. However, its application to space invention comes with legal uncertainties as patent law typically applies within the borders of the countries granting the patent. When it comes to the invention that is deployed on the International Space Station ISS, which orbits the Earth and involves collaboration from multiple

23 *Ibid.*

countries, legal uncertainties arise. The ISS operated under a unique legal framework governed by the Intergovernmental Agreement (IGA)[24], which stipulates that each partner state retains jurisdiction over its elements and personnel. Although this agreement allows for the application of national laws to specific areas of the space station, it offers a potential model for resolving jurisdictional issues. However, it's not being comprehensive and an ultimate solution as it does not extend to other space environments such as private space stations, lunar bases, or asteroid mining operations. Moreover, at present, ISS is between government agencies, but in the future, space activities will involve private companies operating independently or in collaboration with multiple nations.[25]

The patent landscape in space technology is particularly complex due to the interdisciplinary nature of space innovations, which often involve advances in materials science, propulsion systems, life support technologies, communications, and computer systems. Many space technologies also have dual-use applications, serving both civilian and military purposes, which can complicate patent protection strategies as companies must balance the benefits of patent disclosure with national security considerations. The long development cycles typical of space technologies also present challenges for patent protection, as the 20-year patent term may not provide adequate protection for innovations that take decades to develop and deploy. Furthermore, the international nature of many space projects means that patent protection must be secured in multiple jurisdictions, creating significant costs and administrative burdens for companies operating in the space sector.

The enforcement of patent rights in space presents even greater challenges than their initial protection. Traditional patent enforcement mechanisms rely on the ability of courts to issue injunctions, calculate damages, and impose penalties within their territorial jurisdiction. However, space-based patent infringement may occur in locations where no terrestrial court has clear jurisdiction, making it difficult or impossible to obtain effective legal remedies. For instance, if one company's patented technology is used without permission on another company's lunar mining operation, it may be unclear which court system has jurisdiction to hear the dispute and what remedies would be available. The practical difficulties of gathering

24 *Ibid.*

25 Md Jewel Ali, "From Earth to Orbit: Converging Space Law and Intellectual Property Rights to Safeguard Innovation Beyond Earth" 6(5) *International Journal of Legal Science and Innovation* 210-228 (2021).

evidence, conducting inspections, and enforcing judgments in space further complicate patent enforcement efforts. These challenges are likely to become more significant as space commercialisation expands and the number of potential patent disputes increases.

It gives rise to ambiguity whether an invention created is to be governed by the national laws of the inventor's state or the state responsible for the module where the work occurred. If an invention is protected only in the state responsible for where the work occurred, then its protection extends only to that nation, leaving its use in space or other nations' space programs potentially unprotected unless additional patents are filed in other jurisdictions.[26] Similarly, Copyright is also being territorial, creating questions about the protection of works created within a country's jurisdiction. This creates questions about the protection of works created in space, such as computer software, databases, or artistic works made aboard spacecraft or space stations.

Global space economy projected to reach $1.8 trillion by 2035, up from $630 billion in 2023.[27] This figure includes both backbone applications, such as those for satellite, launchers, services like broadcast television or GPS, space tourism, satellite communication, etc. Companies like Virgin Galactic, SpaceX, and Blue Origin rely on strong brand identities to differentiate their services, making trademark protection critical. However, again, applying terrestrial trademark law to outer space is fraught with challenges. It is unclear which country's laws will apply to trademark infringement on a multinational space station, as determining the applicable jurisdiction is complex. Without clear jurisdictional rules, patent holders may find it difficult to enforce their rights in space, creating a legal grey area that could deter innovation.

Conclusion

The analysis presented in this study reveals a fundamental and urgent need for comprehensive legal reform to address the growing incompatibility between traditional intellectual property frameworks and the unique challenges of space commercialisation. Space commercialisation cannot be disconnected from IP protection, as space activities are strongly associated

26 *Ibid.*

27 The space economy is projected to reach $1.8 trillion by 2035, *available at:* https://www.mckinsey.com/featured-insights/themes/the-space-economy-is-projected-to-reach-1-8-trillion-by-2035 (last visited on May 07, 2025).

with space technology.[28] The application of IP to outer space can be well illustrated from the perspectives of patent rights and copyrights. The former aims at protecting scientific and technical innovations, while the latter intends to safeguard data generated by satellites and applied widely to telecommunications, remote sensing, and navigation. The rapidly evolving field of space exploration and commercialisation brings with it unique challenges to the traditional understanding and application of IP laws.[29] The pressing need of today is to align international treaties dealing with outer space with domestic laws. Existing international agreements, primarily designed for state-led activities, are insufficient to address modern challenges and not sufficient to deal with commercial space activities.

The core tension between the res communis principle of international space law and the exclusivity requirements of intellectual property protection represents more than a technical legal challenge, it constitutes a fundamental philosophical divide about the nature of innovation, ownership, and equity in the extraterrestrial domain. The 1967 Outer Space Treaty's declaration that space is the "province of all mankind" was crafted during an era of bipolar superpower competition and government-dominated space activities, creating a framework that is increasingly inadequate for addressing the complex realities of contemporary commercial space ventures. The absence of specific provisions for intellectual property rights in existing space treaties has created a legal vacuum that threatens to undermine both innovation incentives and the equitable sharing of space-derived benefits. This vacuum is particularly problematic given the projected growth of the space economy to $1.8 trillion by 2035,[30] representing a transformation from a niche government activity to a major sector of the global economy that requires sophisticated legal protections to sustain continued growth and innovation.

Space commercialisation cannot be separated from IP protection, as space activities are closely linked to space technology. The application of IP to outer space can be well illustrated from the perspectives of patent rights and copyrights. The former aims to protect scientific and technical innovations, while the latter seeks to safeguard data generated by satellites and applied widely to telecommunications, remote sensing, and navigation. The rapidly evolving field of space exploration and commercialisation

28 *Supra* note 14.

29 *Ibid.*

30 *Supra* note 26.

brings with it unique challenges to the traditional understanding and application of IP laws. The pressing need today is to align international treaties governing outer space with domestic law. Existing international agreements, primarily designed for state-led activities, are insufficient to address modern challenges and not sufficient to deal with commercial space activities.

Thus, Intellectual creativity will undoubtedly be an integral driver of outer space exploration, especially upcoming activities such as space tourism, asteroid mining, microgravity R&D, and lunar or Mars settlements involving increased private participation alongside public agencies. With limitations in international space laws on protecting IP exclusively used or created in space environments highlighted in preceding sections, tailored sui generis models are imperative to balance recovery of risk investments, access for utilisation, especially by developing countries and preserving collective stakeholding in global commons defined under principles like common heritage and province of humankind.

Protection of intellectual property in space should be based on the existing international space agreements, on the extension of national law, and international precedents relating to intellectual property issues in space. Liability for the existing intellectual property infringement in space should be addressed through the existing international norms of IP regimes like TRIPS under the WTO. The TRIPS agreement is a highly reputable agreement for the protection of intellectual property law, and it always acts in support of the intellectual property issues that arise at times. Globalising jurisdiction for outer space activities is the most preferable solution to address issues relating to IPR in outer space. A single worldwide IPR legislation is needed for space activities.

Chapter 17

Intellectual Property Beyond Borders: Navigating Intellectual Property Law in Commercialized Space Tourism

---

-Rajini BV

Abstract

Space tourism is a part of the aviation sector, known for its commercial and recreational activities carried out by either a government or a private entity of a nation, offered to mankind irrespective of whether they are professional astronauts or members of spaceflight. Virgin Galactic, a private company, offered space tourism tickets at $450k in 2023. Despite such high rates, it has already seen approximately 800 bookings. Thus, space tourism by public-private entities increases economic growth. India has yet to debut in this sector; however, in 2024, Indians began their space journey with Blue Origin, a private company. This could also lead to complex legal and jurisdictional issues, as well as lacunae in applying Intellectual property laws to outer space creations and infringements.

The International instruments dealing with space laws include the Outer Space Treaty (1967), Liability Convention (1972), Registration Convention (1974), Rescue and Return Agreement (1968), The Moon Treaty (1979), etc. However, these instruments do not specifically deal with Intellectual property laws governing space tourism. According to the Liability Convention and Registration Convention, the jurisdiction over the spaceflight and liabilities against personnel and any damage caused to outer space objects could lie with the launching state. This chapter explores the emerging areas of commercialised space tourism for the non-professionals by intersecting areas of Intellectual Property and Space tourism, the need to address the gaps in the current National and International instruments in dealing with the uncertainty for innovations and inventions in space vehicles and space during space travel, the future ethical and environmental impact of granting IP to space inventions. It suggests a new uniform international instrument for international cooperation, a separate space registry to specifically address IP rights created in tourism beyond Earth, and the establishment of basic principles for domestic countries to adapt. This chapter recommends the adoption of a harmonised international legal instrument to foster innovation and invention, particularly in space activities, by balancing legal and ethical considerations to boost the domestic economy.

Keywords: Space Tourism, Space Exploration, Public-Private entities, International Instruments, Ownership, Liabilities, Jurisdiction, Environmental Impact.

Space Tourism

Space tourism is the recent recreational activity taken up by many private companies, states and citizens to explore space. Space tourism primarily deals with Orbital space tourism, and Suborbital space tourism, Lunar, Martian zone tourism, etc. Orbital tourism reaches a higher altitude than suborbital tourism. The first crewed orbital flight was in 1961. After that, tourism came into the public eye, especially after Dennis Tito's commercial spaceflight. Recently, the SpaceX Dragon spacecraft was launched, and it is believed to be one of the competitors among private companies. After the internationalisation, globalisation, and commercialisation of space exploration, not only engineers and scientists but also people in the research field have been actively taking part in researching the topic.

The first tourist to travel to the orbital zone was Dennis Tito in 2001; the trip was privately funded to the International Space Station. What is to be noted is that the participant has no prior spaceflight experience and is solely doing it for recreational purposes. We have witnessed the success of orbital space tourism and the beginning of suborbital tourism. Considering the cost of travel and investments, suborbital flights are smaller and can be reused after each flight. Orbital tourism can reach up to 160km, whereas suborbital tourism can reach around 100km. However, in orbit, they travel at a higher speed to overcome gravity and reach the orbital zone. Hence, the size and design may vary and be comparatively higher; also, the parts will have to be replaced after each flight. This can be one of the drawbacks, as it is not economically viable compared to suborbital flights. However, research has been conducted on the development of reusable flights.

We can note that the future would hold a much more competitive market to have an improvised safe, high quality and a better experience with prices lower than compared to what is quoted in the present day.

Space Tourism and Economy

Speaking about the importance of space tourism, one cannot neglect the economic benefits that come along with it, as it would not only bring new perspectives to the upcoming space tourist, but it would also result in reusable spaceships, which would again be related to the country's economy without being a burden on its pocket. This is a new era of commercial recreation, through which we can develop the country's economy by billions of dollars in annual revenue. This would result in increased job opportunities and taxes, which would contribute to the nation's economy.[1] This would also result in the development of support industries, indirectly. Tourism being the largest sector when it comes to the world economy and the commercial aspect it is going to be an exotic realm when we go beyond the atmosphere.

Over a period of time, space tourism might result even in a much cheaper flights with less risk. As we also make the usage of reusable space system possible, it would lead to the development of better class of vehicles by the nations, which would result in cautious work and better qualities. As this is not just limited to the government sector, even the public apart from the private spaces would benefit.[2] Finally, the general public has been losing interest in space exploration, but after the introduction of private space tourism, we can see a rise in public enthusiasm for exploring space. It has been noted that when people witness the earth, the black sky and our environmental atmosphere from above, there comes a sense of awareness among the people to protect and conserve the resources of the planet.[3]

Thus, we can summarise and categorise it as both microscopic and macroscopicfinancialissueswhenitcomestospacetourism.Themicroscopic

1 Derek Webber ,*Space tourism: Its history, future and importance,* Acta Astronautica 92 (2013) 138–143, https://www.spaceportassociates.com/pdf/tourism_history.pdf

2 Toivonen, A. K. (2017). *Sustainable planning for space tourism.* Matkailututkimus, 13, 21. Article 1/2.

3 Sam Cole, *Space tourism: prospects, positioning, and planning,*Published in the Journal of Tourism Futures, https://www.emerald.com/insight/content/doi/10.1108/jtf-12-2014-0014/full/pdf?title=space-tourism-prospects-positioning-and-planning

level would be about the new opportunities for entrepreneurship and the funding made to space industries. On the macro level, we can, look into the various job creations, tax generation, and industrial development related changes. It has been noted and observed that the economic multiplier is higher in terms of the space tourism industry when compared to other industries. This might also lead to space infrastructure development. This can lead to the development of the destination area of the launch vehicle and its surroundings, which would attract more terrestrial tourism.[4]

Environmental Issues

Considering the issues with respect to space tourism, the environmental issues would obviously stand out along with the ethical issues, when it comes to sustainable tourist activities. There are various critics as well for space tourism, stating that this would result in serious environmental problems, as the release of carbon and particulate matter emissions would lead to various factors such as environmental, degradation, climate change, global warming, and air pollution. It would result in a lot of debris and garbage and this pollution might also extend to outer space. In terms of resource mass, tourism and transportation usually rely on fuels, fossil oil mineral resources that are naturally obtained from the earth and by using an overdoing this result in depletion of natural resources. Also, there are destination-level critics who criticise the spaceport development; for example, the spaceport in New Zealand has been criticised on the basis of various environmental, cultural, and political challenges. [5]

Space exploration requires many complex technological aspects at the same time. It is adventurous as well. Initially, during the Cold War era, when they had the space race, only the USA and USSR had enough resources to have advanced technologies and ideas. However, as years passed by many new players, such as Japan, Pakistan, India, Australia, France, South Korea, Israel, Iran, et cetera had joined. This is making the industry competitive. The current trend is with respect to exploring space as a part of a tourist or recreational activity by all members, irrespective of their occupation with the entry of many private companies. This is leading to a lot of complicated rules and practices of space studies. The primary reason is because the current international law is not updated enough to fit in all the

4 Yavuz Toraman. (2025) Space Logistics and Risks: A Study on Spacecraft. *Politeknik Dergisi* 28:2, pages 573-584

5 Myles Harris, Patrizia I. Duda, Ilan Kelman & Navonel Glick. (2022) Addressing disaster and health risks for sustainable outer space. *Integrated Environmental Assessment and Management* 19:4, pages 994-1001.

current happenings. So far, only public entities were being governed by the international space law, so this is a new area to be improved and included.

Space law emerged during the years 1950 and 60. There were two main schools of thought. The first one wanted the application of the principles of international law to those space exploration, such as the international conventions, all the general principles by civilisations, the international customs, et cetera. The second School considered space matters to be a separate and unique unit which required new tailor-made loss laws itself to be more specific to deal with matters of jurisdiction enforcement. It is also quite unreasonable and impossible to apply the international law principles to an area beyond the earth where the legal status is not known. The legal status of space is very uncertain currently. UNOOSA United Nations Office for Outer Space Activities is one of the primary bodies. However, it was only to implement the decision of General Assembly. When it comes to adjudication is no separate body with respect to space matters. Thus, letting the countries decide the principles, the principles are usually decided by the regulators pressure at the regional level. For example, NASA in the US, Europeans Space Agency in the European Union, et cetera. Currently, we can see that the international space law is dealt by two ways, namely the treaties and the principles. The treaties commonly referred to as the five United Nations treaties on outer space are as follows:

1. Treaty on Principles Governing the Activities of States in the Exploration and Use of Outer Space, including the Moon and Other Celestial Bodies. It was adopted by the General Assembly in its resolution 2222 (XXI), opened for signature on 27 January 1967, entered into force on 10 October 1967.

2. Agreement on the Rescue of Astronauts, the Return of Astronauts and the Return of Objects Launched into Outer Space. It was adopted by the General Assembly in its resolution 2345 (XXII), opened for signature on 22 April 1968, and entered into force on 3 December 1968.

3. The Convention on International Liability for Damage Caused by Space Objects. It was adopted by the General Assembly in its resolution 2777 (XXVI), opened for signature on 29 March 1972, entered into force on 1 September 1972.

4. Convention on Registration of Objects Launched into Outer Space. It was adopted by the General Assembly in its resolution

3235 (XXIX), opened for signature on 14 January 1975, entered into force on 15 September 1976.

5. The Agreement Governing the Activities of States on the Moon and Other Celestial Bodies. It was adopted by the General Assembly in its resolution 34/68, opened for signature on 18 December 1979, entered into force on 11 July 1984.

The five declarations and legal principles are:

1. The Declaration of Legal Principles Governing the Activities of States in the Exploration and Uses of Outer Space. It was adopted by the UN General Assembly resolution 1962 (XVIII) of 13 December 1963.

2. The Principles Governing the Use by States of Artificial Earth Satellites for International Direct Television Broadcasting. It was adopted by the General Assembly resolution 37/92 of 10 December 1982.

3. The Principles Relating to Remote Sensing of the Earth from Outer Space, adopted by the General Assembly resolution 41/65 of 3 December 1986.

4. The Principles Relevant to the Use of Nuclear Power Sources in Outer Space, adopted by the General Assembly resolution 47/68 of 14 December 1992.

5. The Declaration on International Cooperation in the Exploration and Use of Outer Space for the Benefit and in the Interest of All States, Taking into Particular Account the Needs of Developing Countries. It was adopted by the General Assembly resolution 51/122 of 13 December 1996. This was primarily declared to enhance international cooperation, especially in space exploration. This led to the developing countries contributing to their basic exploration activities. The countries notably India, Pakistan, Iran, South Korea etc. The states adopt only those international agreements that suit their own needs. [6]

6 https://www.unoosa.org/oosa/en/ourwork/spacelaw/treaties.html , (last reviewed on 14-05-2025).

Issues with Application of International Space Law to space Tourism?

The instruments of international law that cover space law are not comprehensive enough to include the commercial aspects of space flight. Article 6 of the Outer Space Treaty, 1967, states that the state would bear international responsibility for all activities undertaken on the moon or other celestial bodies. This also to ensure that the activities are done according to the provisions of the treaty.[7] However, the issues concerning the article are jurisdiction and liability. When a multinational company with shareholders from various countries launches a commercial spaceflight, the jurisdiction is unclear. For example, the Virgin Galactic Corporation, which is incorporated in California, is a subsidiary of companies in England and thus arises under various jurisdictions. If a space light is launched from international waters, the Arctic zone Audi Antarctic zone. The jurisdiction again remains in question. However, little insight can be gained from reading Article 17 of the same convention, which states that the aircraft usually bears the nationality of the state where it has been registered. The other issue would lie in the liability of the nations or the safety of the passengers, which would lead to significant insurance issues. The liability treaty is found to be silent in some aspects of safety and Precautions that are ought to be taken by the launching stage and the term astronauts covered under the rescue agreement does not mention private tourists, which leads to a lot of chaos and uncertainty in applying such international conventions and treaties on space to the commercial space tourism industry.

Intellectual Property and Space Tourism

An emerging aspect of space tourism is the issue of intellectual property and its applicability to outer space, as most laws, whether enforceable or territorial in nature, require the sovereignty of a nation, which is currently limited to the earth's surface.

USC105 (2003) one logical way of interpreting Intellectual Property Laws to the space object would be to interconnect it with the laws of the launching state.

However, in situations like the International Space Station, where there is joint ownership by the US, Russia, Europe, and Japan, the laws are silent on creations or inventions made in the space station or other outer space

7 Raimi L. (2025). *Examining the Relevance and Adequacy of the Outer Space Treaty as an International Legal Instrument for Space Tourism Entrepreneurship (STE): A Systematic Literature Review*. Journal of Infrastructure. 1(1), 1–20.

objects. It also remains quiet on matters such as infringement and remedies relating to intellectual property. The significance of intellectual property and basic exploration lies in the basic concept that space exploration is a science based on creativity, with strong interconnectivity with Intellectual Property Rights. [8]

The various conventions during with Intellectual property rights are quite when it comes to space exploration. Article 5 of the Paris Convention,1883 states that in matters of patents in transit, the patent rights usually request upon the country which statement was registered. It is again Generally, discussed with respect to ships and other transporting vessels remaining silent on outer space objects, and space stations.

The Patent Cooperation Treaty (PCT), and the World Intellectual Property Organisation (WIPO), which are meant to harmonise the cooperation of Patents at the international level, have, so far, not taken much effort to deal with matters of IP rights in outer space.

The US, however, has formulated Section 105 of the Patents Act, 2003, which addresses patents in outer space.

In *Brown v Duchesne* (16 US 19 HOW.183 (1856) the Supreme Court decided that the patent would not extend to another port. If it is entering a foreign state, the jurisdiction of the laws of the nation and the exclusive rights over the Patent would also cease to exist. Later in the Supreme Court case of *Hughes Aircraft Company v US* (29 FED Cl 201) the applicant received compensation around $4 billion from the government over his patent used for having control over the attitude of spin-stabilised spacecraft titled "Velocity Control and Orientation of a Spin-Stabilised Body". Thus, when a patent extends to the whole body of spacecraft, the launch of the spacecraft would result in the utility of the Patent.

In the two cases, it is evident that there are various interpretations of the extendibility of IP rights beyond the jurisdiction of national laws. However, lacuna still prevails over the extension of IP rights beyond Earth.

In terms of IP protection, we can divide the activities into three types, namely the space activities that are performed in outer space which could be in the moon or any other bodies, secondly the activities that are performed in spacecraft, flying vehicle or an object, finally space activities

8 Dr. Chitra B. T., Ankitha Shet, *Space Law and Intellectual Property Rights: Issues and Challenges,* Shodhshauryam, International Scientific Refereed Research Journal, Volume 7, Issue 4, July-August-2024, Page Number: 23-36

or any other activities relating to outer space that are performed within a state not exceeding the territorial limits of the country.

When it comes to activities that are performed within the country, the application of laws becomes very easy as jurisdiction of the nation for the regulation of the activities would either be the concerned domestic law or any multilateral treaty. There is no international treaty or an instrument that deals with space tourism and IP so far. [9]

According to Article 5 of the Convention on the High Seas, 1958, the concept of the "law of the flag" would apply to be the jurisdiction of the nation in which the vessel was registered. The flag nation would have the jurisdiction over the ship and the people, including the activities that have been carried, on board on high seas. On comparison, according to Article 8 of the Outer Space Treaty, 1967, a state which is a party to the treaty and has also registered the launch vehicle would have jurisdiction and control over the body. The ownership would continue even when the spaceflight goes beyond the earth to the outer space.

From this, we conclude that in terms of jurisdiction, more importance is given to the state of registry than that of the launching state and by applying the concept of Quasi-Territoriality, we can even apply jurisdiction to an object and people even after reaching the outer space.

As mentioned in Article 5 of the Paris convention, the rights over the patent would still prevail even in terms of aircraft. It is uncertain on whether it would apply to a spacecraft. We can conclude that upon registration of the space objects and the space by the state, one can protect their rights, including that of their Intellectual Property Rights. Even when the object features of the space. This has not been expressly stated with respect to IP right in space tourism but could be arrived upon liberal interpretation of the existing laws. Framing new regulations with respect to commercial space exploration and IP rights would provide more clarity eliminating loopholes.

When it comes to activities that are performed after reaching outer space, it shall be treated as if the activity were created in the country of the registered vehicle. According to Article 21 of the International Space Station Intergovernmental Agreement (IGA), "Doctrine of Temporary

9 Ritesh Mehra, *Intellectual Property Protection in Outer Space – An Overview*, ILI Law Review Vol. II Winter Issue 2019 144

Presence" eliminates cases of immediate infringement of IP by the other states due to mere presence during transit.

Applying the Doctrine of Quasi-Territoriality, we have observed that even the domestic laws could be extended to outer space by the state of registry. Apart from these principles, Berne Convention of copyright also protects and the spirit of national treatment and it also offers automatic protection to the works created, this could be interpreted to be applied even to other space subject once the issue of jurisdiction is clearly demarcated. WIPO copyright treaty also has its applicability when it comes to works transmitted to and from an aircraft which can also be extended to space flights, though are not expressly dealt with currently. Article 25 of the TRIPS Agreement which talks about Patents and the grant of which has to be allocated without any discrimination as to the place of invention, interpreting this we can conclude that there shall be no discrimination in extending the jurisdiction of patents beyond Earth. According to WIPO there are certain issues when it comes to intellectual property and its applicability in space. Firstly, when the jurisdiction is not clearly marked by the existing laws, interpretation can lead to complexities, thereby making the applicability of IP laws to outer space bodies difficult. Secondly, the enforceability of IP laws when it comes to protecting the exclusive use as well as granting remedies for infringement, in outer space body again becomes an issue as ownership and entitlement of creations and inventions is ambiguous. Outer space IP provisions are not yet clearly defined in any of the national or international instruments as it involves a lot of complexities with respect to jurisdiction ownership, etc. The role of arbitration and mediation is to be tailored to fit the outer space disputes which might result from such ambiguities and complexities. The Doctrine of Temporary Presence read with Article 5ter of the Paris Convention,1883, excluding the infringement of Patent during temporary presence in a foreign state, only mentions aircraft and transporting vessels. It does not specifically mention space lights and commercial space supplies that are flown to the outer space.[10]

Conclusion

Commercial space tourism marks the future development for a wide range of industries. Updating existing laws, such as the Outer Space Treaty and the Moon Treaty, which currently do not allow the appropriation

10 Intellectual Property and Space Activities Issue paper prepared by the International Bureau of WIPO April, 2004, https://www.wipo.int/documents/d/patents/docs-en-topics-outer-space-ip_space_wipo-contribution_oecd_2004.pdf (last viewed on 14.05.2025)

of space objects, could be done to sustain future space exploration and commercialised space tourism. Though it raises environmental concerns about debris and particulate matter, et cetera, space travel would also help protect the earth's resources and atmosphere, leading to a more inclusive and sustainable environmental development. Expanding IP rights in commercial outer space exploration would not only boost tourism, but it can also be helpful in boosting the investments to our country, to R&D department, in granting employment opportunities, increases the amount of innovations and creations extended beyond the earth's atmosphere, protecting such rights and balancing the fair use by the government for any private party to the space. Clarity in the legal framework would create a sense of security and accountability and help attract more investment, resulting in the betterment of society and the future of science, technology, and innovation.

Bibliography

Meenakshi Harith

This selected bibliography brings together major academic books, journal articles, reports, and online resources published between 2020 and 2025 on the intersection of Intellectual Property (IP) and Space Law, highlighting recent scholarship and legal developments in the space economy.

"An Evaluation of Intellectual Property Rights Protection in Space Activities." *International Journal for Multidisciplinary Research*, vol. 5, no. 6, Nov.–Dec. 2023. *(IJFMR).*

"From Earth to Orbit: Converging Space Law and Intellectual Property Rights to Safeguard Innovation Beyond Earth." *International Journal of Law, Society & Innovation*, Oct. 2024. https://ijlsi.com/wp-content/uploads/From-Earth-to-Orbit-Converging-Space-Law-and-Intellectual-Property-Rights-to-Safeguard-Innovation-beyond-Earth.pdf.

"Intellectual Property Challenges in the Space Economy." *The Space Review*, 2024. https://www.thespacereview.com/article/5009/1.

"No Space for Intellectual Property Rights in Space?" *The IP Press*, 20 June 2024. https://www.theippress.com/2024/06/20/no-space-for-intellectual-property-rights-in-space/.

"The Law Applicable to Military Strategic Use of Outer Space." *New Technologies and the Law of Armed Conflict*, edited by Hitoshi Nashu and Robert McLaughlin, T.M.C. Asser Press, 2014, pp. 115–142.

Aahaan, Anand. "The Role of AI in Space Mission Planning and Simulation: Transforming Space Exploration with Advanced Computing." *International Journal of Computing and Artificial Intelligence*, vol. 5, no. 2, 2024, pp. 220–224.

Abeyratne, Ruwantissa. *Space Law and Global Governance.* Springer, 2021.

Adhikari, Malay. *Legal Regulation of Private Actors in Outer Space: India's Role.* KW Publishers Private Limited, 2017.

Adhikari, Malay. *Legal Regulation of Private Actors in Outer Space: India's Role.* KW Publishers Private Limited, 2017.

Alberts, Anton de Waal. "The Degree of the Lack of Regulation of Space Debris Within the Current Space Law Regime and Suggestions for a Prospective Legal Framework and Technological Interventions." *Space Security and Legal Aspects of Active Debris Removal,* edited by Annette Froehlich, Springer, 2019, pp. 93–106.

Alberts, Anton de Waal. "The Degree of the Lack of Regulation of Space Debris Within the Current Space Law Regime and Suggestions for a Prospective Legal Framework and Technological Interventions." *Space Security and Legal Aspects of Active Debris Removal,* edited by Annette Froehlich, Springer, 2019, pp. 93–106.

Alexander, William Salter. "Space Debris: A Law and Economics Analysis of the Orbital Commons." *Stanford Technology Law Review,* vol. 19, 2016, pp. 221–238.

Alexi, Arbatov, and Vladimir Dvorkin, editors. *Outer Space: Weapons, Diplomacy, and Security.* KW Publishers, 2010.

Al-Turki, Rawan. "Intellectual Property Challenges in Satellite-Based Innovation." *Journal of Space Technology & Policy,* vol. 4, no. 1, 2024, pp. 55–70.

Alves, Pericles Gasparini. *Prevention of an Arms Race in Outer Space: A Guide to the Discussions in the Conference on Disarmament.* United Nations Institute for Disarmament Research (UNIDIR), 1991.

Aoki, Setsuko. "Law and Military Uses of Outer Space." *Routledge Handbook of Space Law,* edited by Ram S. Jakhu and Paul Stephen Dempsey, Routledge, 2017, pp. 197–224.

Azevedo, Joao Pedro Marques de. *The Principle of Common Heritage of Humankind in the Law of Outer Space.* Ph.D. dissertation, Universidade NOVA de Lisboa, 2021.

Baiden, Jerome K. "International Cooperation, Intellectual Property Rights, and the New Space Economy." *Global IP Review,* vol. 12, no. 2, 2023, pp. 112–129.

Bamakan, Seyed Mojtaba, Nasim Nezhadsistani, Omid Bodaghi, and Qiang Qu. "Patents and Intellectual Property Assets as Non-Fungible Tokens: Key Technologies and Challenges." *arXiv Preprint*, 2 Mar. 2023. https://arxiv.org/abs/2304.10490.

Bandyopadhyay, S., and R. Kadam. "Patentability of Space Manufacturing Technologies: A Critical Study." *Indian Journal of Intellectual Property Law*, vol. 18, 2023, pp. 201–223.

Baratto, Eduardo Bressel. "Peacekeeping Operations in Outer Space: Contradictions in Article IV of the Outer Space Treaty." *A Fresh View on the Outer Space Treaty*, edited by Annette Froehlich, Springer, 2017, pp. 39–48.

Bhat, Sandeepa B. "National Space Law for India: A Reality Check." *SSRN Electronic Journal*, 7 July 2024. https://papers.ssrn.com/sol3/papers.cfm?abstract_id=4887689.

Blake, Ducan. "Military Strategic Use of Outer Space." *New Technologies and the Law of Armed Conflict*, edited by Hitoshi Nashu and Robert McLaughlin, T.M.C. Asser Press, 2014, pp. 97–114.

Blanc, Alexis A., et al. *Chinese and Russian Perceptions of and Responses to US Military Activities in the Space Domain.* RAND Corporation, 2022.

Boothby, Bill. "Space Weapons and the Law." *International Law Studies*, vol. 97, 2017, pp. 179–214.

Boothby, William H. *Weapons and the Law of Armed Conflict.* Oxford University Press, 2016.

Bosco, Joseph A. "International Law Regarding Outer Space—An Overview." *Journal of Air Law and Commerce*, vol. 55, 1990, pp. 609–651.

Bowen, B. E. *War in Space: Strategy, Space Power, Geopolitics.* Edinburgh University Press, 2020.

Brockmann, Kolja, and Dmitry Stefanovich. *Hypersonic Boost-Glide Systems and Hypersonic Cruise Missiles: Challenges for the Missile Technology Control Regime.* SIPRI, Apr. 2022.

Bushnell, Dennis M. *Commercial Space in the Age of "New Space," Reusable Rockets and the Ongoing Tech Revolutions.* Langley Research Center, 2018. https://ntrs.nasa.gov/citations/20180008444.

Cannon, Jennifer A. "Targeting Dual-Use Satellites: Lessons Learned from Terrestrial Warfare." *Air and Space Operations Review*, vol. 2, no. 2, Summer 2023, pp. 37–52.

Cassandra, Steer. "Sources and Law-Making Processes in Space Activities." *Routledge Handbook of Space Law*, edited by Ram S. Jakhu and Paul Stephen Dempsey, Routledge, 2017, pp. 3–24.

Cassandra, Steer. "Sources and Law-Making Processes in Space Activities." *Routledge Handbook of Space Law*, edited by Ram S. Jakhu and Paul Stephen Dempsey, Routledge, 2017, pp. 3–24.

Cassese, Antonio. "The Martens Clause: Half a Loaf or Simply Pie in the Sky." *European Journal of International Law*, vol. 11, no. 1, 2000, pp. 187–216.

Chabert, Valentina. "The Exploitation of Mineral Resources of the Moon and Celestial Bodies in International Law and Practice." *The Irish Yearbook of International Law*, vol. 16, 2021–2022, pp. 36–58.

Challenges to Security in Space: Space Reliance in an Era of Competition and Expansion. U.S. Defence Intelligence Agency, Mar. 2022.

Challenges to Security in Space: Space Reliance in an Era of Competition and Expansion. U.S. Defence Intelligence Agency, Mar. 2022.

Chen, Kuan-Wei, and Bayer Goswami. "Publication of the World's First Manual on International Law Applicable to Military Uses of Outer Space." *Indian Journal of International Law*, vol. 62, nos. 1–2, Jan.–June 2022, pp. 84–107.

Chen, Zhijie, and Yun Zhao. "Intellectual Property Protection in Outer Space: Conflict in Theory and Application in Practice." *Space Policy*, vol. 61, 2022. https://doi.org/10.1016/j.spacepol.2022.101484.

Chen, Zhijie. *Application of Intellectual Property Rights to Outer Space Activities: An Adaptive Regulatory Approach in the Context of Space Commercialization*. Ph.D. thesis, 2018.

Cheng, Bin. "Properly Speaking, Only Celestial Bodies Have Been Reserved for Use Exclusively for Peaceful (Non-Military) Purposes, but Not Outer Void Space." *International Law Studies*, vol. 75, 2000, pp. 81–117.

Chesterman, Simon. "Intellectual Property Rights and Generative AI." *Policy and Society*, vol. 44, no. 1, 2025, pp. 1–23. https://doi.org/10.1093/polsoc/ppa-7606572.

Chitra, B. T., and Ankitha Shet. "Space Law and Intellectual Property Rights: Issues and Challenges." *Shodhshauryam: International Scientific Refereed Research Journal*, vol. 7, no. 4, 2024. https://shisrrj.com/SHISRRJ24744.

Christol, Carl Quimby. *The Modern International Law of Outer Space.* Pergamon Press, 1982.

Chung, Gordon. "Jurisdiction and Control Aspects of Space Debris Removal." *Space Security and Legal Aspects of Active Debris Removal*, edited by Annette Froehlich, Springer, 2019, pp. 31–48.

Clerc, Philippe. "French Law Approach Around the Topic 'Legal Implications/Aspects of Active Debris Removal.'" *Space Security and Legal Aspects of Active Debris Removal*, edited by Annette Froehlich, Springer, 2019, pp. 179–187.

Crockett, Jameson W. "Space Warfare in the Here and Now: The Rules of Engagement for U.S. Weaponized Satellites in the Current Legal Space Regime." *Air Law and Commerce Journal*, vol. 77, 2012, pp. 671–700.

Dan, L. Burk. "Patents in Outer Space." *Harvard Journal of Law & Technology*, vol. 35, no. 1, 2021, pp. 1–42.

Dasgupta, Arjun. "Outer Space and the Principle of Common Heritage of Mankind: An Indian Perspective." *Astropolitics*, vol. 19, no. 3, 2021, pp. 216–233.

De Penning & De Penning. "IPR for Outer Space Activity: Clarity Is a Necessity for Its Development." *Mondaq*, 23 Nov. 2023. https://www.mondaq.com/india/intellectual-property/1482886/ipr-for-outer-space-activity.

Deplano, Raffaele. "The Artemis Accords: Evolution or Revolution in International Space Law?" *International and Comparative Law Quarterly*, vol. 70, 2021.

Deplano, Rossana. "Technological Innovation and the Transformation of International Law: Artificial Intelligence and Space Law." *International and Comparative Law Quarterly*, vol. 71, no. 4, 2022, pp. 835–861.

Diederiks-Verschoor, I. H. Ph., and Vladimir Kopal. *An Introduction to Space Law.* 4th ed., Wolters Kluwer, 2018.

Dixon, James. "Commercial Space Mining: Legal and Policy Challenges." *Air and Space Law Review*, vol. 48, no. 2, 2023, pp. 101–125.

Dolzer, Rudolf, and Christoph Schreuer. *Principles of International Investment Law.* 3rd ed., Oxford University Press, 2022.

Drake, Jennifer N. "Cross-Licensing and IP Protection in the New Space Economy." *Journal of Intellectual Property Law & Practice*, vol. 18, no. 6, 2023, pp. 455–469.

Duchek, Anke. "Strategic Management of Intellectual Property in Emerging Space Markets." *International Journal of Innovation Management*, vol. 27, no. 2, 2023, pp. 221–240.

Ehrlich, Sean. "Trade-Related Aspects of Intellectual Property Rights in Outer Space Commerce." *World Trade Review*, vol. 22, no. 1, 2023, pp. 75–98.

Eisen, Michael. "Satellite Data, Ownership, and Intellectual Property Rights." *Journal of Space Law*, vol. 47, no. 2, 2021, pp. 59–92.

El Khatib, Omar. "Ownership, Patents, and Space Resources: Reconciling Territoriality in IP Law." *Arab Journal of International Law*, vol. 7, no. 3, 2024, pp. 45–59.

Elvis, Martin, et al. "Legal Frameworks for Asteroid Mining and the Protection of Intellectual Property." *Space Policy*, vol. 63, 2023, pp. 101–123.

European Commission – Intellectual Property Helpdesk. *IP and Space Activities: Guidance Note.* 29 Apr. 2021. https://intellectual-property-helpdesk.ec.europa.eu.

Farrand, Benjamin. "From TRIPS to the Stars: The Interface Between Intellectual Property and Space Commercialization." *European Intellectual Property Review*, vol. 46, no. 4, 2024, pp. 281–298.

Fernandez, José. *Intellectual Property Governance in Global Commons: Lessons from Outer Space and the Deep Sea.* Routledge, 2023.

Finkelstein, Ariel. "Digital Replication and IP Protection in Space Manufacturing." *Stanford Technology Law Review*, vol. 26, no. 1, 2023, pp. 47–69.

Finnemore, Martha, and Duncan B. Hollis. "Constructing Norms for Global Space Governance." *Journal of Conflict & Security Law*, vol. 28, no. 1, 2023, pp. 1–29.

Forster, Robert A. "Space Sustainability and IP Incentives: A Legal Nexus." *Journal of Air and Space Law*, vol. 98, no. 3, 2023, pp. 315–337.

Frakes, Michael D., and Melissa F. Wasserman. *Patent Office and the Innovation Economy.* Oxford University Press, 2023.

Freeland, Steven. "Cybersecurity, Satellites, and Space Law: Emerging Challenges." *Annals of Air and Space Law*, vol. 47, 2022, pp. 1–23.

Froehlich, Annette. *Space Law Dimensions of the Moon Agreement: Opportunities for Renewed Global Cooperation.* Springer, 2022.

Gabrynowicz, Joanne Irene. *The Development of International Space Law and the Role of Soft Law Instruments.* Routledge, 2023.

Gangmeih, Poujiabthai, and Ravi K. Mishra. "The Relationship Between Outer Space Activities and Intellectual Property Laws." *Educational Administration: Theory and Practice*, vol. 30, no. 1, 2024, pp. 741–748. https://doi.org/10.53555/kuey.v30i1.5456.

García, Elena. "Patenting Space Technology: Balancing Innovation and Access." *European Intellectual Property Review*, vol. 45, no. 8, 2023, pp. 501–520.

Garrison, Sean R. "The Space Economy and Intellectual Property: Legal Mechanisms for Innovation." *Journal of Business Law*, vol. 27, no. 2, 2022, pp. 215–243.

Gavrilović, Nenad. "Legal Regimes for Data Ownership in Outer Space." *Air and Space Law*, vol. 48, no. 1, 2023, pp. 35–54.

Ghosh, Anupam. "The Future of Space Law and Intellectual Property: Trends and Challenges." *Indian Journal of International Law*, vol. 64, nos. 1–2, 2024, pp. 87–108.

Ghosh, Shubha. *Intellectual Property: Private Rights, the Public Interest, and the Regulation of Creative Activity.* 3rd ed., Cambridge University Press, 2023.

Gibson, Sarah L. "Intellectual Property Licensing in Multi-National Space Collaborations." *International Review of Law, Computers & Technology*, vol. 38, no. 1, 2024, pp. 78–97.

Gleeson, Patrick. "Satellite Broadcasting and IP Law: A European Perspective." *Media Law Review*, vol. 45, no. 3, 2022, pp. 145–162.

Goh, Gerard. "Blockchain, Smart Contracts, and Space-Based IP Transactions." *Computer Law & Security Review*, vol. 51, 2024, pp. 1–18.

Gomes, Eduardo Silva. "Protecting Inventions Developed in Outer Space: Revisiting the Jurisdictional Question." *Journal of Space Law*, vol. 48, no. 1, 2023, pp. 33–59.

Gonzalez, Marta. "The Interplay Between IP Law and Space Law in the Context of Artificial Intelligence." *AI & Society*, vol. 38, no. 3, 2023, pp. 659–676.

Gopalakrishnan, N. S. *Intellectual Property and the New Frontiers: Biotechnology, AI, and Space.* LexisNexis, 2022.

Gupta, Rishabh. "Protection of Trade Secrets in Space Missions: Legal and Practical Issues." *International Journal of Space Law Studies*, vol. 3, 2024, pp. 77–95.

Haesler, Julian. "Protecting Intellectual Property Rights in International Space Stations." *Space Policy*, vol. 61, 2022, pp. 101–119.

Hall, Trevor I. "Commercial Space Innovation: Incentivizing IP While Preserving Global Access." *Journal of Intellectual Property Law & Practice*, vol. 18, no. 3, 2023, pp. 210–226.

Harris, Melinda. "Space Data as Intellectual Property: Ownership and Licensing Issues." *Air and Space Law*, vol. 48, no. 2, 2023, pp. 121–143.

Harrison, James, and Julia Dorn. *Intellectual Property in Global Commons: Space, Deep Seabed, and Antarctica.* Routledge, 2023.

Hassan, Riaz. "Space Commercialization and IP Law in Developing Economies." *Asian Journal of Comparative Law*, vol. 19, no. 1, 2024, pp. 101–127.

Hedman, Sven. "Cybersecurity, AI, and the Regulation of Space-Based Data under IP Law." *Journal of Law, Technology & Policy*, vol. 2023, no. 2, 2023, pp. 77–95.

Helm, Kristina. "Patent Jurisdiction for Inventions Made Aboard Orbital Platforms." *European Space Policy Review*, vol. 12, no. 2, 2022, pp. 89–110.

Hernández, Laura. "Public-Private Partnerships in Space Technology: IP Sharing Models." *Journal of Business Law and Innovation*, vol. 8, no. 4, 2024, pp. 345–366.

Herron, Michael, et al. *International Space Traffic Management: Legal and Policy Challenges.* RAND Corporation, 2023.

Hertzfeld, Henry G. *Space Economics and Intellectual Property: Policy and Practice.* Palgrave Macmillan, 2022.

Hobe, Stephan, and Kai-Uwe Schrogl, editors. *Space Law and Policy in the 21st Century.* Nomos, 2023.

Hobe, Stephan, et al., editors. *Cologne Commentary on Space Law.* Carl Heymanns Verlag, 2020–2024.

Hoffman, Erika. "Legal Aspects of IP Protection in Outer Space Activities." *German Journal of Air and Space Law*, vol. 71, no. 1, 2023, pp. 1–18.

Holmes, Daniel. "Licensing Innovations in Space Exploration: IP Frameworks for Public Benefit." *Stanford Law Review Online*, vol. 75, 2023, pp. 201–220.

Horowitz, David. "IP Management in Collaborative Satellite Projects." *Space Policy*, vol. 65, 2023, pp. 1–12.

Howard, Emily. "Space Mining and the Intellectual Property Paradox." *Journal of Space Law*, vol. 48, no. 2, 2023, pp. 101–132.

Huang, Yufan. "China's IP Policy and Space Innovation Strategy." *Asian Journal of WTO & International Health Law and Policy*, vol. 18, no. 2, 2023, pp. 67–90.

Hughes, Jane. "Regulating Orbital Innovation: Intellectual Property in Private Space Missions." *Journal of Air and Space Law*, vol. 97, no. 4, 2023, pp. 412–435.

Iftikhar, Saad. "Space as the Next Frontier of IP Disputes." *Pakistan Journal of International Law*, vol. 9, no. 1, 2024, pp. 33–54.

Iida, Reiko. "Patentable Subject Matter and the Space Industry: Lessons from Japan." *Tokyo University Law Review*, vol. 19, 2022, pp. 245–268.

Iliev, Dobromir. "The Role of IP in International Cooperation for Lunar Exploration." *Astropolitics*, vol. 21, no. 2, 2023, pp. 105–125.

International Trademark Association. *Intellectual Property in Space: White Paper.* INTA Research Project, May 2023. https://www.inta.org.

Iqbal, Nadeem. "Legal Challenges to Protecting Space-Generated Data as Intellectual Property." *Space Policy*, vol. 64, 2023, pp. 201–223.

Irwin, Jennifer. "Commercial Satellites, Data Rights, and Intellectual Property Law: A Modern Dilemma." *Journal of Space Commerce*, vol. 9, no. 1, 2025, pp. 33–58.

Iskander, Amira. "Open Science vs. Proprietary Research in Space: Balancing Access and IP." *Science and Public Policy*, vol. 51, no. 3, 2024, pp. 312–330.

Ivanova, Daria. "Artificial Intelligence and IP in Space Missions." *AI and Society*, vol. 39, no. 2, 2024, pp. 499–514.

Jackson, Peter. "Sovereignty, IP, and Space Governance." *Journal of International Law and Policy*, vol. 45, no. 1, 2023, pp. 15–38.

Jain, Rahul. "Space-Based Innovation and India's IP Legal Framework." *Indian Journal of Law and Technology*, vol. 19, 2023, pp. 201–225.

Jakhu, Ram S., and Paul Dempsey, editors. *Routledge Handbook of Space Law.* Routledge, 2022.

Janikowski, Adam. "Investment Impacts of Space Resources Legislation." *Space Policy*, vol. 65, 2024.

Jensen, Marta. "Technology Transfer and IP Rights in Space Collaborations." *Journal of World Intellectual Property*, vol. 27, no. 4, 2024, pp. 376–394.

Johnson, Rachael. "Protecting IP Rights for Commercial Lunar Projects." *Air and Space Law Review*, vol. 48, no. 4, 2024, pp. 289–311.

Jones, David R. "Intellectual Property and the Privatization of Space." *Yale Journal on Regulation*, vol. 40, no. 2, 2023, pp. 255–281.

Jorgensen, Lars. "Data Licensing and IP Rights in Satellite Networks." *Information & Communications Technology Law*, vol. 33, no. 2, 2024, pp. 155–173.

Kamal, Noor. "Balancing Open Innovation and IP Enforcement in Space Technology." *Journal of Intellectual Property Rights*, vol. 29, no. 1, 2024, pp. 21–44.

Kang, Sunhee. "Lunar Resources and IP Ownership in the Republic of Korea's Space Policy." *Korean Journal of International Law*, vol. 62, no. 1, 2023, pp. 87–112.

Kapoor, Anjali. "Emerging Trends in Space IP Litigation." *Indian Journal of International Economic Law*, vol. 15, 2024, pp. 77–98.

Keller, Richard. "The Role of WIPO in Space-Related IP Protection." *World Intellectual Property Organization Journal*, vol. 11, no. 3, 2022, pp. 145–166.

Kennedy, Alice M. "Space Patents and International Harmonization." *Journal of Patent and Trademark Office Society*, vol. 105, no. 4, 2023, pp. 301–326.

Khoshyari Haji Baba, R., S. Koosha, H. Al-Kajbaf, and A. Mahmoudi. "Intellectual Property in Space Tourism: Gaps in International Law and the Need for New Regulations." *Interdisciplinary Studies in Society, Law & Politics*, vol. 5, no. 2, 2026, pp. 1–12. https://doi.org/10.61838/kman.isslp.391.

Kim, Jiyoung. "Comparative Analysis of National Space IP Regimes: The U.S., EU, and Japan." *Astropolitics*, vol. 20, no. 4, 2023, pp. 275–297.

Klein, Peter. "The Commons Revisited: Intellectual Property and Space Mining." *Environmental Law Review*, vol. 25, no. 1, 2023, pp. 65–85.

Koellner, Ed. "Harmonizing Intellectual Property Law for the Expanding Space Economy." *SSRN Electronic Journal*, July 2025. https://papers.ssrn.com/sol3/papers.cfm?abstract_id=5441476.

Koenig, Tobias. "Cross-Border IP Disputes in the Space Industry." *European Intellectual Property Review*, vol. 45, no. 9, 2023, pp. 602–620.

Koosha, S. "Protecting the Intellectual Property Rights of Tourists and Advancing the Space Tourism Industry." *Journal of Law and Political Studies*, vol. 4, no. 1, 2024, pp. 84–97.

Kovacs, Natalia. "Ethical Dimensions of IP in Space Exploration." *Journal of Ethics and Law*, vol. 15, no. 2, 2024, pp. 89–107.

Krishna, S. R. *Space Commerce, Innovation, and IP Law: A New Legal Paradigm*. Sage Publications, 2023.

Kumar, Ajay. "IP Protection and the Indian Space Research Ecosystem." *Indian Journal of Law and Technology*, vol. 20, 2024, pp. 155–178.

Kuo, Ming-Hua. "Satellite Data and Intellectual Property: An East Asian Perspective." *Asia Pacific Journal of Environmental Law*, vol. 27, no. 1, 2024, pp. 12–31.

Lang, Oliver. "IP in Space Tourism Ventures." *Tourism and Law Review*, vol. 19, no. 2, 2024, pp. 199–219.

Laurentis, Paolo. "Copyright and Creative Works Produced in Space Stations: A Jurisdictional Examination." *European Intellectual Property Law Review*, vol. 46, no. 4, 2024, pp. 287–301.

Lee, Min. "AI-Driven Space Missions and Patent Law Reform." *Computer Law & Security Review*, vol. 50, 2024, pp. 1–20.

Liu, Han. "Data Ownership and Intellectual Property in China's Commercial Space Programs." *Chinese Journal of International Law*, vol. 23, no. 1, 2024, pp. 45–70.

Liu, Yang. "Emerging IP Governance Models in the Space Industry." *Asian Journal of International Law*, vol. 15, no. 2, 2023, pp. 211–234.

Lyall, Francis, and Paul B. Larsen. *Space Law: A Treatise.* 3rd ed., Routledge, 2024.

Macdonald, Fiona. "Innovation Incentives and IP in the Space Sector." *Journal of Intellectual Property Law & Practice*, vol. 18, no. 7, 2023, pp. 587–606.

Mahajan, Neha. "IP Regulation for Space Startups: India's Legal Challenges." *Indian Journal of Intellectual Property Law*, vol. 15, no. 1, 2023, pp. 123–142.

Mahmoud, Omar. "IP Rights and Satellite-Based Services: Emerging Legal Issues." *Journal of Space Law*, vol. 49, no. 1, 2024, pp. 27–55.

Malhotra, Rina. "Space Resources and Patent Law: A Comparative Study of U.S. and EU Approaches." *Space Policy*, vol. 64, 2024, pp. 34–53.

Malhotra, Ritu. "Patenting Space Technologies Developed Under International Partnerships." *Journal of Air and Space Law*, vol. 98, no. 1, 2024, pp. 33–58.

Mandal, Anirban. "Protecting Space-Based AI Software Under Copyright Law." *AI and Law Journal*, vol. 14, no. 2, 2024, pp. 97–116.

Mani, Ravindra. "IP Commercialization in the New Space Economy: A Policy Framework for Developing Countries." *Indian Journal of Intellectual Property Law*, vol. 16, 2023, pp. 147–172.

Marboe, Irmgard. *Legal Aspects of Space Resource Utilization: From Celestial Bodies to Intellectual Property Rights.* 2nd ed., Springer, 2022.

Marboe, Irmgard. *Soft Law in Outer Space: The Function of Non-Binding Norms in International Space Law.* Springer, 2023.

Mariani, Luca. "From Space Mining to IP Rights: Who Owns Extraterrestrial Innovation?" *Space Policy*, vol. 63, 2023, pp. 201–218.

Markoff, Samuel. "AI and Autonomous Spacecraft: Challenges for IP Ownership." *Journal of Law, Technology and Policy*, vol. 2023, no. 1, 2023, pp. 89–113.

Martin, Laura J. "Legal Dimensions of Data Sharing in Space Missions." *International Data Privacy Law*, vol. 13, no. 2, 2023, pp. 121–142.

Martinez, Diego. "Artificial Intelligence, IP, and Autonomous Spacecraft." *Journal of Space Law*, vol. 48, no. 2, 2023, pp. 135–155.

Masson-Zwaan, Tanja, and Mahulena Hofmann, editors. *Introduction to Space Law.* 5th ed., Wolters Kluwer, 2022.

McDougall, Walter A. *Space and the American Imagination.* 3rd ed., Johns Hopkins University Press, 2023.

McGill, David. "Space Mining, Innovation, and Patents: The Next Frontier of IP Law." *Harvard Journal of Law & Technology*, vol. 36, no. 3, 2023, pp. 413–441.

McGill, Sarah. "Collaborative Research and IP Management in Space Science." *Science and Public Policy*, vol. 51, no. 4, 2024, pp. 451–472.

McKeown, Benjamin. "Safety Zones and Long-Term Use in the Artemis Accords." *Space Policy*, vol. 61, 2022.

McKinnon, Oliver. "IP and Data Rights in Remote Sensing Satellites." *Air and Space Law Review*, vol. 48, no. 1, 2023, pp. 55–78.

Mensah, Ben. "Public-Private Partnerships and IP Management in Space Projects." *Acta Astronautica*, vol. 13, 2024, pp. 95–112.

Merchant, Phil. "Intellectual Property Challenges in the Space Economy." *The Space Review*, 23 June 2025. https://www.thespacereview.com/article/5009/1.

Meyer, Günter. "The Outer Space Treaty and Technological Innovation: Balancing IP with Public Interest." *Zeitschrift für Luft- und Weltraumrecht*, vol. 73, no. 2, 2024, pp. 87–109.

Mishra, Anjali. "Legal Status of Intellectual Property in Orbital Platforms." *Journal of Intellectual Property Rights*, vol. 29, no. 4, 2024, pp. 305–328.

Mishra, Devika. "Space Commercialization and IP: The Legal Framework for India." *Indian Journal of International Law*, vol. 64, no. 2, 2024, pp. 189–210.

Mohamed, Aisha. "IP Ownership in International Lunar Missions." *African Journal of International and Comparative Law*, vol. 32, no. 2, 2024, pp. 215–233.

Mohanty, Sanjay K. "Open Science in Space Research and Its Impact on IP Regulation." *Science and Public Policy*, vol. 51, no. 2, 2024, pp. 219–237.

Morales, Javier. "Open-Source Technology and IP in Space Exploration." *Technology and Innovation*, vol. 27, no. 1, 2024, pp. 12–32.

More, Aumirah. "Role of Patents in Advancement of Space Exploration." *India Intellectual Property / Mondaq*, 12 Nov. 2024. https://www.mondaq.com.

Morgan, Daniel. "Defining Property Rights Beyond Earth: Law and Policy Challenges." *Georgetown Journal of International Affairs*, vol. 25, no. 1, 2024, pp. 99–120.

Morin, Jean-Pierre. *Intellectual Property and Innovation in Outer Space: The Global Commons Challenge*. Routledge, 2022.

Mousavi, Reza. "Iran's Approach to IP and Space Law." *Asian Journal of International Law*, vol. 15, no. 1, 2023, pp. 33–53.

Mukherjee, Pallavi. "The Future of IP Enforcement in Outer Space." *NUJS Journal of International Law and Policy*, vol. 18, no. 1, 2024, pp. 201–222.

Mukherjee, Rashmi. "Copyright and Data Protection in Satellite Imagery." *Computer Law Review International*, vol. 25, no. 1, 2024, pp. 12–33.

Müller, Andreas. "Satellite Constellations and IP Licensing Frameworks." *European Intellectual Property Review*, vol. 46, no. 5, 2024, pp. 331–352.

Nair, Deepa. "India's Position on Space Intellectual Property and Technology Transfer." *Indian Journal of International Law*, vol. 64, nos. 3–4, 2024, pp. 221–243.

Nair, P. S. "Data Ownership and IP Rights in Earth Observation Satellites." *Remote Sensing Legal Journal*, vol. 8, no. 1, 2023, pp. 12–34.

Nakamura, Hiroshi. "Innovation, IP, and Japan's National Space Policy." *Japan Review of International Affairs*, vol. 37, no. 1, 2023, pp. 1–19.

Nanda, Meera. "Developing Nations and Access to Space IP." *Third World Quarterly*, vol. 45, no. 3, 2024, pp. 501–520.

Narayanan, S. "Protection of Industrial Designs in Space Manufacturing." *Indian Journal of Intellectual Property Law*, vol. 16, 2024, pp. 155–174.

Nath, Aranya, and Srishti Roy Barman. "Legal Regime of Patent Protection to Outer Space Activities in India and USA: A Comparative Study." *Journal of Legal Studies*, vol. 6, no. 1, 2025. https://cnlu.ac.in/wp-content/uploads/2025/07/Legal-Regime-of-Patent-Protection-To-Outer-Space-Activities-in-India-and-USA-A-Comparative-Study-by-Aranya-Nath-Srishti-Roy-Barman.pdf.

Ncube, Chipo. "Patent Regimes and International Space Cooperation." *African Journal of International and Comparative Law*, vol. 32, no. 2, 2024, pp. 167–186.

Ndiaye, Oumar. "African Space Policy and IP Law Development." *African Journal of Legal Studies*, vol. 13, no. 2, 2024, pp. 117–139.

Nelson, Andrew. "Private Ownership of Data from Outer Space: Emerging Legal Norms." *Space Policy*, vol. 65, 2023, pp. 233–254.

Nguyen, Linh. "Commercial Satellites, Data Ownership, and IP Disputes in ASEAN." *Asian Journal of International Law*, vol. 14, no. 3, 2024, pp. 333–357.

Nguyen, Thanh. "Outer Space and IP Disputes: Jurisdictional Challenges." *Asia-Pacific Journal of International Law*, vol. 27, no. 1, 2023, pp. 44–63.

Nirmala, S. "Patentability of AI-Generated Space Technologies." *Indian Journal of Law and Technology*, vol. 20, 2024, pp. 245–269.

Norton, Joshua. "Patent Law Beyond the Atmosphere." *Harvard Journal of Law & Technology*, vol. 36, no. 2, 2023, pp. 121–148.

O'Brien, John. "Licensing Models for Space Start-Ups and SMEs." *Journal of Business Law and Innovation*, vol. 19, no. 3, 2024, pp. 159–182.

O'Brien, Michael. "Cross-Border Enforcement of Space-Related IP Rights." *Journal of World Intellectual Property*, vol. 27, no. 2, 2024, pp. 145–168.

O'Connell, Sarah. "Space Sustainability and Licensing Regimes." *Air and Space Law*, vol. 48, no. 3, 2023, pp. 223–247.

Oberlin, Claire. "Patents for Space-Based Biotech: Ethical and Legal Concerns." *Biotechnology Law Report*, vol. 42, no. 2, 2023, pp. 97–115.

Oestmann, Christoph. "The Interface Between IP and Export Controls in Space Technology." *German Law Journal*, vol. 25, no. 1, 2024, pp. 77–96.

Okafor, Amara. "Sovereignty, IP, and the Ownership of Orbital Inventions." *Air and Space Law Review*, vol. 49, no. 2, 2024, pp. 88–109.

Okafor, Chika. "The African Space Industry: IP and Innovation Challenges." *African Journal of Science, Technology, Innovation and Development*, vol. 16, no. 4, 2024, pp. 315–333.

Oliveira, Renata. "Environmental Protection, Space Activities, and IP Responsibilities." *Environmental Law Review*, vol. 26, no. 2, 2024, pp. 165–183.

Orlova, Tatiana. "Space Law Harmonization in the Eurasian Region." *Eurasian Law Review*, vol. 11, no. 3, 2023, pp. 245–262.

Owen, Joshua P. "The IP Dimension of Space Debris Technology." *Journal of Environmental Law & Policy*, vol. 45, no. 1, 2024, pp. 63–85.

Pagallo, Ugo. *The New Laws of Outer Space: Ethics, Legislation, and Governance in the Age of AI.* Hart Publishing, 2024.

Pal, Ramesh. "Space Patents and India's Strategic IP Roadmap." *Indian Journal of International Economic Law*, vol. 16, 2024, pp. 123–144.

Panda, Dipti. "Legal Aspects of Protecting IP in Outer Space: Indian Perspective." *Indian Journal of International Law*, vol. 63, nos. 1–2, 2023, pp. 45–68.

Park, Jihyun. "The Korean Approach to IP Rights in Space Exploration." *Korean Journal of International and Comparative Law*, vol. 12, no. 1, 2024, pp. 31–55.

Park, Joon. "Digital Twins, IP Law, and Space Engineering." *Computer Law & Security Review*, vol. 51, 2024, pp. 201–221.

Patel, Kavita. "Patent Enforcement in Outer Space: An Emerging Legal Frontier." *International Review of Intellectual Property and Competition Law (IIC)*, vol. 55, no. 3, 2024, pp. 241–259.

Patel, Priya. "India's Draft Space Activities Bill and IP Rights Implications." *Journal of Air and Space Law*, vol. 99, no. 1, 2024, pp. 87–106.

Patidar, Kapila, Sakar Joshi, and Aditya Awasthi. "IPR in Outer Space: Issues, Challenges, Legal Framework and Future Considerations." *Research & Reviews: Journal of Space Science & Technology*, vol. 13, no. 3, 2024, pp. 21–26. https://journals.stmjournals.com/rrjosst/article%3D2024/view%3D181559/.

Patil, Vinay. "Balancing Innovation and Access in Space Technologies." *Technology Law Review of India*, vol. 10, no. 2, 2024, pp. 61–80.

Pelton, Joseph N., and Firoz Khan. *New Frontiers in Space Law and Policy.* Springer, 2021.

Pereira, Maria. "Space Data and Intellectual Property: Balancing Innovation and Accessibility." *European Space Policy Review*, vol. 4, no. 2, 2023, pp. 61–80.

Peters, Laura. "Ownership of Lunar Resources and IP Implications." *Astropolitics*, vol. 21, no. 3, 2023, pp. 215–234.

Petrovic, Luka. "Space Mining Patents and the Commons Dilemma." *Journal of World Intellectual Property*, vol. 27, no. 2, 2024, pp. 183–203.

Pop, Virgiliu. *Who Owns the Moon? Extraterrestrial Aspects of Land and Mineral Resources Ownership.* Springer, 2020.

Popova, Elena. "The Role of IP Law in Regulating Mega-Constellations." *European Journal of Space Policy*, vol. 17, no. 1, 2023, pp. 33–51.

Prasad, Sanjay. "Patent Rights and Liability in Space Collaborations." *Indian Journal of Intellectual Property Law*, vol. 16, 2024, pp. 211–232.

Qureshi, Hina. "IP Law and Ethical AI in Space Exploration." *AI and Ethics*, vol. 5, no. 2, 2024, pp. 245–263.

Qureshi, Imran. "Revisiting the Legal Framework for IP Protection in Space-Related Research." *International Journal of Intellectual Property Law and Practice*, vol. 18, no. 2, 2024, pp. 123–145.

Rahman, Tariq. "Space-Based Innovations and the IP–Security Nexus." *Journal of Law, Technology & Policy*, vol. 2024, no. 1, 2024, pp. 33–56.

Rajeswari, A. "Cyberspace and Intellectual Property: Evaluating Legal Frameworks through the Lens of Space Transition Theory."

International Journal of Law, Management & Humanities, vol. 7, no. 2, 2024, pp. 3938–3947. https://doi.org/10.10000/IJLMH.117478.

Rao, Ananya. "Women Entrepreneurs and IP in the Space Economy." *Indian Journal of Gender Studies*, vol. 31, no. 1, 2024, pp. 99–118.

Rao, Arvind K. "IP Rights and the Global Commons in Space Law." *Space Policy*, vol. 65, 2024, pp. 91–109.

Raza, Aqa, and Ghayur Alam. "IP Case Law Development." *SSRN Electronic Journal*, 9 Feb. 2024. https://papers.ssrn.com/sol3/papers.cfm?abstract_id=4885511.

Reddy, Ananya. "AI-Generated Space Inventions and Patentability Challenges." *Journal of Artificial Intelligence & Law*, vol. 32, no. 1, 2024, pp. 71–93.

Reddy, Sunil. "IP Rights and the Commercialization of Satellite Services in India." *Indian Journal of Intellectual Property Rights*, vol. 29, no. 3, 2024, pp. 199–223.

Rees, Jonathan. "Space Technology Exports and IP Governance." *World Trade Review*, vol. 22, no. 4, 2023, pp. 411–430.

Reinhardt, Mark. "Cross-Border Enforcement of IP in Outer Space." *Michigan Journal of International Law*, vol. 46, no. 2, 2025, pp. 203–227.

Rossi, Maria. "European Legal Developments in Space IP Protection." *European Intellectual Property Review*, vol. 46, no. 2, 2023, pp. 157–175.

Roth, Lisa. *Intellectual Property in the Age of Private Space Enterprises.* Cambridge University Press, 2024.

Saikia, Koushik, and Pritam Deb. "Intellectual Properties Derived in Space Exploration: Issues and Scopes." *Journal of Intellectual Property Rights*, vol. 29, no. 2, 2024. https://or.niscpr.res.in/index.php/JIPR/article/view/61.

Sarabdeen, J. "Intellectual Property Law Protection for Energy-Efficient Technologies in Saudi Arabia." *Journal of Intellectual Property and Innovation*, 2024. https://www.sciencedirect.com/science/article/pii/S2405844024060110.

Sato, Hiroshi. "Japan's Legal Framework on Space Innovation and IP Rights." *Japanese Yearbook of International Law*, vol. 67, 2024, pp. 155–177.

Schneider, Thomas. "The Interrelation Between IP Law and Space Resource Governance." *German Law Journal*, vol. 25, no. 1, 2024, pp. 201–223.

Scott, Karen. *Space Law and Environmental Protection: Legal Responsibilities and IP Implications.* Edward Elgar, 2023.

Sen, Amrita. "Open Access Data in Space Research: Reconciling IP and Scientific Collaboration." *Journal of World Intellectual Property*, vol. 27, no. 3, 2024, pp. 311–333.

Shankar, Roshini. "Patenting the Final Frontier: Intellectual Property Challenges in Space Exploration." *International Journal of Intellectual Property Law*, vol. 9, no. 2, 2023, pp. 89–107.

Shaw, Malcolm N. *International Law.* 9th ed., Cambridge University Press, 2023.

Shawkat, Nadia. "The Future of Space IP Law: Innovation, Sovereignty, and Global Governance." *Astropolitics*, vol. 20, no. 1, 2024, pp. 34–56.

Singh, Rajdeep. "India's Emerging Space Economy and IP Challenges." *Indian Journal of Law and Technology*, vol. 20, no. 1, 2024, pp. 71–94.

Smith, Aaron T. "Protecting AI-Generated Inventions in Space: Patent Law at a Crossroads." *AI and Technology Law Review*, vol. 6, no. 1, 2024, pp. 55–78.

Smith, Oliver. "IP Rights in Satellite Networks and Constellations." *Telecommunications Policy*, vol. 48, no. 2, 2024, pp. 229–246.

Sood, Nupur. "Space Patents and Global Commons: Legal and Ethical Dilemmas." *Indian Journal of International Economic Law*, vol. 16, no. 1, 2024, pp. 55–78.

Sood, Raunak. "An Analytical Study of Intellectual Property Regime in Outer Space with Special Reference to India." *Bennett Journal of Legal Studies*, vol. 6, no. 1, June 2025, pp. 89–108. https://www.bennett.edu.in/wp-content/uploads/2025/06/5.-Raunak-Sood.pdf.

Sousa, Catarina. "EU Space Programme and IP Regulation: The Case of Copernicus and Galileo." *European Law Review*, vol. 49, no. 3, 2024, pp. 412–431.

Sposito, Benjamin. "The Space Race to Uniformity: The Intersection of Patent Law and Space Law." *Loyola Maritime Law Journal*, vol. 24, Summer 2025, pp. 87–107. https://loyolamaritimelawjournal.scholasticahq.com/article/143817.pdf.

Stevens, Richard. "Private Space Enterprises and the IP Landscape." *Air and Space Law*, vol. 49, no. 1, 2024, pp. 1–24.

Su, Jinyuan. "The Legal Status of Private Actors in Outer Space." *Chinese Journal of International Law*, vol. 21, no. 4, 2022, pp. 965–988.

Subramanian, Leela. "Space Technology Transfer and the Role of IP in South–South Cooperation." *Journal of International Trade Law and Policy*, vol. 23, no. 2, 2024, pp. 98–118.

Sundaram, K. "Patentability of AI-Based Space Inventions: Legal Considerations." *Artificial Intelligence and Law Review*, vol. 11, no. 1, 2024, pp. 59–79.

Tanaka, Yuki. "IPR Enforcement and Jurisdiction in Low Earth Orbit." *Asian Journal of Air and Space Law*, vol. 5, no. 2, 2024, pp. 87–103.

Taylor, Matthew. "Commercial Space Launches and Patent Protection." *Journal of Law, Innovation and Technology*, vol. 16, no. 1, 2024, pp. 101–125.

Thompson, Eleanor. "International Cooperation and IP Ownership in Multi-Nation Space Missions." *Space Policy*, vol. 65, 2024, pp. 133–151.

Torres, Gabriel. "Protecting IP in Space Manufacturing and 3D Printing." *Additive Manufacturing Law Review*, vol. 7, no. 2, 2023, pp. 77–96.

Trivedi, Ashok. "Indian Legal Framework for Space IP Rights and Innovation." *National Law School Journal*, vol. 36, no. 1, 2023, pp. 145–164.

United Nations. *Treaty on Principles Governing the Activities of States in the Exploration and Use of Outer Space (Outer Space Treaty).* United Nations, 1967. https://www.unoosa.org.

Valencia, Julia. "Global Governance and IP Challenges in Space-Based Data Sharing." *Space and Society Journal*, vol. 2, no. 1, 2024, pp. 51–73.

van Fenema, Paul. "Cybersecurity and Space Law: Overlapping Regimes in the New Frontier." *Space Policy*, vol. 63, 2023, pp. 17–29.

Vasquez, Miguel. "Commercial Exploitation of Space Resources: IP and Treaty Obligations." *Journal of World Trade and Investment*, vol. 25, no. 2, 2024, pp. 167–190.

Verma, Neha. "Copyright Challenges in Satellite Broadcasting and Streaming." *Media and Communications Law Review*, vol. 30, no. 2, 2023, pp. 201–219.

Vidaurri, Monica R., and Alexander Q. Gilbert. "Environmental Considerations in the Age of Space Exploration: The Conservation and Protection of Non-Earth Environments." *arXiv Preprint*, 2023. https://arxiv.org/abs/2308.03241.

Vikram, Arjun. "IP Protection in Space Start-Ups: The Indian Perspective." *Indian Journal of Intellectual Property Law*, vol. 17, 2024, pp. 123–143

von der Dunk, Frans G. *Advanced Introduction to Space Law.* Edward Elgar, 2020.

Wachowicz, M. E. "Space Technology Transfer Problems in the Context of Patent Protection." *Space Policy*, 2017–2020.

Wang, Yilin. "China's Space Law and the Integration of IP Rights." *Chinese Journal of International Law*, vol. 23, no. 3, 2024, pp. 355–379.

Weber, Claudia. "International Enforcement of IP Rights in Space Contexts." *Global Intellectual Property Review*, vol. 11, no. 2, 2024, pp. 99–118.

White, Daniel. "The Future of IP and Space Commercialization." *Journal of Business and Technology Law*, vol. 20, no. 2, 2024, pp. 191–211.

Williams, Andrew. *Space Commerce, Law, and Intellectual Property: A Global Handbook.* Routledge, 2023.

Williams, Thomas. "Private Space Mining and the Commercialization of Asteroid Resources: IP Implications." *Space Policy and Law Quarterly*, vol. 11, no. 2, 2024, pp. 101–118.

Wong, Celia. "International Collaboration and IP Sharing in Space Science." *Asia-Pacific Journal of International Law*, vol. 27, no. 3, 2024, pp. 289–309.

World Intellectual Property Organization. *World Intellectual Property Report.* WIPO, 2024. https://www.wipo.int.

Xu, Lijuan. "Patentability of Space Technologies under Chinese Law." *Tsinghua China Law Review*, vol. 16, no. 2, 2024, pp. 157–177.

Yadav, Priya. "The Role of IP in India's Space Innovation Ecosystem." *Indian Journal of Law and Technology*, vol. 21, no. 1, 2025, pp. 33–59.

Yamamoto, Kei. "Space Debris Removal Technologies and Related IP Rights." *Japanese Journal of Space Law*, vol. 9, 2024, pp. 71–92.

Zamora, Luis. "International Harmonization of Space IP Law." *International Review of Intellectual Property and Competition Law (IIC)*, vol. 56, no. 2, 2025, pp. 111–134.

Zhang, Lei. "Inventorship and Attribution Issues in Autonomous Robotic Space Missions." *Journal of Robotics and Space Law*, vol. 3, no. 1, 2025, pp. 19–41.

Zhang, Wei. "Intellectual Property Protection for Space Data in the Digital Age." *Computer Law & Security Review*, vol. 52, 2025, pp. 1–22.

Zhao, Yun. "Reconciling Territoriality of Intellectual Property with Non-Territoriality in Outer Space." *Queen Mary Journal of Intellectual Property*, vol. 7, 2017, pp. 137–162.

Zhen, Mei, and Yu Zhao. "AI and Autonomous Satellites: Legal Challenges in Outer Space." *Journal of World Trade and Space Law*, vol. 15, no. 2, 2025, pp. 98–117.

Index

K

L

M

N

O

P

W

Z

www.ingramcontent.com/pod-product-compliance
Lightning Source LLC
Chambersburg PA
CBHW031321230926
51848CB00001B/43
9789347436826